Outstanding Leadership in Special Educational Needs

This book provides new and experienced Special Educational Needs Coordinators (SENCOs) with a critical approach to understanding the importance of outstanding leadership of Special Educational Needs and Disabilities (SEND) and how to effectively meet the current SEND policy requirements.

Closely informed by the statutory guidance for SENCOs, this book covers all aspects of this challenging leadership role within the school. It provides a principled approach to understanding the challenges and complexity of SEND within the current context. Through concise summaries of policy and current research, critical discussions, reflective activities, case studies as well as practical examples, it helps the reader engage more deeply in critical thinking about the effectiveness of current practices in their own school setting and ways to develop them further for the future. Alison Ekins and Lorna Hughes establish that outstanding leadership in special educational needs is not something that can be achieved just by a single individual. The SENCO has a key role in enabling and empowering everyone in their school setting to understand SEND and engage actively in the development of more inclusive systems to meet the needs of diverse pupils.

Outstanding Leadership in Special Educational Needs will, therefore, support everyone involved in education to develop their understanding of SEND. It is key reading for teachers, educational leaders and policymakers.

Alison Ekins is Director of SEND in a Multi-Academy Trust and Senior Lecturer at Canterbury Christ Church University, UK. She has previously authored *The Changing Face of Special Educational Needs* (2015) for Routledge.

Lorna Hughes is Principal Lecturer in SEND and Inclusion at Canterbury Christ Church University, UK.

Outstanding Leadership in Special Educational Needs

Principles, Policy and Practice

Alison Ekins and Lorna Hughes

Routledge
Taylor & Francis Group

LONDON AND NEW YORK

Designed cover image: © Getty Images

First published 2024
by Routledge
4 Park Square, Milton Park, Abingdon, Oxon OX14 4RN

and by Routledge
605 Third Avenue, New York, NY 10158

Routledge is an imprint of the Taylor & Francis Group, an informa business

© 2024 Alison Ekins and Lorna Hughes

The right of Alison Ekins and Lorna Hughes to be identified as authors of this work has been asserted in accordance with sections 77 and 78 of the Copyright, Designs and Patents Act 1988.

All rights reserved. No part of this book may be reprinted or reproduced or utilised in any form or by any electronic, mechanical, or other means, now known or hereafter invented, including photocopying and recording, or in any information storage or retrieval system, without permission in writing from the publishers.

Trademark notice: Product or corporate names may be trademarks or registered trademarks, and are used only for identification and explanation without intent to infringe.

British Library Cataloguing-in-Publication Data
A catalogue record for this book is available from the British Library

Library of Congress Cataloging-in-Publication Data
Names: Ekins, Alison, 1974- author. | Hughes, Lorna, 1976- author.
Title: Outstanding leadership in special educational needs : principles, policy and practice / Alison Ekins and Lorna Hughes.
Description: Abingdon, Oxon ; New York, NY : Routledge, 2024. | Includes bibliographical references and index. |
Identifiers: LCCN 2023034239 (print) | LCCN 2023034240 (ebook) | ISBN 9780367471071 (hardback) | ISBN 9780367471156 (paperback) | ISBN 9781003033554 (ebook)
Subjects: LCSH: Special education. | Educational leadership. | Education and state. | Students with disabilities--Education.
Classification: LCC LC3965 .E42 2024 (print) |
LCC LC3965 (ebook) | DDC 371.9--dc23/eng/20230804
LC record available at https://lccn.loc.gov/2023034239
LC ebook record available at https://lccn.loc.gov/2023034240

ISBN: 978-0-367-47107-1 (hbk)
ISBN: 978-0-367-47115-6 (pbk)
ISBN: 978-1-003-03355-4 (ebk)

DOI: 10.4324/9781003033554

Typeset in ITC Galliard Pro
by KnowledgeWorks Global Ltd.

Contents

About the authors   vi

1. Introduction   1
2. Understanding SEN/SEND   13
3. SEND statutory responsibilities   30
4. Outstanding leadership of SEND   45
5. Whole-school approaches to SEND   67
6. Identifying difference and needs   88
7. Co-ordinating provision effectively   105
8. Planning and delivering effective intervention   128
9. Developing effective working relationships with teaching assistants   147
10. Working with pupils: developing effective person-centred planning   166
11. Effective partnership working with parents/carers   186
12. Working effectively with other agencies   203
13. Concluding comments   223

Index   243

About the authors

Alison Ekins is the Director of SEND in a Multi-Academy Trust, working with both primary and secondary schools, including schools with a Specialist Resource Provision for pupils with Education, Health and Care Plans (EHCPs). She is also Senior Lecturer at Canterbury Christ Church University and has responsibility for the delivery of the statutory National Award for SEN Coordination and doctoral supervision in the areas of SEND and Inclusion.

Lorna Hughes is Principal Lecturer in Special Educational Needs and Inclusion at Canterbury Christ Church University. She teaches the National Award for SEN Coordination and Postgraduate Certificate in Dyslexia. Her PhD studies focus on the role of parents and schools in the co-production of Education Health and Care Plans for children.

1 Introduction

> In this chapter, we provide an introduction to the book as a whole, including the following aspects:
>
> - An overview of the policy context to date
> - Principles underpinning the discussions
> - A note on language
> - Overview of the structure of the book

We are living and working in a time of unprecedented change. The Special Educational Needs (SEN) and Disability Code of Practice (DfE/DoH, 2014, 2015) introduced 'potentially the most significant reforms to the SEND system' (House of Commons Education Committee, 2019: 6) since the Warnock Report (Warnock, 1978) and the subsequent educational reforms (DES, 1981). The proposed reforms were said to be 'ambitious and transformative' (House of Commons Education Committee, 2019: 6).

Since 2014, schools have, however, experienced a significant period of development and re-learning, needing to respond, often overnight, to changing regulations and priorities as schools experienced the first national closures, the provision of Hubs for vulnerable pupils (including those with Special Educational Needs and Disability [SEND]), the demands of online learning and provision and the constantly shifting reality of pupil and staff absences, self-isolation periods and COVID-testing processes.

Whilst the planned five-year review of the SEN and Disability Code of Practice (DfE/DoH, 2014, 2015) was delayed by the impact of Brexit and then the global pandemic, we have now reached a point, in 2023, where the review of the new SEND reforms (DfE/DoH, 2014) has been completed, with a new SEND and Alternative Provision Improvement Plan published to set out the direction of travel moving forward (DfE, 2022; DfE/DoHSC, 2022; DfE/DoHSC, 2023).

These documents, along with other reports and reviews that preceded them, review the current state, and challenges, of the existing SEND and education systems, and provide frameworks and proposals for priority and action moving forward.

Effective and principled leadership of SEND is a matter for everyone, not just the SENCO. This not only includes the statutory responsibilities that all teachers hold in respect of meeting the needs of all children, including children with SEND, but also includes senior leaders and headteachers having the knowledge and understanding of SEND to

DOI: 10.4324/9781003033554-1

ensure that planning for the needs of children with SEND is at the heart of whole-school planning and priorities.

It also includes, as is seen in the recent reviews of the current SEND system (House of Commons Education Committee, 2019; DfE/DoHSC, 2022), leadership and understanding of consistent and effective SEND systems at a local authority level to ensure that the systems and processes that are used are fit for purpose and effective.

At such a time, the role of the SENCO as strategic leader, informed about the current SEND system – where it has come from, how it works and the plans for the future, is therefore crucial. This book is therefore written at a critical time to provide SENCOs and those working and interested in meeting the needs of pupils with SEND with a principled, values-led guide to understanding effective ways to provide outstanding leadership of SEND within a range of different school contexts.

The policy context

Following the critical review of the SEND system from 2006 to 2014 (House of Commons Select Committee, 2006; OFSTED, 2010; DfE, 2011), the publications of the SEND reforms and new SEN and Disability Code of Practice (DfE/DoH, 2014) were intended to provide a more consistent framework for setting out the statutory responsibilities for SEND. Notably, the new SEN and Disability Code of Practice (DfE/DoH, 2014) was jointly published by the Department for Education and the Department for Health, indicating an intention to increase statutory responsibilities and accountability for the SEND framework.

In January 2015, an updated SEN and Disability Code of Practice (DfE/DoH, 2015) was published with minor additions to the original 2014 version relating to implementation of the new guidance from 1 April 2015. In April 2020, further guidance was added related to EHC needs assessments and plans due to the coronavirus.

Whilst the SEN and Disability reforms and Code of Practice (DfE/DoH, 2014, 2015) were supposed to be based on three years of evidence gathered about effective systems and approaches to embed the new reforms through the SEN Pathfinder projects, unfortunately, little direct reference to the evaluations of those projects has been used to inform the direction of practices moving forward: 'Pathfinders did not substantially inform policy changes, as they operated in tandem with, rather than prior to, the consultation and implementation timescale for the new framework' (Hellawell, 2019: 5).

Five years on from the publication of the SEN and Disability Code of Practice (DfE/DoH, 2014, 2015), however, significant issues with the implementation and accountability for the statutory responsibilities laid out in 2014/2015 were identified:

- 'We have found a general lack of accountability within the system. The absence of a rigorous inspection regime at the beginning set the tone of a hands-off approach. This has been perpetuated by the fact that those required, or enabled, to "police" the system have been limited in part by an apparent unwillingness to grapple with unlawful practice, while others are limited by the narrowness of their remit' (House of Commons Education Committee, 2019: 3)
- 'The lack of heed taken to the warnings during the legislative scrutiny process has resulted in the failure of the aspirations of this policy to be realised' (House of Commons Education Committee, 2019: 25)

- '50.0% – proportion of inspected local authority areas that Ofsted and the Care Quality Commission had assessed as underperforming at July 2019' (NAO, 2019: 4)
- 'In practice, the number of cases being taken to tribunal increased by 80.5%, from 3,147 in 2014/15 to 5,679 in 2017/18' (NAO, 2019: 8).

Whilst the 2014 SEND reforms were therefore largely identified as being the 'right ones' (House of Commons Education Committee, 2019: 3), it is the lack of accountability that has proved challenging for effectively embedding those key reforms into practice, leading to calls from the House of Commons Education Committee Report for the need for a 'systemic cultural shift on the part of all parties involved' (House of Commons Education Committee, 2019: 12).

Key to this is the way that government departments work together to ensure that the SEND reforms really do bring together Education, Health and Social Care in meaningful and effective ways. Unfortunately, due to differences in accountability and prioritisation for the SEND reforms in each of those government departments, the focus has largely remained educational, with very limited effective progress being made in engaging Health and Social Care in meaningful ways – see also Chapter 12 – Working with other Professionals.

As will be seen in Chapter 3, the House of Commons Education Committee Report (2019), as well as The Office for Standards in Education (OFSTED) and Care Quality Commission (CQC) have also identified major failings in the ability of local authorities to fully and effectively interpret and apply the national guidance and SEND reforms into meaningful practice to support the children with SEND and their families in their area.

Fundamentally, and sadly, as the House of Commons Education Committee (2019: 3) bluntly states:

> The Department did not need to preside serenely over chaos for five years to see that things were not quite going as planned. The distance between young people's lived experience, their families' struggles and Ministers' desks is just too far.

In 2023, the government summarised the key challenges facing the SEND system as follows:

- The system is failing to deliver improved outcomes for children and young people with SEND. Children and young people with SEND are not consistently being helped to fulfill their potential.
- Parents' confidence in the system is in decline. Too many parents have lost faith in a system that is not sufficiently responsive to them, which is increasingly adversarial, and in which they face long waiting times to access information and support for their children, including accessing therapists and mental health support.
- Despite substantial additional investment, the system has become financially unsustainable. The government has increased investment in high needs by over 50% from 2019–20 to 2023–24, with no marked improvement in outcomes or experiences (DfE/DoHSC, 2023: 16).

The DfE/DoHSC (2023) highlighted the 'vicious cycle of late intervention, low confidence and inefficient resource allocation' (DfE/DoHSC, 2023: 16), noting that 'It is time to deliver a more dignified experience for children and young people with SEND and to restore families' confidence in the system' (DfE/DoHSC, 2023: 3).

The DfE/DoHSC (2023) therefore plan to 'establish a new national SEND and alternative provision system with the mission to:

- fulfill children's potential: children and young people with SEND (or attending alternative provision) enjoy their childhood, achieve good outcomes and are well prepared for adulthood and employment;
- build parents' trust: parents and carers experience a fairer, easily navigable system (across education, health and care) that restores their confidence that their children will get the right support, in the right place, at the right time;
- provide financial sustainability: local leaders make the best use of record investment in the high needs budget to meet children and young people's needs and improve outcomes, while placing local authorities on a stable financial footing' (DfE/DoHSC, 2023: 5).

These improvements will be built on the foundation of the new 'evidence-based National Standards', which will 'improve early identification of needs and intervention, and set out clear expectations for the types of support that should be ordinarily available in mainstream settings' (DfE/DoHSC, 2023: 5).

To achieve this, the DfE/DoHSC (2023) have identified 'three approaches to delivery:

1 *Support and stabilise*: we will support and stabilise the system, getting local areas working in the best possible way within the current system to ensure that the needs of children and young people are met, without escalating costs, and to ensure that local authority deficits are brought under control. This includes supporting local authorities with financial deficits through the Delivering Better Value and the Safety Valve programmes. Further information on these programmes is set out in Chapter 6
2 *Delivering capacity to address supply issues*: in the short to medium term, we will take action to address supply issues – ensuring that there is sufficient support available for children and young people when they need it, in the most efficient way. This includes investing £2.6 billion between 2022 and 2025 to deliver new places and improve existing provision for children and young people with SEND or who require alternative provision, reducing the need for costly independent provision
3 *Design and test for systemic reform*: our £70 million Change Programme will create up to nine Regional Expert Partnerships that will test and refine longer-term, systemic reforms including developing and testing National Standards, strategic partnerships and inclusion plans, the proposed alternative provision service and tailored lists. This will help guard against unintended consequences and build a strong evidence base to inform future funding and legislation' (DfE/DoHSC, 2023: 19).

A principled approach

The most important feature of this book is that it is not intended as a simplistic 'how-to' guide. Outstanding practice and leadership of SEND does not happen in that way. Instead, the focus is on developing a deeper understanding of and reflection on the key principles underpinning the approaches that underpin the SEND systems within which we work.

The key principles underpinning the focus of the discussions running throughout this book are purposefully presented below as a cycle of interlocking circles as we do not see this as a linear list but as dynamically interconnected key principles (see Figure 1.1). We see that some of these will take precedence and be of more importance than others for some key issues, and particularly, when considered and applied within the context of each unique school setting. Throughout the book, we therefore invite readers to consider ways that they will use these underpinning key principles and the critical questions that we pose relating to them in each chapter to inform the development of meaningful and values-led reflection and development.

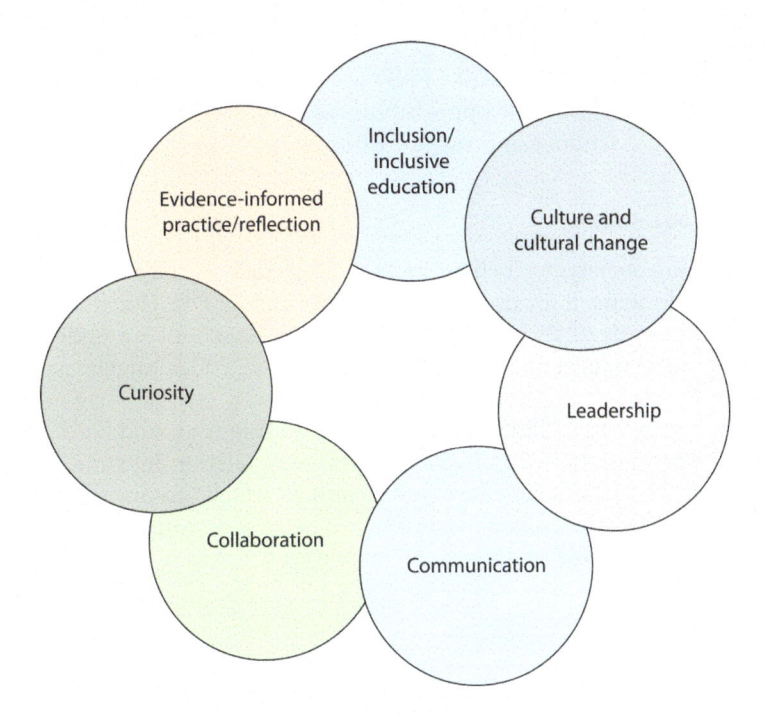

Figure 1.1 Key principles model

Underpinning all of the key principles is the importance of genuine respect – respect in leadership, communication and collaboration to meaningfully value the contributions, participation and different perspectives of all, and find ways to effectively embrace and welcome diversity as a way to build stronger understandings and practices.

Each chapter will explore these key principles in relation to the focus of the chapter, but here we outline our understanding and perspective on each of the key principles and why they are so important to underpin the development of outstanding SEND practice.

Inclusion/inclusive education

Whilst this is a book focused on SEND and the development of effective SEND practices, we see this to sit centrally within an approach that is focused on inclusion and inclusive education. The importance of the individual child at the centre of planning for provision and practice; the celebration of diversity; and recognising and addressing exclusionary practices is at the heart of our approach to SEND.

We believe that inclusion and the development of inclusive practices is an ongoing and dynamic process, not something that can simply be 'achieved'. It is fundamentally concerned with the identification and removal of barriers, and the presence, participation and achievement of ALL pupils (UNESCO, 2021).

6 *Introduction*

We support the position of the Education Endowment Foundation (EEF), which noted in the EEF (2020) SEN in Mainstream Schools Guidance Report that:

- 'The starting points for educating all pupils are the same: an acceptance of diversity, pupils' rights, and the knowledge that all pupils can learn if they receive good teaching' (EEF, 2020: 4)
- 'In an inclusive school, pupils with SEND are not just *in* the school, they are *part* of the school – they have the same opportunities as their peers to benefit from the highest quality teaching the school can provide' (EEF, 2020: 12).

Culture and cultural change

In an ever-changing society, we believe in the importance of the embedded culture in a school setting, and the need for ongoing review and change/development of that culture to ensure that the needs of the whole community of the school are understood and appropriately supported (Corbett, 2001; Booth & Ainscow, 2002; Kugelmass, 2004; Ekins, 2017).

School culture is literally defined as 'the way we do things around here' (Fullan, 2020: 70) – it is everywhere, in the attitudes, values, practices, relationships and communication embedded in the school. Challenging school cultures which are not inclusive and where cultural change may be needed is difficult but, we believe, essential in ensuring an equitable society and education for all.

Leadership

To effect the culture change that is required demands strong strategic leadership. Leadership that is embedded with inclusive values, with a knowledge and understanding of the change process, and ways to enable and empower all staff working within the school context to understand, own and take responsibility for the changes to practice, provision, attitude and approach to SEND that is required.

This is why the notion of the SENCO as a strategic leader has become so important, and why the strategic leadership skills and abilities of the SENCO need to be considered as paramount to the development of effective SEND practice and provision within the school context.

Whilst there is a specific chapter devoted to the notion of Leadership, the key skills and responsibilities of SENCO as a strategic leader are therefore embedded across all of the discussions in all of the chapters. Fundamentally effective SEND provision and practice cannot move forward until and unless SENCOs are supported to be central to the whole school development processes as strategic leaders, working closely and dynamically with other senior leaders in the school to ensure that SEND is considered centrally at the heart of all in-school planning (curriculum, pastoral, provision, extra-curricular). By ensuring that SEND is considered and addressed at the heart of whole school development work, rather than sitting separately or alongside other whole school developments, schools will be able to fully meet the statutory duties of the 2014 reforms, establishing and embedding knowledge and understanding of SEND at the heart of the practice of the whole school.

As will be seen in Chapter 4, leading SEND is not about being a 'lone ranger' (Fullan, 2020: 3) – even a passionate and enthusiastic one. Effective SEND leadership is about positive collaboration and meaningful relationships and communication to ensure that all are engaged – staff, pupils, parents/carers in reviewing and developing practice. It is also about the development of meaningful leadership at all levels – to include pupil leadership.

Communication

Effective communication and relationships need to embed everything that we do. All too often communication systems are not fit for purpose for the people (pupils, parents/carers, colleagues, other professionals) that we need to include.

In some cases, communication can be more challenging, especially when we are supporting vulnerable pupils or supporting families experiencing very challenging circumstances. It is essential that we are sensitive to this and adopt ethics of care (Noddings, 2012) as central to undertaking any difficult conversations.

This level of sensitivity and empathy is required to ensure that everyone is involved. Shared understanding – based on effective communication systems – is therefore essential.

Collaboration

As we have already identified, building effective inclusive schools requires a move away from the 'lone ranger' (Fullan, 2020: 3) approach into a collaborative one where all are equally involved in and understand the developments being made. Collaborative practice indicates a commitment to working together, in some cases, for pupils with more complex SEND this is fundamental to be able to support their progress. Ensuring that there are genuine and meaningful collaborative approaches which seek to involve and include everyone in appropriate ways is therefore key to the development of outstanding SEND practices in our schools.

Curiosity

For us, professional curiosity is a central factor in the development of inclusive practices and schools. In our work in schools, there is therefore a need to develop professional curiosity. This helps us to challenge existing or embedded assumptions – leading us to ask questions rather than base new ideas on pre-existing knowledge and 'truths', which may actually not reflect the actual situation or reality for the pupils, families and colleagues with whom we work.

As a curious practitioner, we should always be open to exploring and questioning/reflecting on evidence bases, as well as seek to always stand back and reflect anew on familiar practices within our own school settings.

In this, we have found the concepts of 'making the familiar unfamiliar' (Delamont & Atkinson, 1995) and 'principled interruptions' (Ainscow et al., 2006) really important (Ekins, 2015, 2017).

Evidence-informed practice and reflection

Linked to the principles of curiosity above, underpinning inclusive school practices there needs to be a willingness to engage in meaningful reflection – to continually 'make the familiar unfamiliar' (Delamont & Atkinson, 1995) and engage in 'principled interruptions' (Ainscow et al., 2006), which deepen critical reflection of whether existing practices/assumptions are still effective or whether they need to be challenged/changed.

Where change is needed, and to support with the reflection, evidence-informed approaches and practices, which consider the research evidence about what works in what type of setting and under what conditions, are really important. Here, we support the EEF's focus on the importance of evidence-*informed* practices – with the emphasis on supporting active engagement by professionals in reflecting on the appropriateness of evidence within the context of their practices; rather than the traditional focus on 'evidence-*based* practice', which suggests a less dynamic response to interrogating ways that evidence can inform the development of effective, situated practices.

Fundamentally, there is a need for more effective, principled approaches to understanding how to address the concerns that have been raised for so many decades about the existing SEND system and ways to effectively and inclusively meet the needs of children with SEND.

We therefore support the work of the Education Endowment Foundation (EEF), and the range of evidence-informed Guidance Reports that have been published to support schools in developing more engaged and evidence-informed approaches to different aspects of practice.

For us, the Special Educational Needs in Mainstream Schools Guidance Report (EEF, 2020), and other linked EEF Guidance Reports supports all of the work that we have been doing in schools and with the SENCOs with whom we work, and throughout the book, we will draw on elements from the SEN in Mainstream Guidance Report as well as others that provide useful access to evidence bases to inform the development of thinking and practice:

- Making Best Use of Teaching Assistants (EEF, 2018a)
- Working with Parents to Support Children's Learning (EEF, 2018b)
- Putting Evidence to Work – A School's Guide to Implementation (EEF, 2019)
- Effective Professional Development (EEF, 2021).

A note on language

As the EEF (2020) has identified in their Special Educational Needs in Mainstream Schools Guidance Report, 'language matters' (EEF, 2020: 5) and we agree that it is really important that practitioners consider carefully the language that is used to talk about pupils with SEND.

Whilst we acknowledge that for some areas of SEND, e.g. autism, there is a growing sense within the community that autistic people feel that as autism is central to their identity, it is important to reflect this by positioning this in the way that they identify – e.g. identity first; yet for the broader discussions about SEND, we firmly believe that it is important to value a person-first approach to understanding and describing needs – it is not helpful to talk about 'SEND pupils' – as this devalues the individual pupil and suggests that needs are homogenous, which they certainly are not in such a broad definition of SEND.

In this book, we have chosen to use the term SEND (Special Educational Needs and Disabilities) as this is the term currently used by the government in recent publications (DfE/DoHSC, 2022; DfE/DoHSC, 2023) even though the current SEN and Disability Code of Practice (DfE/DoH, 2015) has not yet been updated and still uses the term SEN. However, it is important to recognise the distinct definitions of both SEN and Disability as defined in legislation and the current SEN and Disability Code of Practice (DfE/DoH, 2015). Pupils may have SEN, a disability or both.

We have chosen to use the term 'pupils' throughout to ensure consistency and we have adopted a strengths rather than deficit-based approach to understanding and exploring learning differences rather than learning difficulties.

Overview of the book

Whilst the book is not intended as a simplistic 'how-to' guide for SENCOs and practitioners in school, it is intended to support deeper reflection and review of existing knowledge and current practices, by providing concise and clear summaries of current evidence bases, research and policies. The aim is for readers to be able to reflect further on their own understandings and practices and therefore practical examples, case studies and templates are used to enable the reader to immediately reflect on ways to apply new learning and understandings to their own school setting.

Throughout the book, therefore, a similar structure will be followed in each chapter to help readers to engage with the issues that are introduced and discussed. Throughout all of the sections, reflective activities and templates to support reflection and application of the ideas being introduced will be used. The first and second sections are brief, providing a brief overview of the key issues and policy/research context, whilst the third section forms the main part of each chapter, focusing on planning for practice.

Key issues

At the start of each chapter, a summary of the key issues relevant to the focus of the chapter will be provided. This will introduce and discuss key critical issues impacting on the effective implementation and development of effective practices relating to the area being discussed in the chapter as a whole.

Current policy/research

This section provides a clear overview of up-to-date policy and research to ensure that the reader has direct access to key policies, evidence bases and research that is informing the development of current practices and policy priorities. The discussions in this section therefore provide a background context to the next key section of each chapter.

Planning for practice

In each chapter, this is the largest and most important section, as it draws on the overview of key critical issues and current research/policy developments presented in the preceding sections to then consider the practical and strategic implications of this for reflecting on, reconsidering and developing aspects of practice within the school setting.

In this section, key principles that will aid effective implementation and development of ideas and practices will be introduced. A range of case studies, written by practitioners from different roles and professional perspectives, and reflective activities, as well as example formats or models are presented to aid engagement with the key principles for practice being discussed.

The discussions in this section will link back to the core principles that have already been introduced and which underpin the book as a whole.

Concluding comments and reflections

At the end of each chapter, some brief concluding comments are provided and a simple format to support and encourage the reader to reflect on their learning/understanding and then use those reflections to support planning for next steps/actions is provided.

Table 1.1 provides an overview of the key context covered in each chapter.

10 Introduction

Table 1.1 Table of all chapter contents

Chapter 1	Introduction	• An overview of the policy context to date • Principles underpinning the discussions • A note on language • Overview of the structure of the book
Chapter 2	Understanding SEN/SEND	• Reductionist interpretations • Reviewing the definition • Medical and social models • New National Standards for SEND • National standardisation and digital systems for EHCPs • SEN Support and EHCPs • Embedding Continuing Professional Development (CPD) to develop understanding of SEND • The four areas of SEN/SEND • Effective support strategies
Chapter 3	SEND statutory responsibilities	• Statutory SEND responsibilities for Government, local authorities, OFSTED and other agencies • Accountability and checking of statutory responsibilities • SEND Law • The local offer • Local inclusion plans and tailored lists
Chapter 4	Outstanding leadership of SEND	• Understanding leadership • Successful school leadership • Leadership of change • The SENCO as a strategic leader • The National Award for SEN Coordination and the development of the SENCO National Professional Qualification (NPQ) • Tools to support the management of change • Developing understanding of the role of the SENCO and implications of this for practice
Chapter 5	Whole-school approaches to SEND	• Inclusive school cultures • Teacher and staff self-efficacy and confidence levels • Training in SEND • Whole-school inclusive pedagogy • High-quality teaching • Inclusion by design • Scaffolding and adaptation
Chapter 6	Identifying difference and needs	• The challenges of identification • Inclusive approaches to identifying needs • Screening assessments • Solution-focused approaches • Communication systems – Class Profile of Needs • Identifying SEND • SEND register • SEND referral systems
Chapter 7	Co-ordinating provision effectively	• Effective, accessible systems • Models to support the coordination of provision • The Graduated Approach • Tiered approaches to planning provision • Provision Mapping • Individual Class Inclusion Maps • Evaluating provisions

(Continued)

Table 1.1 (Continued)

Chapter 8	Planning and delivering effective intervention	• Key principles underpinning effective provision • Ways to evaluate the effectiveness and impact of interventions • Evidence-informed approaches and research relating to interventions • Digital technology to support interventions • Interventions based on the SEND areas of need
Chapter 9	Developing effective working relationships with teaching assistants	• Changes in the teaching assistant workforce in schools • Research relating to the effectiveness of teaching assistants • Continuing Professional Development (CPD) and training approaches for teaching assistants • Communication between teachers and teaching assistants • Models for effective deployment of teaching assistants
Chapter 10	Working with pupils: developing effective person-centred planning	• Understanding person-centred planning • Involving and valuing everyone's individual voice • Exploring pupil participation and engagement • Investment and resources for person-centred planning • Embedding person-centred planning across the school • Frameworks to support person-centred planning
Chapter 11	Effective partnership working with parents/carers	• The importance and value of meaningful parental partnership with parents/carers • Recognising and challenging persistent inequalities • The impact of social capital • Trust • Communication skills • Relationships • Removing barriers for parents/carers • Participation models • Stages of co-production
Chapter 12	Working effectively with other agencies	• Professional identity and differences • Stretched services • Structural issues and systemic silos • Communication • Levels of participation • Interpreting and using professional reports • Embedding multi-professional working in practice

Chapter 13	Concluding comments	• A summary of the current situation and challenges
		• Ways to move forward – a timeline for the new proposals
		• Models to implement change
		• Use of evidence-informed practice:
		    Action Research
		    Lesson Study
		    EEF Guidance Reports
		• Use of Continuing Professional Development (CPD)
		• Principled approaches to the development of effective practices

References

Ainscow, M., Booth, T. and Dyson, A. (2006) *Improving schools, developing inclusion.* Abingdon: Routledge.

Booth, T. and Ainscow, M. (2002) *Index for inclusion: Developing learning and participation in schools.* Bristol: Centre for Studies on Inclusion in Education.

Corbett, J. (2001) *Supporting inclusive education: School concerns.* London: Routledge Falmer.

Delamont, S. and Atkinson, P. (1995) *Fighting familiarity: Essays on education and ethnography.* Cresskill, NJ: Hampton Press.

DES (1981) *Education Act.* London: DES.

DfE (2011) *Support and aspiration: A new approach to special educational needs and disability: A consultation.* Norwich: TSO.

DfE (2022) *Opportunity for all: Strong schools with great teachers for your child.* London: HMSO.

DfE/DoH (2014) *Special Educational Needs and Disability Code of Practice for 0 to 25 year olds.* London: TSO.

DfE/DoH (2015) *Special Educational Needs and Disability Code of Practice for 0 to 25 year olds* (available from https://www.gov.uk/government/publications/send-code-of-practice-0-to-25).

DfE/DoHSC (2022) *SEND review: Right support, right place, right time* (available from https://www.gov.uk/government/consultations/send-review-right-support-right-place-right-time).

DfE/DoHSC (2023) *Special Educational Needs and Disabilities (SEND) and Alternative Provision Improvement Plan – Right support, right place, right time.* London: HMSO.

EEF (2018a) *Making best use of teaching assistants.* London: EEF.

EEF (2018b) *Working with parents to support children's learning.* London: EEF.

EEF (2019) *Putting evidence to work – A school's guide to implementation.* London: EEF.

EEF (2020) *SEN in mainstream schools guidance report.* London: EEF.

EEF (2021) *Effective professional development.* London: EEF.

Ekins, A. (2015) *The changing face of special educational needs impact and implications for SENCOs, teachers and their schools* (2nd Edition). Abingdon: Routledge.

Ekins, A. (2017) *Reconsidering inclusion – Sustaining and building inclusive practices in schools.* Abingdon: Routledge.

Ekins, A. and Grimes, P. (2009) *Inclusion: Developing an effective whole school approach.* Maidenhead: Open University Press.

Fullan, M. (2020) *Leading in a culture of change* (2nd Edition). Hoboken, NJ: Jossey-Bass.

Hellawell, B. (2019) *Understanding & challenging the SEND code of practice.* London: SAGE Publications Ltd.

House of Commons Education Committee (2019) *Special Educational Needs and Disabilities.* London: House of Commons.

House of Commons Select Committee (2006) *Special Educational Needs: Third report of session 2005–2006.* London: TSO.

Kugelmass, J. (2004) *The inclusive school: Sustaining, equity and standards.* New York, NY: Teachers College Press.

Leithwood, K., Harris, A. and Hopkins, D. (2008) 'Seven strong claims about successful school leadership'. *School Leadership and Management* 28(1), 27–42.

NAO (2019) *Support for pupils with special educational needs and disabilities in England.* London: House of Commons.

Noddings, N. (2012) *Philosophy of education* (3rd Edition). Boulder, CO: Westview Press.

Norwich, B. (2007) *Dilemmas of difference, inclusion and disability: International perspectives and future directions.* Oxon: Routledge.

OFSTED (2010) *The SEN and disability review: A statement is not enough.* Manchester: Crown Copyright.

UNESCO (2021) *Reaching out to all learners – A resource pack for supporting inclusion and equity in education.* Geneva: International Bureau of Education.

Warnock, M. (1978) *Warnock report: Special Educational Needs, report of the Committee of Enquiry into the education of handicapped children and young people.* London: HMSO.

2 Understanding SEN/SEND

> In this chapter, we critically examine and explore the following key aspects of SEN/SEND:
>
> - Reductionist interpretations
> - Reviewing the definition
> - Medical and social models
> - New National Standards for SEND
> - National standardisation and digital systems for EHCPs
> - SEN Support and EHCPs
> - Embedding Continuing Professional Development (CPD) to develop understanding of SEND
> - The four areas of SEN/SEND
> - Effective support strategies

Key issues*

Whilst this is a book focused on Special Educational Needs and Disability (SEND) and the effective leadership of SEND within our schools, we do not see the concept of SEND as a simple one. Rather, we see it as a deeply problematic and interpretable concept which can conflict with broader principles of inclusion and inclusive principles.

We remain committed to ensuring that the needs of children with SEND are understood and met through inclusive practices and this chapter therefore explores and highlights the challenges inherent in the concept of SEND, before then providing guidance on effective ways forward.

The concept of Special Educational Needs (SEN) was first introduced in 1978 by the Warnock Report. Before that time, children with a range of different needs, from mild difficulties with speech and language to more profound and complex needs were deemed 'ineducable' and were often denied access to an educational setting (Warnock, 1978; Warnock, 2005).

The introduction of a concept of special educational needs was therefore initially a positive and significant step in moving thinking and practice beyond the dismissal of the rights of a significant proportion of the population to have an education and placed the focus of thinking and planning for children with a range of learning differences into the school setting.

Whilst the concept initially referred largely to the simple 'integration' of children into education settings (DES, 1981), gradually over time the concept and practices have evolved,

---

* Due to the changing terminology of SEN/SEND in government legislation over the decades, in this chapter we have used the appropriate version of the terminology to reflect the context and key issues we are writing about.

DOI: 10.4324/9781003033554-2

14 *Understanding SEN/SEND*

if not fully certainly to some extent, into a deeper understanding of inclusion and children's right to an inclusive education.

However, despite the term SEN (and more recently SEND) being embedded within education policy and practice for over four decades, the term remains a problematic and interpretable concept, with a lack of shared consistent understanding and meaning. Three key issues are central to this, and will be explored in this chapter:

1 Problems with reductionist interpretations of SEND
2 Challenges with embedding clear and consistent thresholds for identifying what SEND actually means and to which needs it should apply
3 The need for shared understanding about the different levels of SEN/SEND and consistent expectations about the implications for the levels of provision that are required to meet those needs.

The discussions in this chapter also links closely with those that are developed in Chapter 6 relating to the Identification Dilemma (Norwich, 2007) and inherent challenges to the development of an inclusive society and education system from a practice which emphasises 'difference' based on expectations of a false sense of what is 'normal' and that those who do not fit within that artificial concept are therefore different and thus labelled as having SEND (see Chapter 6 for further discussion).

Current policy/research context

The problems with a reductionist view of SEND

Whilst SEN/SEND is a concept now firmly embedded in our education system, it is not a concept that is unproblematic and that should be simply accepted without question. Indeed, the label itself – reduced to the acronym SEN/SEND is deeply problematic, with discourse across schools largely focusing on the acronym without deep understanding of the meaning behind the label. The NASUWT (2018) therefore identified difficulties with the 'general nature of the information provided. For example; 'often no more information is given other than "*SEN*". No information available as to the specific SEN or strategies' (NASUWT, 2018: 6).

SEN/SEND is therefore largely referred to by the acronym which reduces the impact and understanding of exactly what we are referring to by using the acronym. SEN/SEND refers to us making a judgement that a child has 'special educational needs'. This is a significant judgement to make, but is often not respected as such when the term is reduced to a simplistic label' 'SEN/SEND'.

Using the reductionist acronyms of 'SEN/SEND' also reduces discussions and suggests a homogeneity which is not the case for pupils with SEND, who have very different and individual profiles of needs and strengths. As the DfE (2017: 15) identifies 'children and young people with SEND show a huge variety of individual needs, and it is not normally useful to assume that "all" those with a particular need will require the same type of support'. They note the advice of Mitchell (2014 – cited in DfE, 2017: 15) that any approach should be based on 'develop[ing] a repertoire of such strategies nested within your own philosophy … professional wisdom, and above all knowledge of the characteristics and needs of your students'.

Linked to this is also the need to ensure a clear focus on the pupil as an individual, rather than just a label. Whilst there are separate very important perspectives on the use of identity versus person first labels for some communities – e.g. autistic people and disabled people, within school, we need to avoid the homogenous labelling and grouping together of groups of pupils with very different needs and abilities. Practice in schools should therefore emphasise the person first, with the use of SEN/SEND as a clarifying feature rather than the descriptor – e.g. 'pupils with SEND' rather than 'SEND pupils' (EEF, 2020). Such an approach prioritises inclusive values and serves as a helpful reminder and prompt that pupils with SEN/SEND are children first, no matter how complex their needs and presentation may be at times, and therefore need to be understood developmentally as children rather than as a completely separate group.

Challenging reductionist interpretations of the concept of SEN/SEND also need to acknowledge that SEN/SEND is not an absolute fixed concept. Rather it needs to be recognised and understood as a social construct – one which is socially imagined and reimagined and not one where there is a clear and consistent diagnostic basis.

We saw this clearly in practice with the implementation of the SEN and Disability Code of Practice (DfE/DoH, 2014) where 'overnight' children who were previously on the SEND Register at School Action no longer met the criteria for the new SEND levels of SEN Support and EHCP and were therefore no longer defined as having SEND or included on the SEND Register.

The needs, including the support needs of those children, had not changed overnight with the implementation of the SEN and Disability Code of Practice (DfE/DoH, 2014) and new levels of SEND, yet many pupils then no longer had 'SEND'.

Currently, we are seeing a similar shift in thresholds around SEND, with needs that were previously considered more severe and complex now being seen to be more common and to be expected within the mainstream context. The shift in what is considered to be 'predictable needs' and those that are considered 'exceptional needs' is therefore changing, currently without a clear framework around those shifting thresholds.

As we will explore in more detail in Chapter 6, we do also need a critical approach to examining why we have a system that is based on a need to 'label' and highlight differences, rather than celebrate diversity.

Understanding of and consistent thresholds for identifying SEND

Ensuring that everyone within the school community has a clear understanding of the different levels and areas of SEND and the implications of them for developing practices which support children with SEN/SEND is essential. Yet, it is not as straightforward as we may hope from the simplistic way that it is set out in the SEN and Disability Code of Practice (DfE/DoH, 2015). One of the greatest challenges in the SEND system therefore is, and always has been, embedding a consistent shared understanding of what the term SEND actually means and who it should be applied to. As respondents to the NASUWT Survey (2018) noted – there remain concerns about inconsistent understandings of thresholds for what needs the concept and term 'SEND' actually applies to.

Over 40 years on from the introduction of the term SEN by the Warnock Report (Warnock, 1978), we are still using the same broad definition set out in the 1981 Education Act, despite the significant societal changes that have occurred since that time (House of Commons Select Committee, 2006).

> **Definition of SEN**
>
> A child or young person has SEN if they have a learning difficulty or disability which calls for special educational provision to be made for him or her.
>
> A child of compulsory school age or a young person has a learning difficulty or disability if he or she:
>
> - has a significantly greater difficulty in learning than the majority of others of the same age, or
> - has a disability which prevents or hinders him or her from making use of facilities of a kind generally provided for others of the same age in mainstream schools or mainstream post-16 institutions.
>
> For children aged two or more, special educational provision is educational or training provision that is additional to or different from that made generally for other children or young people of the same age by mainstream schools, maintained nursery schools, mainstream post-16 institutions or by relevant early years providers. For a child under two years of age, special educational provision means educational provision of any kind.
>
> (DfE/DoH, 2015: 15–16)

Since the term SEN was originally introduced in 1981, problems have evolved as a result of the circuitous definition of SEN that is used, which is too open to interpretation and which can therefore mean different things to different people (House of Commons Select Committee, 2006; OFSTED, 2010; DfE, 2011; NASUWT, 2018; House of Commons Education Committee, 2019).

The definition of SEN/SEND that is currently used, rather than providing clarity and consistency, continues to cause confusion due to differences in understanding and interpretation depending on the context within which it is applied.

We therefore currently do not have a clear threshold or understanding of what that 'greater difficulty in learning than the majority of others of the same age' actually looks like in practice and therefore as a result, decisions about identifying and labelling SEN/SEND can become too contextually impacted.

For example, the threshold of what may signify a 'greater difficulty in learning than the majority of others of the same age' may be significantly different in different schools due to the nature of the needs of their cohort as a whole.

Whilst we have basically had the same definition of SEN/SEND for over 40 years, the interpretation and application of the definition has shifted over time and different government priorities between largely medical-based models of SEND and more social-based models of SEN, and, to an extent, back towards a more medical diagnosis-led model of SEND through the focus on identification of SEND 'from birth' that was originally mooted in the DfE Green Paper – Support & Aspiration (DfE, 2011).

Medical models of SEND primarily emphasise a diagnosis led model of practice – one which is focused on identifying a need/deficit within an individual and labelling that need/deficit.

The term and concept of SEN (and later SEND) was an attempt to move away from a focus just on difficulties or disabilities, and into a broader understanding of the child as a whole where the child is 'seen not in terms of a particular disability which a child may be judged to have, but in relation to everything about him, his abilities as well as his disabilities – indeed all factors which have a bearing on his educational progress' (DES, 1978: 37).

Social models of SEND have aimed to move on from that deficit-led model into one that recognises and acknowledges the impact of contextual factors (the environment, relationships and interactions, the curriculum) on the barriers to learning and participation that a child may experience. Social models of SEND focus on the responsibility of society to identify and remove barriers to learning and participation, rather than just seeing the 'problem' as being a 'within-child' problem.

Too often, the term SEN is given the status of a diagnosis, yet without the rigour and clear threshold criteria that a diagnosis affords.

Whilst we completely recognise the challenges of implementing clear threshold criteria for a concept such as SEND, where the needs are experienced so individually by children with SEND, some form of consistent national framework and criteria which provides examples of the type of level of need and support requirements to meet the threshold of SEND would be helpful and may address the continuing issues of inconsistency.

The DfE/DoHSC (2023: 5) have acknowledged these challenges and have now planned the introduction of 'new evidenced-based National Standards [which] will improve early identification of needs and intervention, and set out clear expectations for the types of support that should be ordinarily available in mainstream settings'.

The National Standards will therefore 'set clear and ambitious expectations for what good looks like in identifying and meeting needs, and clarify who is responsible for delivering provision and from which budgets, across the 0–25 system' (DfE/DoHSC, 2023: 8), thereby hopefully improving the consistency of understanding and practice in relation to what 'SEND' is and how the needs of pupils with SEND are to be supported.

Yet, whilst the proposed National Standards (DfE/DoHSC, 2023) will hopefully provide some consistency and shared understanding about the different predictable and exceptional levels of need, even if the definition of SEND was more fully defined, the concept and labelling of pupils with SEN would still be problematic as, as the EEF (2021: 5) identify, 'SEND is not a fixed or permanent characteristic …. Pupil's development is not linear. As pupils age, the complexity of their needs will change. Some pupils might not have SEND to begin with but will develop SEND as they mature. Others who are considered to have SEND at the beginning of their lives may no longer have these needs later in life'.

In addition to clarity about the thresholds of SEND and expectations about levels of provision, the SEND and Alternative Provision Improvement Plan (DfE/DoHSC, 2023: 37) also identifies a focus on improving the consistency and quality of the statutory paperwork around EHCPs. The government therefore plan to:

Standardise the templates and processes around EHCPs to improve consistency and best practice, improving experiences for families and children and young people seeking plans

Digitise EHCPs, to reduce the burden of administrative process in the system, improve the experience and satisfaction of parents, carers and professionals and improve our ability to monitor the health of the SEND system.

(DfE/DoHSC, 2023: 37)

The new EHCP format is planned to utilise a digital system as the DfE/DoHSC (2023: 38) identify that: 'digital systems can deliver better experiences for both families and professionals and enable them to continuously improve their services – focusing staff time on working with families rather than managing bureaucracy'.

Whilst there is therefore a commitment to review and standardise the EHCP system and formats, there is also recognition of the need to reflect existing differences in 'circumstances and the needs of local communities' (DfE/DoHSC, 2023: 38) and the fact that the needs of children with EHCPs are complex and that therefore a standardised EHCP format should not compromise the individualised planning needed to truly understand, reflect and meet the needs of the individual.

Understanding of different levels of SEN/SEND and expectations for levels of provision

Our current SEN and Disability Code of Practice (DfE/DoH, 2015) identifies two levels of SEN:

- SEN Support
- SEN with an Education, Health and Care Plan (EHCP).

National data (https://explore-education-statistics.service.gov.uk/find-statistics/special-educational-needs-in-england/2021-22) does show that the numbers of pupils identified as having SEND has been rising over recent years, following the initial drop in 2015–2016 to respond to the new levels of SEN/SEND in the new SEN and Disability Code of Practice (DfE/DoH, 2015) (see Table 2.1).

Table 2.1 National SEND data

	2014–2015	2015–2016	2016–2017	2017–2018	2018–2019	2019–2020	2020–2021	2021–2022
SEN Support	12.6%	11.6%	11.6%	11.7%	11.9%	12.1%	12.2%	12.6%
EHCPs	2.8%	2.8%	2.8%	2.9%	3.0%	3.3%	3.7%	4.0%
Total SEND	15.4%	14.4.%	14.4%	14.6%	14.9%	15.4%	15.9%	16.6%

Source: (DfE, 2022).

Despite the system around levels of SEN having been simplified – from the five different levels of the original SEN Code of Practice (DfE, 1994) to just two different levels, possibly in order to 'reduce the number of children who were labelled as having special educational needs' (House of Commons Education Committee, 2019: 32), yet there are still challenges of understanding and interpretation of these levels, and this continues to cause confusion and inconsistency across the country.

Whilst pupils with an EHCP will have gone through a statutory assessment process that formally identifies their special educational needs and the statutory provision and outcomes that are required to support them through each stage of their education, concerns continue to be raised about practices in relation to supporting pupils at SEN Support. As the House of Commons Education Committee (2019: 45) identify, 'the definition of support is too fluid, and many schools are tempted to keep the level of support low due to the lack of funding'.

There remain concerns that processes and systems to support pupils at SEN Support have been 'neglected' (House of Commons Education Committee, 2019: 15) with low-quality and inconsistent practices in relation to provision at SEN Support as a result of the intense pressure to transfer Statements into Education Health and Care Plans. This, the House of Commons Education Committee (2019: 15) identified, drives down parental confidence in the SEND system and has led to 'an increase in parents applying for Education Health and Care Plans because they appear to be the only way to open doors for access to support that has become rationed and difficult to access'. This, in turn has 'led to an increase in applications, which has further strained a system already under pressure from the introduction of Education Health and Care Plans and the transition process which was much more complex than had been imagined' (House of Commons Education Committee, 2019: 15).

As Chris Harrison, the Director of SEND4Change, told the Education Committee, as 'SEN Support often does not include input from health and social care, … EHCPs [become] more "magnetic" to parents. He suggested that there is a lack of consistency around what is provided for pupils at SEN Support, and that if parents saw a plan with consistent features and some rigour, they would be less inclined to request an EHCP. Local authority representatives agreed that parents seeing EHCPs as the only way to meet their child's needs was concerning' (House of Commons Education Committee, 2019: 45).

Yet, even if EHCP's are seen as the 'magic wand' or magic solution to parents/carers to ensure that their child's needs are understood and supported, EHCPs remain far from effective in their development and implementation.

The quality of EHCPs, after all of the time that it has taken to transfer them from Statements of SEN to the new Education, Health and Care Plans has therefore been seen to be a cause for concern (House of Commons Education Committee, 2019). Again, it is concerning that the wealth of evidence generated through the SEN Pathfinder Projects (2011–2014) was not utilised to immediately provide clear consistent examples of the formats to be used, as this could have reduced the amount of time that has been wasted on the development of vastly differing interpretations and quality of the statutory processes and formats.

Concerningly, the House of Commons Education Committee (2019: 47) identified that:

New advice was disregarded, and that the contents of existing documents (such as statements or reports) were copied and pasted into a new document. We heard that there was no quality assurance, and that there was a lack of specificity in reports, outcomes and provision. We heard that local authorities used out of date assessments and information and named provision that bore no relation to need. We were told that some young people lost provision or support that had been detailed in their Statements, or that local authorities attempted to remove it during the transfer process.

Concerns have consistently been raised (House of Commons Education Committee, 2019; and OFSTED & CQC Inspections of local authorities) about the ability of local authorities to rewrite and update the EHCPs, leading to poor quality and school staff having to spend an inordinate amount of time (still) rewriting and updating EHCPs so that they are accurate, meaningful and fully reflect the needs of the child.

As we have already discussed, it is hoped that the new National Standards, as well as the standardised digital EHCP format may help to address the inconsistencies in understanding, interpretation of national guidance and, fundamentally, the quality of provision and statutory documentation (DfE/DoHSC, 2023).

Planning for practice

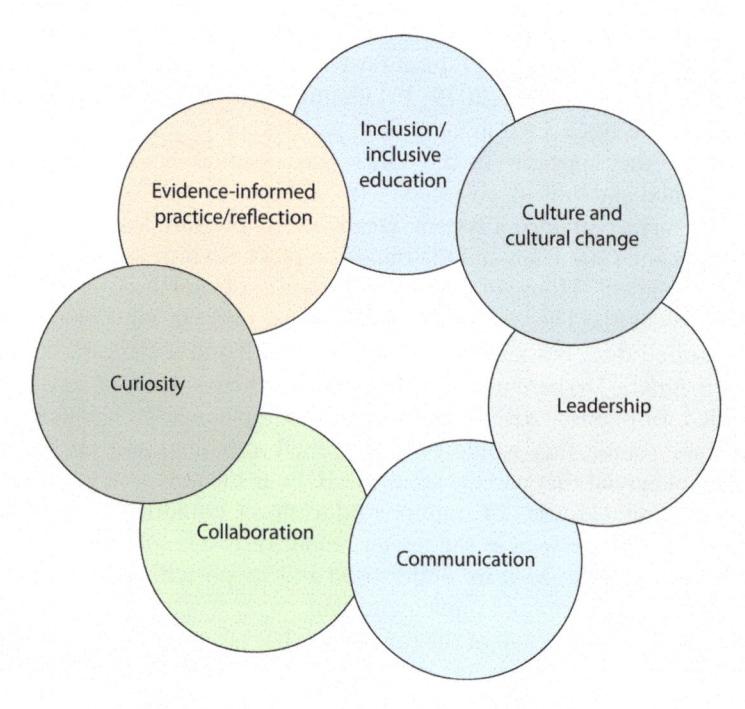

Figure 2.1 Key principles model

Developing and embedding shared, and nuanced, understandings of SEND as a problematic and social construct, rather than as a deficit, medical-based label is essential in our school settings in order to take forward the respectful, dignified approach to meeting SEND that is referred to in the SEND and Alternative Provision Improvement Plan (DfE/DoHSC, 2023).

To do this, will require effective *leadership* of SEND, based on *inclusive values* and understandings, meaningful *communication and collaboration* with others, *curiosity* to expose and challenge/question embedded assumptions and *evidence-informed* approaches.

Tackling reductionist interpretations of SEND

One of the most fundamental issues to address within schools is how to appropriately and effectively identify SEND so that this directly tackles reductionist interpretations of SEND. This needs to start with developing a clear and shared understanding of what SEND is. The first step is to introduce an open dialogue about what people think SEND means and how/why they think this. This helps to introduce *curiosity* to challenge existing and embedded assumptions and beliefs. The following Case Study provides an example of how this can be achieved.

Case Study – Exploring SEND

Context

The activity described in this Case Study has been used in a variety of situations as a really quick way to encourage individual and collective reflection about what the term SEND actually means. It has therefore been used with a range of different groups of people, including Initial Teacher Education (ITE) and Postgraduate Certificate in Education (PGCE) students; teachers; SENCOs; support staff; governors as a way to enhance shared understanding and expose any embedded assumptions.

Activity

- Provide participants with individual post-it notes
- Provide the prompt – 'What does SEND mean to me?'
- Ask the participants to write down the first three words or short phrases that came to mind when asked what 'SEND' means to them
- Tell the participants to not record their name on the piece of paper
- Give the participants one minute to record their responses
- Collect in the post-it note responses and collate using a word cloud or similar.

Notes

Providing a very quick response time of one minute is important in this activity as the activity is about capturing people's immediate 'gut feelings' and responses, rather than prepared 'right' answers.

Review and discussion of the words and phrases that are shared, helps to start a reflective discussion about the implications of the different interpretations of SEND on the effective development of a shared understanding of SEND within the school context.

Issues such as the focus on 'difficulty', 'support', 'difference' can all be identified and supportively challenged through an open discussion of the terms that had been collectively chosen and used.

Different terminology relating to inclusive principles, the concept of 'diversity' and 'practices relating to' 'labelling' can also be explored.

The inclusion of the phrase 'Special Educational Needs' in the responses is also a really interesting point for discussion, as it helps to encourage participants to reflect on what 'SEN/SEND' actually means. All too often in our discussions today, the term is abbreviated and used without thinking, and taking time to reflect on what it actually means – that the child has a 'Special Educational Need' is really important in developing people's understanding.

22 *Understanding SEN/SEND*

> **Reflective Activity**
>
> - What three words or short phrases would you use to define 'SEND'?
> - Review and reflect on them – what does this say to you about your own current understanding of the concept of 'SEND'?
> - Does this expose any reductionist interpretations of SEND?
> - How could this be addressed?
> - Think about ways the staff in your setting currently think about SEND
> - Are there ways that you could use or develop the activity above for use in your own school setting?

Understanding of and consistent thresholds for identifying SEND

> **Reflective Activity**
>
> Look again at the definition of SEN provided earlier.
> Read the statements slowly and carefully.
>
> - What do they actually mean?
> - How do they help clear and consistent identification of which children have SEN/SEND and at what time?
> - What, for example, does a 'greater difficulty in learning than the majority of others of the same age' actually mean? What is that greater difficulty, and against which peers is the judgement applied?
> - How is the term understood and applied in your school setting?
> - Is it consistently understood and applied?
> - Do you think that there is consistency across schools in your local area? Nationally?

The SEN and Disability Code of Practice (DfE/DoH, 2015) identifies four different Areas of Need:

- Cognition and Learning
- Communication and Interaction
- Social Emotional and Mental Health difficulties
- Sensory and/or physical needs

> **Reflective Activity**
>
> - How confident are you that all members of staff in your school setting (senior leaders, teachers and support staff) know about and understand the different levels of SEND and the different SEND Areas of Need?
> - How are decisions made about whether a child should be identified as needing SEN Support?

- What criteria/threshold is used for making those judgements?
- Where have the criteria/threshold come from?
- How is understanding about the different Areas of Need used to support planning for meeting the individual and collective needs of children with SEND within a class, year group or school cohort?

Case Study – Understanding the Four Areas of Need

Context

A Multi-Academy Trust comprising both primary and secondary schools.

As part of a key focus on SEND, staff within each school were asked to write down their response to 'What are the SEND Areas of Need?'

Despite high levels of focus on SEND and the four SEND Areas of Need within the schools, it was very interesting, and concerning, to see that very few members of staff could actually correctly name the four SEND Areas of Need (Cognition and Learning; Communication and Interaction; Social Emotional and Mental Health; Sensory and/or physical needs). Whilst many people were able to name 'types' of SEND – e.g. Dyslexia, ASC, ADHD – they were unable to automatically relate this to the four SEND Areas of Need from the SEN and Disability Code of Practice (DfE/DoH, 2015).

Interestingly, it also highlighted further misconceptions and embedded assumptions about SEND – with some people identifying aspects such as Medical Needs or English as an Additional Language as a SEND Area of Need.

This very simple and extremely quick activity therefore showed a really clear need to be even more explicit in the training and development work with staff to ensure that this important concept is fully understood and embedded in practice with everyone, ensuring that everyone would be able to confidently fulfil all of their statutory responsibilities for SEND (see also discussions in Chapter 4).

This is therefore a good example of a really quick and easy activity, taking just one minute to complete, to encourage individual review and reflection and then shared meaning making and understanding of central concepts that need to be embedded in practice.

To develop understanding of the four SEND Areas of Need further, the EEF (2020) provides a really useful model for the four SEN Areas of Need identified in the SEN and Disability Code of Practice (DfE/DoH, 2015), reflecting that categorising needs is not as simple as purely identifying one need type. Every child with SEND will have a slightly different presentation of needs, reflecting their individual differences, and often pupils with SEND have overlapping or co-occurring needs.

The model in Figure 2.2 (EEF, 2020: 7) is therefore a useful one to use to help to develop our own understanding, and the understanding of other staff members in the school setting about the different areas of SEND:

SPECIAL EDUCATIONAL NEEDS IN MAINSTREAM SCHOOLS
Plotting overlapping needs for pupils with SEND

The terms used within SEND are not universally agreed, either within legislation or by the individuals with those needs. However, the following terms and categorisations come largely from the SEND Code of Practice (2015) and are therefore a useful guide. This document is not an attempt to list all types of need, merely to provide a starting point to understanding the breadth of needs that fall within SEND.

Cognition and learning

This area includes moderate learning difficulties (MLD), severe learning difficulties (SLD), profound and multiple learning difficulties (PMLD) and specific learning difficulties (SpLD).

PMLD is when a person has a severe learning disability and other disabilities that significantly affect their ability to communicate and be independent. Someone with PMLD may have difficulties seeing, hearing, speaking and moving. They may have complex health and social care needs due to these or other conditions.

SpLDs include: dyslexia (difficulties with reading and spelling), dyscalculia (difficulties with number and calculation), and dyspraxia* (or 'developmental coordination disorder' - difficulties with motor planning). People with one or more SpLDs may have a 'spiky profile' of attainment, with areas of strength and areas of need.

Sensory and/or physical needs

This area includes sensory impairments, such as visual impairment (VI), hearing impairment (HI) and multi-sensory impairment, as well as physical conditions such as cerebral palsy. These children will usually access support from a specific local team, which may be a combination of education and health services.

These children do not necessarily have difficulties with their cognitive functioning, which may be average or above average.

Communication and interaction

This area includes speech, language and communication needs (SLCN), such as Developmental Language Disorder (DLD). A learner with SLCN may have difficulties with speech production, with understanding language, with using language to express themselves or with a combination of all three. It also includes difficulties with the social use of language.

Children with a diagnosis of Autistic Spectrum Condition, including Asperger's Syndrome**, will have needs in this area.

Children who find communication and interaction challenging may or may not also have difficulties with cognitive functioning.

Social, emotional and mental health

Challenging behaviours are displayed for many reasons, which may be indicative of underlying mental health difficulties (such as anxiety or depression) or emotional issues (such as attachment needs). Some children have conditions such as ADHD (Attention Deficit Hyperactivity Disorder) or ADD*** (Attention Deficit Disorder), which may affect their behaviours in school.

It is crucial to look for the underlying causes of any behaviour and/or emotional state, and aim to support these, rather than just dealing with the presenting behaviour.

For some children with SEMH needs, the nature of these difficulties will affect their successful access to the curriculum, either temporarily or in the long term.

*With many types of SEND, a learner's difficulties will not be restricted to one area. A dyspraxic learner's difficulties in school may overlap into 'Sensory and/or Physical needs'; for example SEND Code of Practice (2015) classification is being used in this case.
**Though no longer recognised as a term in the International Classification of Diseases manual (ICD-11), some children will identify as having Asperger's, hence its inclusion here.
***ADD is no longer recognised as a term within the ICD-11 manual, though it is mentioned in the SEND Code of Practice (2015).

This resource supports the *Special Educational Needs in Mainstream Schools* guidance report

Education Endowment Foundation

Figure 2.2 EEF – SEND Areas of Need
Source: Accessed 4.1.2023: https://d2tic4wvo1iusb.cloudfront.net/eef-guidance-reports/send/EEF-Plotting-overlapping-needs-for-pupils-with-SEND.pdf?v=1672852715

This model is helpful in understanding the four Areas of Need (Cognition and Learning; Communication and Interaction; Social Emotional and Mental Health; Sensory and/or physical) not as completely separate and distinct areas, but instead as overlapping areas which will impact each individual in differing ways. This helps us to view the child more fully as an individual rather than in relation to a simplistic category of need. Models such as the Bronfenbrenner Model (EEF, 2020) also supports the development of our shift away from a simplistic 'medical model' approach to understanding SEN, which is simply focused on diagnoses, into a more nuanced social model of SEN – which recognises the impact and influence of contextual factors on a child's development – see Chapter 6.

Embedding the EEF (2020) model of the overlapping needs for pupils with SEND (see Figure 2.2) will also hopefully help to move thinking from a traditional reductionist model of homogeneous needs and deficit difficulties. However, more does need to be done to positively address understandings and any embedded misconceptions about SEND. Whilst the challenges around the lack of quality training for teachers are recognised, with the DfE (2017: 14) identifying that, teachers 'receive minimal information through initial teacher training to fully understand the concept of SEN', it is therefore vital (as we will explore further in Chapter 5) that we address this in our schools through a whole-school approach to inclusive practice and pedagogy and prioritise support and training with our staff to address this.

The challenge of when and how to fit in the direct support and development that staff need to be able to better understand the needs of individual pupils and have strategies to support them is one that needs to be carefully considered.

At a time when directed Continuing Professional Development (CPD)/professional learning time is often at a premium in schools, with so many competing priorities, it is helpful to reflect on ways that you are able to provide information in accessible and effective ways to staff to ensure that everyone is kept up to date about any changing needs of key pupils.

Reflective Activity

- How many bespoke SEND training/development sessions have been provided in your school setting?
- How effective have they been?
- How do you know?
- How are updates about individual pupil needs and key strategies communicated effectively to all staff?
- How are developments in understandings about SEND and different Areas of Need supported through effective CPD and development opportunities?
- How effective has that been?
- What more is needed?
- How could this be taken forward?

Consider looking at the EEF (2021) Effective Professional Development Guidance Report to support your thinking and understanding about the most effective ways to embed professional learning opportunities for your staff.

Also consider the following Case Study, which provides details of one schools approach to developing a range of different opportunities for staff to be supported to increase their knowledge and understanding of the needs of individual pupils and SEND Areas of Need.

- Are there any aspects from this case study that would be useful for you to take forward in your own practice?
- How could you do that? What would it look like in your own school setting?

Case Study – Delivering Quality CPD to Support Staff Understanding of SEND

Anthony Walmsley

Context

In order to deliver quality CPD in a hectic, busy school environment the SEND team had to devise a way of supporting staff in a quick and effective manner. We had a number of barriers to overcome namely time restrictions, staff knowledge of SEND presentations in pupils and the level of engagement of staff in the process of changing their mindset of SEND.

Implementation

We decided that staff would need a greater 'pull' to the sessions than 'push' to ensure full engagement in the CDP. With this in mind, we designed Tea and Toast Tuesdays, Wednesday Workshops and CPD shorts. All of these sessions were planned as very short (15–30 minute), practical inputs with resources and information shared that could be immediately be utilised by staff and put into practice. They sit outside the longer directed CPD/Professional Learning sessions for staff, but we hoped that as they were so practically focused and brief, staff would engage with them and find them useful.

Tea and Toast Tuesday sessions were introduced as brief before-school inputs focused on providing key information about individual pupils – particularly those with more complex needs. We produced a summary of the pupils profile of needs as a handout given directly to the staff who taught those pupils. To encourage positive engagement, these brief inputs were delivered in the staffroom and accompanied by tea and toast.

In addition to this we realised that staff needed specific training on understanding and supporting with particular needs in the classroom. This developed into SEND Wednesday Workshop sessions which was a solution-based approach to strategies that can be employed in the classroom to support pupils.

These SEND Wednesday Workshop sessions were brief after-school sessions, accompanied by tea/coffee and a cookie. Whilst the sessions were planned to last 30 minutes (3.30–4.00 pm), in reality, many colleagues took the opportunity to stay longer to continue to discuss the aspects that had been shared, and work with the SEND team to develop their own resources and strategies to implement in practice in relation to the Area of Need that had been discussed.

Staff were also provided with a certificate of attendance to CPD on each session. This allowed staff to show they had participated in additional CPD for their appraisal and was an additional 'pull' factor for attendance when the school calendar became incredibly busy for everyone.

In order to ensure that the sessions that we planned met the needs of our staff, we surveyed the staff knowledge of SEND needs and presentations in the classroom and this information then helped us to target the training to the staff requirements.

Impact

From those sessions we were able to identify that the greatest impact was when staff were able to see practical strategies with working examples of successful applications with students, they were able to identify with. Staff feedback highlighted that the most productive sessions were ones where they could see how they could personalise the strategies to their classroom environment and relate it to specific pupils. They also found sessions more engaging when they could see how a 'school directive' related to their own teacher responsibilities rather than 'just another directive from the senior team'.

When staff could see how non-engagement in the feedback process for provision plan support or record of outcome reviews negatively impacted on their own classroom behaviour management strategies they engaged more readily and positively. An understanding of the 'Assess, Plan, Do, Review' process meant that staff acknowledged their role in supporting pupils with SEND. They felt that quality practical advice through the training initiatives benefited their own pedagogy and therefore allowed them to show high-quality inclusive teaching approaches.

If the teachers could see how they could improve their teaching and outcomes for pupils in practical ways, they were much more engaged and invested in the training initiatives.

Understanding of different levels of SEN and expectations for levels of provision

Whilst we have acknowledged the challenges of 'labelling' children and their needs and a reductionist approach to SEND, it is important that an evidence-informed approach is taken to reviewing effective strategies and interventions that can be used to provide support for different Areas of Need. Here, **evidence-informed** and **reflective practices** needs to be prioritised, providing opportunities for all members of the school community, not just the SENCO, to engage with research and evidence-bases about approaches that work to support different needs. This needs to be linked to the changing cohorts and patterns of need that have been identified in the school context so that planning for provision and needs is fully needs led, rather than based on outdated assumptions about what has worked (see also discussions in Chapters 6 and 7).

The DfE (2017) Rapid Evidence Assessment Research Report and the EEF Guidance Reports and materials provide some very accessible and useful information to support review and reflection of evidence-informed approaches to meeting needs.

Reflective Activity

Take some time to review the overview below of some of the evidence-informed strategies, approaches and provisions from the DfE Rapid Evidence Assessment Research Report (DfE, 2017) and EEF Guidance Reports (2019–2021).

RAG-rate the strategies and provisions that are listed to identify which are already fully embedded (Green); in place but not yet consistent (Amber); not used (Red) in your school context currently (Table 2.2).

Consider ways that you could implement this to support the development of practices in your own setting:

- What are the key action points/key principles that you need to consider?
- How can you implement this and take it forward?

Table 2.2 Evidence-informed strategies by Area of Need

Broad Area of Need	Key evidence-informed strategies/provisions	RAG* rating – what is in place in your school setting currently?
Cognition and Learning	**Reading and spelling differences:** • Individual or small group teaching • Word mats, key word lists • Strategies to develop enjoyment and build confidence	
	Concentration differences: • Consider seating plans • Fidget toys/tools • Breaking tasks into manageable chunks • Consider language used and how this impacts on the pupils ability to concentrate and attend to instructions	
Communication and Interaction	**Speech, language and communication differences:** • Referral to a Speech and Language Therapist • Use of language modification techniques • Visual aids • Use of assistive technology	
Social Emotional and Mental Health	**Anxiety:** • Use of a 'trusted' or 'key' adult provision • Use of Safe space • Meditation • Breathing exercises • Referral to outside professionals, e.g. CAMHS/ChYPMHS or Educational Psychologists	
	Challenging behaviour • Refer to and use school's behaviour policy • Focus on understanding the causes of behaviour • Remove distraction • De-escalation techniques • Safe spaces • Building positive relationships	
Sensory and/or physical needs	**Fine motor control differences:** • Chunky pencils/specialist pens • Activities to build fine motor skills – e.g. threading beads, Lego • Use of assistive technology	

* Red = Not evident in practice; Amber = some aspects evident in practice; Green = Fully evident in practice.

Further examples of evidence-informed interventions that can be used and developed within the school setting are provided in Chapter 8.

Concluding comments and reflections

The terms SEN/SEND are well-embedded into our professional discourses in schools but yet, as we have seen in this chapter the concept is not a simple one, it is fraught with inconsistency and subjectivity which impacts on the consistent understanding and application of practices to meet the needs of all pupils.

As this book reinforces, at the heart of all practice must be an inclusive understanding and appreciation of the individual, rather than a simplistic and reductionist following of distinct strategies linked to separate diagnoses – but to do that requires a deeper understanding of the concept and problems inherent in the concept of SEND by everyone within the school setting.

Individual Reflection

- What new information/learning have you gained from this chapter?
- What are your key reflections?
- What are your next steps/actions as a result?

References

DES (1978)) *Special Educational Needs* (The Warnock Report). London: HMSO
DES (1981) *Education Act*. London: DES.
DfE (1994) *Special Educational Needs Code of Practice*. London: DfE.
DfE (2011) *Support and aspiration: A new approach to special educational needs and disability: A consultation*. Norwich: TSO.
DfE (2017) *SEN Support: A rapid evidence assessment research report*. Coventry: Coventry University.
DfE (2022) *Special educational needs in England: National statistics*. London: DfE (available from https://www.gov.uk/government/statistics/special-educational-needs-in-england-january-2022).
DfE/DoH (2014) *SEN and Disability Code of Practice*. London: Crown Copyright.
DfE/DoH (2015) *Special Educational Needs and Disability Code of Practice for 0 to 25 year olds* (available from https://www.gov.uk/government/publications/send-code-of-practice-0-to-25).
DfE/DoHSC (2023) *Special Educational Needs and Disabilities (SEND) and Alternative Provision Improvement Plan – Right support, right place, right time*. London: HMSO.
EEF (2020) *SEN in mainstream schools guidance report*. London: EEF.
EEF (2021) *Effective professional development*. London: EEF.
House of Commons Education Committee (2019) *Special Educational Needs and Disabilities*. London: House of Commons.
House of Commons Select Committee (2006) *Special Educational Needs: Third report of session 2005–2006*. London: TSO.
NASUWT (2018) *Special Educational Needs (SEN), Additional Learning Needs (ALN) and Additional Support Needs (ASN)*. England: NASUWT.
Norwich, B. (2007) *Dilemmas of difference, inclusion and disability: International perspectives and future directions*. Oxon: Routledge.
OFSTED (2010) *The special educational needs and disability review: A statement is not enough*. Manchester: Crown Copyright.
Warnock, M. (1978) *Warnock report: Special Educational Needs, report of the Committee of Enquiry into the education of handicapped children and young people*. London: HMSO.
Warnock, M. (2005) *Special Educational Needs: A new look*. Salisbury: Philosophy of Education Society of Great Britain.

3 SEND statutory responsibilities

In this chapter, we critically examine and explore the following key aspects:

- Statutory SEND responsibilities for government, local authorities, OFSTED and other agencies
- Accountability and checking of statutory responsibilities
- SEND law
- The local offer
- Local inclusion plans and tailored lists

Key issues

Statutory responsibilities for Special Educational Needs and Disability (SEND) are essential to protect the rights of all children with SEND to receive effective educational provision and support to meet their individual needs and to ensure that this is consistently applied across the country rather than it being dependent on the interest or prioritisation in different settings/areas.

Yet, challenges deeply embedded in our current systems and processes remain, meaning that what should be clear and consistent is still not so (House of Commons Select Committee, 2006; OFSTED, 2010; DfE, 2011; House of Commons Education Committee, 2019; NAO, 2019; DfE/DoHSC, 2022, 2023).

Specifically, the issues around understanding and implementing statutory responsibilities for SEND can be seen to be linked to three fundamental issues:

1. Understanding of the *reach* of statutory responsibilities
2. Commitment to, and checking of, the consistent implementation of statutory responsibilities
3. Full understanding of SEND law and the statutory responsibilities.

This chapter explores the implications of this for local authorities and other bodies working with schools to ensure that statutory responsibilities for SEND are fully met, and also provides information about SEND law directly relevant to schools. The following chapter then focuses on the importance of developing whole-school understanding and approaches to meeting the statutory responsibilities for SEND.

DOI: 10.4324/9781003033554-3

Current policy/research context

Understanding of the reach of statutory responsibilities

Statutory responsibilities for SEND are complex and wide-reaching. It is essential to embed deep understanding that to meet those statutory responsibilities requires an approach where **everyone** is responsible and accountable for the full and consistent implementation of those responsibilities.

The responsibility therefore does not just sit with the SENCO, or even just with the school, but needs to be understood and applied at all levels – starting with the government, local authorities, OFSTED and other agencies. As the House of Commons Education Committee Report (2019: 4) identified:

> Special educational needs and disabilities must be seen as part of the whole approach of the Department's remit, not just an add-on. The Department for Education has an approach which is piecemeal, creating reactive, sticking-plaster policies, when what is needed is serious effort to ensure that issues are fully grappled with, and the 2014 Act works properly, as was intended.

Fundamentally, local authorities should be central in providing localised interpretations of the national guidance for SEND, and checking and holding to account schools and educational settings to ensure that they are fully and effectively meeting their statutory responsibilities for SEND. However, as the NAO (2019) and House of Commons Education Committee (2019) identified, half of all local authorities have themselves not been able to evidence their full understanding of and implementation of the SEND reforms and current statutory responsibilities and, as a result have had to produce a written statement of action to address major flaws in their statutory SEND processes and practices. (For more information about the context and criteria for local authority inspections, see: https://www.specialneedsjungle.com/send-2020-current-state-ofsted-la-inspections/)

Whilst this is a fault of local authorities, and more needs to be done to ensure that local authorities are ambitious in ensuring that all of the statutory responsibilities for SEND are understood and implemented effectively in their areas and through the schools and services in their area, the issue is complex with some of the responsibility for this coming back, again, to the focus, prioritisation and accountability of the government to ensure that the reforms and statutory responsibilities that they have implemented are fully adhered to.

Factors impacting on local authorities' ability to effectively take forward the ambitious SEND reforms and statutory responsibilities for SEND in a consistent and meaningful way, include challenges with workload, time and the effective training and expertise of local authority officers and colleagues (House of Commons Education Committee, 2019), and now the cost of living crisis and planned changes to the national funding formula (DfE/DoHSC, 2023).

'The House of Commons Education Committee (2019) also identified a number of other key issues that had been raised by local authorities and which impact on the effective implementation of the SEND reforms. These included:

- the timescales of the process ... [as] timescales have an impact on quality, and do not allow for co-production, proper consideration of the needs of the child and getting good advice ...'

- the practices of schools and colleges ... [which have] an impact on the quality of the provision that they as local authorities provide, but also the quality of support that children and young people with SEND within the education system.
- [Beliefs that] mainstream schools are not meeting needs early or effectively enough, with insufficient emphasis on the Graduated Approach, or that the approaches of schools to the Graduated Approach were inconsistent.
- funding issues within schools and [a feeling] that schools were seeking extra funding through EHCPs.
- [Frustration at] the fragmentation of the school system, including that they could not intervene in academies' (House of Commons Education Committee, 2019: 52–53).
- 'Lack of clarity or strength of the role and responsibilities of health and social care, in particular pointing to where duties for local authorities are 'must' but for health provision was only 'should'.
- Other sectors ... [being] permitted to reduce the support that they provided, leaving the education budget to pick up the costs.
- That the system was reliant on relationships, but local authorities felt that they do not have the power to ensure partners act as they should (House of Commons Education Committee, 2019: 59–60).

Since 2022, the government have implemented a diagnostic approach through the Delivering Better Value in SEND programme. This programmes helps 'local authorities identify achievable and sustainable changes that can drive high-quality outcomes for children and young people with SEND and equip authorities with the tools to enable them to maintain these changes sustainably, on an ongoing basis' (DfE/DoHSC, 2023: 83). The focus for the government currently is therefore on supporting local authorities to 'refocus their resources and provision to encourage mainstream schools to be more inclusive, ensure needs are met early and appropriately and use available local provision effectively' (DfE/DoHSC, 2023: 83). Research reports sharing case studies and 'examples of positive practice' (DfE/DoHSC, 2023: 83–84) are being shared to help inform practice further.

Importantly, it is recognised that meeting the statutory responsibilities for SEND in our society goes beyond the responsibility of education and schools alone – therefore requiring a shift (which was anticipated with the move to Education, Health and Care Plans) towards more effective collaboration and co-production between different Department and agencies. As the House of Commons Education Committee (2019: 37) reported, 'Integration between the three areas was a crucial aspect of the reforms, but has not really happened'. This is particularly significant in the lack of meaningful engagement, collaboration and accountability for provision in Education, Health and Care Plans, but is also seen to have impacted on the effective development of meaningful local offers (see discussion below about local offers). A number of concerns, however, are levelled at the current lack of effective engagement between different agencies and services:

- 'The absence of a full contribution from those responsible for health and social care has put further pressure on the system and that increased pressure has hindered its capacity to work as it was meant to' (House of Commons Education Committee, 2019: 22)
- 'Partner agencies did not receive any additional funding to "respond to the pressures and expectations of the SEND Reform". It also told us that in its experience health and social care professionals did not fully understand what their respective roles and

responsibilities were or have the necessary infrastructure to cope with the EHCP transfer process' (House of Commons Education Committee, 2019: 37)
- 'Despite the hard work, we were told that in reality health and social care are still not equal partners in the process .... Cuts to health and social care were often unnoticed and unmentioned, and they were undermining the reforms' (House of Commons Education Committee, 2019: 37).

Throughout, there seems to be issues around the lack of engagement, collaboration and consultation between the different services and agencies, and that fundamentally health and social care have lacked the statutory footing to prioritise this at a time when their services are under significant pressure. This has meant that 'the bodies responsible for delivering health and social care did not have the same level of accountability as local authorities' (House of Commons Education Committee, 2019: 38).

Unfortunately, as a result of not putting in place adequate plans to ensure that there is equal responsibility and accountability for ensuring that the ambitious SEND Reforms of 2014 are able to be implemented effectively and fully in practice, we have been left with a situation that continues to breed discontent and unsatisfactory practices which lack the collaboration and creative working together that could have had a potential impact, with the House of Commons Education Committee noting that:

> The Minister of State Care, Caroline Dinenage MP, told us that the situation across the country is much like the siloed working in Government. She said that growing collaboration and joint working between Clinical Commissioning Groups and local authorities was difficult.
> (House of Commons Education Committee, 2019: 38)

Commitment to, and checking of, the consistent implementation of statutory responsibilities

Linked to the key issue above are growing concerns of the lack of accountability for and understanding of the statutory responsibilities, which has led to those statutory responsibilities not being actioned effectively. Fundamentally, we need to move into a system where there is the 'systemic cultural shift' (House of Commons Education Committee, 2019: 84) that has been called for and where all local authorities, services and schools are held accountable to meet those statutory responsibilities.

As was identified in Chapter 1, and as set out below, one of the greatest criticisms of the implementation of the current SEND system has been the lack of accountability and an 'absence of responsibility' (House of Commons Education Committee, 2019: 13) for ensuring that actions are taken and that they are the right ones and are effective:

- 'Nobody appears to be taking any action based on the counting and measuring that is taking place, but even worse, no one appears to be asking anyone to take responsibility for their actions. There appears to be an absence of responsibility for driving any change or holding anyone accountable when changes do not happen' (House of Commons Education Committee, 2019: 13)
- 'We do not think that the Department for Education is taking enough responsibility for ensuring that its reforms are overseen, that practice in local authorities is lawful, that statutory timescales are adhered to, and that children's needs are being met. We are

concerned that the Department has left it to local authorities, inspectorates, parents and the courts to operate and police the system. There is a clear need for the Department to be more proactive in its oversight of the way in which the system is operating' (House of Commons Education Committee, 2019: 15).

These are very strongly worded statements, clearly identifying that the lack of responsibility for 'driving the change or holding anyone accountable' (House of Commons Education Committee, 2019: 13) have undermined the potential for the SEND Reforms that were introduced to be implemented effectively and have the impact that was planned. As the House of Commons Education Committee (2019: 15) therefore identifies, 'more needs to be done by government to ensure that local authorities are complying with the law, given that many local authorities are not'. With local authorities not in a consistent position to be able to hold educational settings and health services to account for their statutory responsibilities for SEND, another body that has been turned to support with the review and checking of statutory responsibilities is OFSTED. As the House of Commons Education Committee Report (2019) identified:

There must be greater oversight—we want to see a more rigorous inspection framework with clear consequences for failure. There should also be a greater focus on SEND in school inspections: at present, children who receive SEN Support are being let down by schools failing to meet their needs at this level.
(House of Commons Education Committee, 2019: 3)

We do not think enough is being done to ensure that every pupil with SEND receives a high standard of education and that all schools are inclusive. Ofsted must deliver a clear judgement, and through this assurance to parents, that schools are delivering for individual children with SEND.
(House of Commons Education Committee, 2019: 85–86)

We were surprised that Ofsted and the Care Quality Commission (CQC) told us that it was not in their remit to report on compliance with the law. We were surprised by their apparent lack of conviction.
(House of Commons Education Committee, 2019: 14)

The government (DfE/DoHSC, 2023: 13) has acknowledged that 'current accountabilities are too weak' and have therefore committed to focus on 'Strengthened accountabilities to enforce statutory responsibilities and drive better outcomes and experiences' (DfE/DoHSC, 2023: 73) in a number of ways, including:

- 'Updated Ofsted/CQC area SEND inspections'
- New responses to poor performance 'so that it can act proactively when areas fail to provide the necessary support to meet the needs of children and young people, including the removal of service control and imposition of a trust or commissioner on local authorities, where required'
- 'holistic new ladder[s] of intervention for local areas, with a focus on creating financial sustainability and improving outcomes for children and young people, based on evidence and data, including data in the new inclusion dashboards and delivery of local inclusion plans alongside inspection outcomes'

- Evaluations of 'the full evidence base of where statutory duties are met and not met across the local SEND and alternative provision system, to consider mechanisms to ensure we are able to be more robust with any partner that fails to meet their statutory responsibilities'.

(DfE/DoHSC, 2023: 74)

Full understanding of SEND law and the statutory responsibilities

A clear and consistent knowledge and understanding of SEND law is essential by all to ensure that the reforms that have been introduced are enacted fully in practice and that statutory responsibilities for SEND are fully met. Concerningly, the House of Commons Education Committee (2019) identified a number of failings for local authorities in terms of their accountability and responsibilities for ensuring that statutory responsibilities for SEND were implemented effectively:

- 'We have found that many local authorities are struggling with the reforms, and in some cases this has led to unlawful practice' (House of Commons Education Committee, 2019: 4)
- 'Local authorities must ensure that they are compliant with the law as opposed to waiting to be caught out by an inspection regime, parents/carers or other professionals' (House of Commons Education Committee, 2019: 15)
- 'We have heard that there is a lack of knowledge about SEND law and local authority procedures which are, in some cases, abused or taken advantage of. This ignorance, wilful or otherwise, serves no one well, least of all the children and young people who the system is intended to support' (House of Commons Education Committee, 2019: 17)
- 'We were told of examples of poor, misleading and unlawful advice being given to schools and parents/carers. We heard that in some cases staff in schools and local authorities do not know the law, give misleading or unlawful advice, and in some cases, publish erroneous information on their website' (House of Commons Education Committee, 2019: 73).

Unfortunately, as we have seen, parental confidence in SEND law is at an all-time low, and there are times when this results in challenges to SEND law through Tribunal processes. Over recent years we have seen an increase in Tribunal cases by over 80% (NAO, 2019). The government have acknowledged difficulties with parental access to mediation and appeals (DfE/DoHSC, 2023). They expect that the new National Standards, which will provide greater clarity about who will provide what and how, will 'prevent disagreements arising in the first place' (DfE/DoHSC, 2023: 76). Whilst increased clarity and training to local authority colleagues in all aspects of SEND law is expected to impact positively on parental experiences of the SEND system, the government propose further amendments to the SEN and Disability Code of Practice (DfE/DoH, 2015) 'so that it is clearer about who is responsible for resolving concerns' (DfE/DoHSC, 2023: 76). In this, the role of the Local Government and Social Care Ombudsman will be reviewed. The DfE/DoHSC (2023: 76) have also identified that mediation will become a 'mandatory part of the Tribunal appeals process' although they note that further consideration is needed to ensure that mediation processes do not simply lengthen the time taken to resolve cases for parents/carers and pupils with SEND.

Planning for practice

Figure 3.1 Key principles model

As we have identified, there are continued challenges in being able to effectively implement the SEND Reforms, and these largely lie around the lack of meaningful collaboration and robust accountability embedded at all layers of the system.

Moving forward, the responsibility for SEND therefore must involve ***communication*** and ***collaboration*** – it must be a shared collaborative endeavour involving significant ***cultural change*** and a deeper understanding and embodiment of ***inclusion***. In this, it is, therefore, not the responsibility of the SENCO alone, or indeed education or schools alone to meet the statutory responsibilities for meeting the needs of children and young people with SEND.

Understanding the reach of statutory responsibilities – the local offer

A significant area relevant to planning for practice is the issue of local offers. The key principles of a clear understanding of ***inclusion*** within the local context; meaningful ***collaboration***; clear and accessible ***communication***; and ***evidence-informed approaches*** are all central here.

The concept and practice of local offers was introduced in the SEN and Disability Code of Practice (DfE/DoH, 2014, 2015) but has been impacted by lack of understanding and interpretation. In some areas, local authorities misinterpreted the guidance and required schools and settings to develop their own individual local offers, instead of understanding that the local offer was supposed to encompass the provision available in a local area/local authority to aid understanding and planning of what is locally available and how that meets the needs of the current cohort of children, young people and adults requiring services and provisions. This is another example of where it would have been very useful for the government to have shared examples of effective local offers when the new SEN and

Disability Code of Practice (DfE/DoH, 2014) was published so that consistency could have been established from the start – ensuring that all parents/carers and professionals across the country have access to high-quality information presented in the local offer.

> **Reflective Activity**
>
> - How effective is the local offer in your area?
> - Where can you find it?
> - How is it developed?
> - Is it accessible and useful to all – school staff, other professionals, parents/carers?
> - How far would you say that the local offer in your area fulfils its requirement to involve co-production, innovation, interactivity and accessibility?
> - What works well?
> - What still needs to be developed?

The intention behind the local offer was a promising one – one of creating greater transparency over what provision and services are available in a local area, being able to be used both as a simple and accessible overview of what is available, and a strategic tool to review, reflect and evaluate on what is available and how that would meet the needs of cohorts with changing needs over time.

Unfortunately, as the House of Commons Education Committee (2019: 24) reported, local offers are now 'difficult to create and difficult to use' becoming 'unusable and useless' (House of Commons Education Committee, 2019: 4).

Parents/carers have also reported difficulties with the local offer, and this is reported not only to the House of Commons Education Committee (2019) but also is a consistent theme in local authority OFSTED/CQC Inspections of SEND provision. The concerns reported are largely around the lack of up to date information, that they are not produced and shared in ways that are accessible enough for parents/carers and that they do not include and contain the ongoing dynamic and strategic analyses of provision to support improvements to be planned and made that the local offer was intended to be. At best, the local offer has therefore come to be seen as a very basic 'directory' of services or links to information on the government website (House of Commons Education Committee, 2019).

Moving forward, the government's SEND and Alternative Provision Improvement Plan (DfE/DoHSC, 2023: 40), has identified how 'new local inclusion plans overseen by the new local SEND and alternative provision partnerships will set out how the needs of children and young people in the area will be met in line with the new National Standards. We will ensure this informs the existing statutory local offer of SEND services and provision, as well as clarifying the graduated SEN Support offer, so parents can clearly see what they can expect in their area'.

There is also new guidance on the development of tailored lists of settings to 'give clear choices to families and better meet the needs of children and young people, while supporting them to manage placements in a way that ensures financial sustainability for the future' (DfE/DoHSC, 2023: 41).

The DfE/DoHSC (2023: 41) acknowledge the concerns of some that the lists will 'reduce choice' and have provided assurances that they will listen to stakeholders and 'test delivery options' (DfE/DoHSC, 2023: 41) to ensure that the change is effective.

To ensure consistency and the quality of the plans and tailored lists, the DfE/DoHSC (2023: 41) have also identified that: 'tailored lists will only be introduced in an area once the local inclusion plan has been quality assured and signed off by the Department for Education's Regions Group as being in accordance with the National Standards'.

> **Reflective Activity**
>
> - How might the new local inclusion plans and tailored lists work in your local area?
> - How can you ensure that you are kept up to date with developments and planning for this?

Commitment to consistent implementation of statutory responsibilities

> **Reflective Activity**
>
> - How is/will consistent implementation of statutory responsibilities be achieved in your local area?
> - What are the processes for this already in place and how involved are you in this?

The new National Standards are planned to help to ensure greater consistency of understanding and implementation of SEND provision – setting out guidance for 'system leaders', including 'multi-academy Trust leaders, governing bodies, headteachers, college principals and chief executive officers, directors of children's services and integrated Care Boards' (DfE/DoHSC, 2023: 27).

The focus here is on ensuring consistency of practices across districts of schools, local areas and authorities and nationally. Peer-to-peer review processes, and processes supported by, for example, the NASEN Whole School SEND approach may be helpful in this in enabling practical tools and processes to support the moderation of understandings and practices in relation to SEND.

> **Reflective Activity**
>
> - What systems and processes are already in place in your local area to support you to moderate your judgements and understandings about SEND and SEND practices?
> - Are there supportive, peer-to-peer review processes in place?
> - How can you access those?
> - How can you support others in your setting to be able to engage with those processes to extend their understanding of SEND?

Local authority updates and SENCO forums are an important source of information and a way in which you can contribute to the conversations taking place regarding changes. Signing up for email updates, or similar mechanisms, will ensure that you have an opportunity to be aware of changes and to possibly be involved in the developments as the proposed changes are implemented.

Understanding SEND law

> **Reflective Activity**
>
> - How much do you already know about SEND law and the implications of this for practice?
> - How far is this understood by others in your school, and in your local authority?
> - Where would you go to find out SEND law?

In addition to the SEN and Disability Code of Practice (DfE/DoH, 2015) which provides additional guidance relating to the laws surrounding SEND, the following documents provide key information about current SEND law:

- The Equality Act (2010)
- The Children and Families Act (2014)
  - Part 3 of the Children and Families Act (2014) includes the relevant information about SEND
- The Special Educational Needs and Disability Regulations (2014)
- The Special Educational Needs and Disability

These are documents that everyone involved in SEND (local authorities, schools and other agencies/departments) should be aware of and ensure are enacted in practice. Whilst there are significant consequences for local authorities in not meeting theory statutory SEND duties, through Tribunals and OFSTED/CQC Inspections, here we focus on understanding of SEND law from a school perspective, and the implications for the school in not meeting duties in relation to pupils with SEND:

> **Case Study – What Are the Legal Consequences of Failing in Your Duties to Pupils with SEND?**
>
> **Simon Shepherd – Schofield Sweeney Solicitors**
>
> There are various consequences of a school not complying with its obligations to pupils with special educational needs and disabilities, not least the detrimental impact on the pupils' education and the likelihood of parental complaints. However, this

section will focus on what legal remedies the pupil and/or parents/carers may have should there be a breach of your obligations.

The legal recourse for parents/carers is to commence proceedings for disability discrimination in the Special Educational Needs and Disabilities Tribunal (Tribunal). In order to commence proceedings in the Tribunal, the pupil must be a disabled person as defined by Section 6 of the Equality Act (2010) (EqA):

A person is defined as having disability if they have a physical or mental impairment that has a substantial and long-term adverse effect on their ability to carry out normal day-to-day activities (https://www.legislation.gov.uk/ukpga/2010/15/section/6 – accessed 15.5.2023).

The first matter that the Tribunal will consider is whether the pupil meets this definition and, if not, the claims of disability discrimination will fail. Not every pupil who is on the SEND Register, or who has an EHCP, will be a disabled person but, as highlighted in the example in Case Study 1, it is often better to assume that the pupil is disabled, unless there is clear medical evidence that they do not meet the definition.

If the pupil is disabled, the Tribunal can then consider any allegations of unlawful disability discrimination. There are various types of disability discrimination and the main claims that affect schools can be summarised as follows:

1 *Direct disability discrimination contrary to S.13 of the Equality Act*
   Direct discrimination would arise where a school treats the pupil less favourably *because of* their disability. For example, because the pupil has ADHD, the school excludes the pupil. Direct disability discrimination is extremely unlikely as this example should never happen but, if direct discrimination does occur, it cannot be justified.
2 *Discrimination arising in consequence of the disability contrary to S.15 of the Equality Act*
   This is where an individual is treated less favourably because of something arising out of their disability. The most obvious example would be a pupil who has been excluded due to behaviour that has arisen in consequence of their ADHD. The pupil has not been excluded because of their ADHD, but due to behaviour caused by ADHD. However, this type of discrimination can be justified. The school would have to show that the treatment, i.e. the exclusion, was a proportionate means of achieving a legitimate aim and that it complied with its duty to make reasonable adjustments. This is considered in case 1 below.
3 *Failure to make reasonable adjustments contrary to Ss. 20 and 21 of the Equality Act*
   This would be where the school has applied a provision, criterion or practice (a PCP) that puts a disabled pupil at a substantial disadvantage compared with pupils who are not disabled, and the school has failed to take such steps as would be reasonable for them to have to take to avoid that disadvantage. The duty to make reasonable adjustments includes the provision of education and access to any benefit, facility or service and includes the provision of auxiliary aids. The duty to make reasonable adjustments can be unlimited.

If a claim is made in the Tribunal, it is important to note that there is no financial compensation should the claim succeed. The risk is more about reputational damage should the parent publicise the decision. The Tribunal can order an apology to be issued and make other recommendations, such as training, or overturn an exclusion.

To highlight some of the issues that schools face, below are two real-life examples which highlight the difficulties that schools can face.

Case Study 1

In this case, following behavioural incidents (including some of a violent nature) the pupil was given several fixed term exclusions, with the length of the exclusions gradually increasing, and he was ultimately permanently excluded. On behalf of the pupil, the parents/carers brought claims for discrimination arising out of a disability contrary to S.15 of the Equality Act and failure to make reasonable adjustments.

The failure to make reasonable adjustments was primarily based on the claim that the school had not properly assessed his needs. The allegation of failure to make reasonable adjustments also included allegations that the school had failed to implement strategies suggested by the Educational Psychologist, which the school had also denied.

This was a complicated case with various facets but one of the main issues that resulted in the finding of disability discrimination was that the school did not consider the pupil to be a disabled person. This was despite the school being aware of behavioural issues and the pupil potentially having ADHD. By the time the Governing Body appeal was heard (and rejected), there was medical evidence that he did have a provisional diagnosis of ADHD. In addition, the pupil had complex needs and medical evidence indicated that he also had Oppositional Defiance Disorder and was on the autistic spectrum.

The school's position was that the pupil acted differently to other pupils it had who did have a diagnosis of ADHD and did not believe that his behaviour related to ADHD and was not therefore disability related.

Due to the school's reluctance to categorise the pupil as a disabled person, reasonable adjustments were not made to the extent they could have been. Reasonable adjustments would normally be to amend the Behaviour Policy to discount all behaviour related to the disability or, alternatively, to vary the school-based responses to the behaviour. Another unusual factor of this case was that the Independent Review Panel stated that the school should have reinstated the pupil but, having considered the decision again, the Governing Body Panel refused to reinstate him.

When the proceedings were issued, the school disputed disability in its defence and maintained this position up to the hearing, requiring the pupil to prove he met the definition of a disabled person. This did not go down well with the Tribunal. The Tribunal considered the complex needs of the pupil and, even though there was still no formal diagnosis of ADHD, found that he was a disabled person.

This immediately put the school in a difficult position. Even though a lot of support had been put in place for this pupil, the fact that disability had been disputed made it very hard to show that *all* reasonable adjustments had been made at the time.

The Tribunal acknowledged that the pupil's negative behaviours had escalated and accepted the difficulty that this had caused the school. The Tribunal acknowledged that protecting the health and safety of staff and pupils was a legitimate aim.

However, the Tribunal found that not all of the recommendations of the Educational Psychologist were followed.

Given that there had been a failure to do this and make reasonable adjustments, the Tribunal found that the fixed term exclusions and the permanent exclusion was unlawful treatment on the grounds of disability and could not be justified as a *proportionate means* of achieving a legitimate aim. Had the school done more, but the behaviour had continued despite additional support, the outcome may have been different.

The lesson to learn from this Case Study is to ensure that all strategies and reasonable adjustments are implemented and regularly reviewed and to assume that the pupil may be a disabled person and act accordingly.

Case Study 2

This case highlights the importance of making reasonable adjustments but also that the Tribunal will acknowledge occasions when there is a failure.

In this case, the pupil had a severe visual impairment. This meant that materials should have been provided in a certain font size and other adjustments had to be made to how work was provided to her. The school was aware of this and all relevant staff were made aware and trained in what this pupil needed. Unfortunately, given the problems with COVID-19, the high number of staff absences resulted in a high number of supply teachers. Although work was often set and it was made clear what the needs of this pupil were, sometimes the supply teachers failed to provide materials in the correct format. Each time this was raised with the teacher, it was rectified.

At the same time, there was a recommendation that a specific piece of software be purchased to enable the pupil's laptop to link to the whiteboard so that whatever was on the whiteboard would be on the pupil's laptop. Due to sickness absence, this fell through the cracks and was not purchased.

The parents/carers commenced proceedings for failure to make reasonable adjustments in the Tribunal. The claim included the failure to buy the software. As soon as the headteacher was made aware of this, the software was immediately purchased and training was provided on the software to the relevant teachers. This was therefore acknowledged in the defence to the claim.

With regard to the failure to produce the materials, the school acknowledged that there had been occasions when the materials had not been provided to the pupil but that reasonable adjustments had been made and these failings were rare and were due to exceptional circumstances.

The Tribunal rejected the claim of failure to make reasonable adjustments regarding the materials. The Tribunal acknowledged the difficult circumstances the school was operating in and acknowledged the steps that the school had taken to ensure that materials were provided in the correct format. Whilst there were occasions when it had not been, the Tribunal accepted this did not mean that there had been a failure to make reasonable adjustments regarding the provision of materials.

However, given the acknowledgment made about not purchasing the software, the Tribunal found that there had been a failure to make reasonable adjustments with regard to the software by not purchasing it earlier.

This meant that whilst a vast majority of the claims brought by the parent/carers were rejected one claim succeeded. Unfortunately, it was this one claim, rather than all of the ones that were rejected by the Tribunal that attracted media attention and therefore did further reputational damage to the school.

Reflective Activity

- Are there any aspects in the example above that have surprised you?
- How can you ensure that understanding of SEND law is embedded into practice and that your setting is fully compliant?
- Are there any areas to focus on for your school setting?
- How will you take this forward?

The Equality Act (2010) is fundamental to teaching and inclusion in schools because it ensures all children are treated fairly and are able to access good quality education regardless of who they are. The Equality Act (2010) requires 'reasonable adjustments' to be made where a pupil, who is disabled, would be at a substantial disadvantage in comparison to someone who is not disabled. For example, examination access arrangements are provided for pupils if it is their normal way of working. Arrangements apply unless there is a specific reason, e.g. a reader cannot read in an English exam that tests reading skills of the pupil.

Reflective Activity

- Are you aware of the key protected characteristics presented in The Equality Act (2010)?
- According to The Equality Act (2010), what is a reasonable adjustment?
- Look at the scenario below and consider the reasonable adjustments you might put in place in class as their normal way of working (and therefore in examinations too):
  A pupil with ADD (Attention Deficit Disorder) who has persistent difficulty concentrating and poor working memory.

Concluding comments and reflections

Despite being nine years on from the publication of the new SEND Reforms (DfE/DoH, 2014), understanding and consistency in relation to statutory responsibilities for SEND and SEND law are still not fully embedded.

As an education system, we have a long way to go to ensure that we develop effective systems to share practices and standardise processes so that they consistently and effectively meet the needs of children with SEND. In this, as the House of Commons Education Committee (2019: 87) identified: 'the Government must see support for SEND as a system-wide issue and ensure that all policies are 'SEND proof'.

> **Individual Reflection**
>
> - What new information/learning have you gained from this chapter?
> - What are your key reflections?
> - What are your next steps/actions as a result?

References

DfE (2011) *Support and aspiration: A new approach to special educational needs and disability: A consultation.* Norwich: TSO.

DfE/DoH (2014) *SEN and Disability Code of Practice.* London: Crown Copyright.

DfE/DoH (2015) *Special Educational Needs and Disability Code of Practice for 0 to 25 year olds* (available from https://www.gov.uk/government/publications/send-code-of-practice-0-to-25).

DfE/DoHSC (2022) *SEND review: Right support, right place, right time* (available from https://www.gov.uk/government/consultations/send-review-right-support-right-place-right-time).

DfE/DoHSC (2023) *Special Educational Needs and Disabilities (SEND) and Alternative Provision Improvement Plan – Right support, right place, right time.* London: HMSO.

House of Commons Education Committee (2019) *Special Educational Needs and Disabilities.* London: House of Commons.

House of Commons Select Committee (2006) *Special Educational Needs: Third report of session 2005–2006.* London: TSO.

NAO (2019) *Support for pupils with special educational needs and disabilities in England.* London: House of Commons.

OFSTED (2010) *The special educational needs and disability review: A statement is not enough.* Manchester: Crown Copyright. Reference no: 090221.

The Children and Families Act (2014) https://www.legislation.gov.uk/ukpga/2014/6/contents (accessed 20.12.2022).

The Equality Act (2010) https://www.legislation.gov.uk/ukpga/2010/15/contents (accessed 15.5.2023).

The Special Educational Needs and Disability (First Tier Tribunal Recommendations Power) Regulations (2017) https://www.legislation.gov.uk/uksi/2017/1306/contents (accessed 20.12.2022).

The Special Educational Needs and Disability Regulations (2014) https://www.legislation.gov.uk/uksi/2014/1530/contents (accessed 20.12.2022).

4 Outstanding leadership of SEND

> In this chapter, we critically examine and explore the following key aspects:
>
> - Understanding leadership
> - Successful school leadership
> - Leadership of change
> - The SENCO as a strategic leader
> - The National Award for SEN Coordination and the development of the SENCO National Professional Qualification (NPQ)
> - Tools to support the management of change
> - Developing understanding of the role of the SENCO and implications of this for practice

Key issues

The culture of the school setting, the 'way we do things around here' (Fullan, 2020: 70) is paramount in the development of effective, inclusive practices and culture, and is inextricably linked with the leadership model embedded within the context.

Outstanding leadership of Special Educational Needs and Disability (SEND) is all about enabling and empowering everyone to have the confidence to be able to recognise and meet the needs of all pupils in positive, participatory and inclusive ways.

Outstanding leaders of SEND are rooted in inclusive values and principles, finding ways to work effectively with others to build confidence and capacity across the setting within which they work.

In this way, having a clear moral purpose is essential in outstanding leadership of SEND. Moral purpose, however, is complex – it is not simply a state to embed. Rather, it is seen as a 'dynamic process' (Fullan, 2020: 37) understood in relation to the 'dynamics of successful change, powerful collaboration, deep knowledge and coherence making' (Fullan, 2020: 37).

Outstanding leadership of SEND is also not just about a sole leader. For leadership in schools to be effective, it needs to be built on collaborative, participatory and distributed leadership approaches which are rooted in the culture, practices and ethos of the school as a whole and intrinsically reflected in the language, relationships and behaviours of everyone.

DOI: 10.4324/9781003033554-4

Outstanding leadership of SEND in schools therefore, whilst centred around the role of the Special Educational Needs Co-ordinator (SENCO) should absolutely not be focused solely just on them – the commitment and understanding of SEND and inclusion needs to be understood and reflected by all school leaders, including the Headteacher, as well as all teaching and non-teaching staff within the school. In this way, every school leader should see themselves as a leader of inclusion, within which leadership of SEND is a key part.

This, therefore, demands high levels of attention to the underlying culture and ethos that is being developed within the school as a whole and ways that staff are motivated, supported and actively engaged to recognise and meet the needs of all pupils, including those with SEND. In this way, by involving and actively engaging all members of the school community through a distributed and participatory leadership approach, creative, positive and innovative approaches that utilise the varying expertise and skills of everyone in the school can be explored and developed.

The key issues for schools to consider in relation to what 'Outstanding leadership of SEND' is therefore include:

1 Understanding leadership
2 Leadership of change
3 The development of the SENCO as a strategic leader.

Current policy and research

Understanding leadership

The importance of successful and effective leadership of SEND continues to be very much emphasised, including in the recent Special Educational Needs and Disabilities (SEND) and Alternative Provision Improvement Plan (DfE/DoHSC, 2023: 52) which notes that: 'reform is not possible without a strong and capable workforce with robust leadership'.

There is a recognition of 'the importance of SEND expertise being held at every level, including senior leaders. Senior leaders play a key role in setting an inclusive culture, in which individual needs are identified and where there are high ambitions for children and young people with SEND' (DfE/DoHSC, 2023: 58).

To take this forward therefore requires an understanding of key principles of effective leadership.

Much has been written about leadership models and school leadership in particular, with many different models and approaches being advocated (Precey & Mazurkiewicz, 2013; Ottesen, 2013; Ruairc et al., 2013; Ekins, 2017). We believe that understanding leadership involves understanding key principles/practices, qualities and attitudes/values that are central to outstanding SEND and school leadership.

Leithwood et al. (2008) identified seven strong claims about successful school leadership from an extensive review of literature and empirical evidence about school leadership. These claims continue to provide a useful basis against which to consider leadership models in our schools now:

1 School leadership is second only to classroom teaching as an influence on pupil learning
2 Almost all successful leaders draw on the same repertoire of basic leadership practices – e.g. to improve employee performance and recognise that that performance is directly

linked to the 'beliefs, values, motivations, skills and knowledge and conditions in which they work that are embedded in the setting' (Leithwood et al., 2008: 29)
3 The ways in which leaders apply these basic leadership practices – not the practices themselves – demonstrate responsiveness to, rather than dictation by, the contexts in which they work
4 School leaders improve teaching and learning indirectly and most powerfully through their influence on staff motivation, commitment and working conditions
5 School leadership has a greater influence on schools and students when it is widely distributed
6 Some patterns of distribution are more effective than others
7 A small handful of personal traits explains a high proportion of the variation in leadership effectiveness (Leithwood et al., 2008: 27–28).

From the literature and research evidence that Leithwood et al. (2008) reviewed, the way that leaders achieve their key leadership task is by:

- **Building vision and setting directions:** involves motivating colleagues; developing shared purpose and shared vision
- **Understanding and developing people:** building the knowledge and skills, but also the dispositions (the 'commitment, capacity and resilience' (Leithwood et al., 2008: 30)) of colleagues through individualised support and 'modeling appropriate values and behaviours' (Leithwood et al., 2008: 30)
- **Redesigning the organisation:** involves establishing effective work conditions, 'building collaborative cultures, restructuring [and reculturing] … the organisation, building productive relations with parents and the community, and connecting the school to its wider environment' (Leithwood et al., 2008: 30)
- **Managing the teaching and learning programme:** creating 'productive working conditions … by fostering organisational stability and strengthening the school's infrastructure' (Leithwood et al., 2008: 30).

As can be seen by the seven strong claims above (Leithwood et al., 2008), effective school leadership is connected with distributed leadership, vision, values, motivating others and principled approaches to understanding and connecting with the particular context of the individual school and the school community as it is experienced at that time.

Leadership, however, is not just about a set of practices. More importantly, leadership is about personal qualities. As Leithwood et al. (2008) identify: 'the most successful school leaders are open-minded and ready to learn from others. They are also flexible rather than dogmatic in their thinking within a system of core values, persistent (e.g. in pursuit of high expectations of staff motivation, commitment, learning and achievement for all), resilient and optimistic' (Leithwood et al., 2008: 36).

Bourke and Titus (2020) identified that 'inclusive leaders share a cluster of six signature traits:

1 **Visible commitment:** They articulate authentic commitment to diversity, challenge the status quo, hold others accountable, and make diversity and inclusion a personal priority.
2 **Humility:** They are modest about capabilities, admit mistakes, and create the space for others to contribute.
3 **Awareness of bias:** They show awareness of personal blind spots, as well as flaws in the system, and work hard to ensure a meritocracy.

4 **Curiosity about others:** They demonstrate an open mindset and deep curiosity about others, listen without judgment, and seek with empathy to understand those around them.
5 **Cultural intelligence:** They are attentive to others' cultures and adapt as required.
6 **Effective collaboration:** They empower others, pay attention to diversity of thinking and psychological safety, and focus on team cohesion' (Bourke & Titus, 2020: np).

At a time when, arguably, the education and school system is at the most challenging (post-pandemic, in the midst of a cost of living crisis and the impact that that has for school budgets and for the pupils and families, not to mention the staff themselves that the school serves) that it has been for some time, perhaps all school leaders will need to draw on the personal traits identified above, as we see the profile of needs within school communities change dramatically in the face of the societal changes that have and are happening. 'Humility, empathy and perspective taking' (Bourke & Titus, 2020: np) are therefore also seen as critical to an effective inclusive leader.

In addition to personal qualities, personal attitudes are key to the effective leadership of inclusion and SEND in schools. Indeed, one of the key factors in the success of inclusive agendas and practices in schools will be the positive attitudes of the leaders to that priority.

The government have set out their commitment to supporting and strengthening the leadership of SEND at all levels, and in the SEND and Alternative Provision Improvement Plan (DfE/DoHSC), have therefore identified that, 'to support excellent SEND leadership we have:

- Committed to setting out the first descriptors for academy trust strength, which will include measures for a high-quality, inclusive education. This will help ensure that trust leaders set the right calm, safe and supportive culture for inclusion and improving the outcomes of pupils with SEND and in alternative provision.
- Begun work on a new MAT CEO development offer, providing leaders with the knowledge, skills and behaviours to lead improvement at scale, with the needs of children with SEND and those requiring alternative provision embedded throughout.
- Introduced a new NPQ for Early Years Leadership to support current and aspiring leaders to develop expertise in leading high-quality early years education and care which meet the needs of all learners, including those with SEND.
- Developed the NPQ for Headship to support teachers and leaders to develop the knowledge that underpins expert school leadership and enables all pupils to succeed, including designing and implementing fair and inclusive policies, making reasonable adjustments and encouraging staff to share best practice on supporting pupils with SEND
- Provided training and capability building to senior strategic leaders in local authorities through the Delivering Better Value Programme, supporting them to design, implement and embed effective change management and evidence-based decision-making.

- Promoted the Local Government Association Leadership Programme, which provides targeted support to senior leaders in local authorities with responsibility for children's social care. SEND is embedded throughout the programme including training, mentoring and bespoke support to deliver targeted interventions to improve their SEND services'.

(DfE/DoHSC, 2023: 58–59)

Leadership of change

We have been living and working in a period of unprecedented change – much of which, with the global pandemic, has happened without time for adequate or any planning and forethought. Now, more than ever, we need to have an understanding and empathy for the significant impact that unplanned change has had on many people – and the breakdown in fundamental trust and respectful relationships that can occur when change processes are not managed as effectively as they could be.

Whilst even implementing simple practice changes may be challenging (because of the basic emotional responses that all humans have to change), implementing cultural change is 'one of the hardest things that humankind faces' (Fullan, 2020: 1). Yet, change is necessary for organisations and practices to develop and evolve in response to changing cohort needs. It is a good thing that the language and practices of the early 1970s and before in relation to SEND and diversity have, largely, changed over time to become more inclusive and understanding.

Change can also be exciting – leading to innovative and creative changes in thinking and practice. Yet, too often, change can be perceived as something to be feared and can cause feelings of stress, anxiety, frustration and upset if not managed and planned in an effective way.

Change, therefore, is a 'double-edged sword. Its relentless pace these days runs us off our feet. Yet when things are unsettled, we can find new ways to move ahead and to create breakthroughs not possible in stagnant societies' (Fullan, 2020: 1). Changing culture is about collaboration and ensuring that people understand the need for change and are on board and supportive of it – that they see themselves aligned with the changes suggested and are part of the leadership of change processes. 'Lone Ranger' leadership styles which dictate and lead without ensuring that everyone else is on board do not work (Fullan, 2020). Instead, significant cultural change must involve the building of relationship and communication. As Fullan (2020) identifies:

- 'The single factor common to every successful change initiative is that relationships improve' (Fullan, 2020: 10)
- 'Leaders must be consummate relationship builders with diverse people and groups – especially with people different from themselves. Effective leaders constantly foster purposeful interactions and problem-solving, and are wary of easy consensus' (Fullan, 2020: 10–11).

The importance of that focus on relationships, effective and meaningful collaborations which value and embrace different perspectives and understandings and powerful communication that works for everyone involved is therefore essential.

As the EEF (2019) identify, by using a range of skills including vision-setting, planning, review and evaluation, school leaders 'create an organisational climate that is conducive to change' (EEF, 2019: 10). This is achieved through working collaboratively with others to ensure a focus on 'dedicated and distributed leadership ... with a culture of shared leadership' (EEF, 2019: 10).

The SENCO as strategic leader

Since the introduction of the role of the SENCO in 1994, the role has increasingly become more of a strategic leadership role.

With the requirements through the Education Act (2008) for SENCOs to be a qualified teacher; to complete a statutory national qualification (the National Award for SEN Coordination) and either be a member of the senior leadership team of the school, or have direct access to a senior leader as their line manager – the role and remit of the SENCO was strengthened further (Passy et al., 2017).

The SEN and Disability Code of Practice (DfE/DoH, 2015) also reinforced this, stating that:

> The SENCO has an important role to play with the headteacher and governing body, in determining the strategic development of SEN policy and provision in the school. They will be most effective in that role if they are part of the school leadership team.
> (DfE/DoH, 2015:108)

The House of Commons Education Committee Report (2019: 17) recognise and highlighted the importance of the role of the SENCO: 'SENCOs play increasingly important roles in schools …. The system is only as strong as the professionals who make up its system, and we want to see greater support provided to them'.

They identified, however, that challenges remain with the amount of time that SENCOs have for their role, including the often part-time nature of the role in many schools and times when SENCOs are 'diverted from their SEND responsibilities by other duties, taking them away from supporting teachers and pupils' (House of Commons Education Committee, 2019: 48) and noted that 'We consider that the role of the SENCO is of such importance that those undertaking that role should have enough pay and knowledge to enable them to do their job well' (House of Commons Education Committee, 2019: 17).

The House of Commons Education Committee (2019: 48) summarises that: 'The pressure on Special Educational Needs Co-ordinators (SENCOs) seemed to be immense, while the level of experience and the status they were afforded in schools varies'.

Since 2008 and the subsequent introduction of the statutory SENCO qualification – the National Award for SEN Coordination, there has been a strengthening of the consistent quality of SENCO knowledge and practices, with research undertaken by Passy et al. (2017) identifying that:

- 'There is statistically-significant evidence that a majority of Award-holders and trainees felt that the Award increased their confidence in some aspects of all three domains of Professional Knowledge and Understanding; Leading and Coordinating Provision; and Personal and Professional Qualities' (Passy et al., 2017: 8)
- 'Trainees reported that they valued Award training specifically for broadening their policy and theoretical knowledge of SEND' (Passy et al., 2017: 9)
- 'The aspects of course delivery that were reported as the 'most helpful' were networking and sharing practice with other SENCOs' (Passy et al., 2017: 38).

The importance of networking, quality training and professional development and valuing the important role that SENCOs have in our schools continues to be highlighted: 'The Government should encourage local authorities, and if necessary provide them with the relevant powers, to bring all SENCOs from all schools in their area together, in order to share best practice, knowledge and training' (House of Commons Education Committee, 2019: 86).

With the new SEND and Alternative Provision Improvement Plan (DfE/DoHSC, 2023: 57) there is now a commitment to bring the SENCO qualification in line with other school leadership qualifications by introducing a new National Vocational Qualification (NPQ) to equip SENCOs to shape their school's approach through a new SENCo NPQ: 'Special educational needs coordinators (SENCOs) play a vital role in setting the direction for their school, coordinating day-to-day SEND provision and advising on the Graduated Approach to providing SEN Support. We want to invest in their training to ensure they are well equipped, valued by their colleagues and the attainment of children with SEND improves' (DfE/DoHSC, 2023: 57).

Some concerns have been raised through the consultation process (DfE/DoHSC, 2022) that NPQs do not have the same high standard of academic quality as the National Award for SEN Coordination (as this is a Post Graduate Certificate qualification) and 'that the current qualification is fit for purpose and that changing the type of qualification risks undermining the SENCO role' (DfE/DoHSC, 2023: 57).

Yet, the government believe that 'introducing a new NPQ sends an important message about the role of the SENCO and the need for it to be "whole-school, senior and strategic" whilst reflecting the complexity of the system and preparing SENCOs for this' (DfE/DoHSC, 2023: 57).

As there continues to be 'strong support for strengthening the mandatory requirement to undertake SENCO training' (DfE/DoHSC, 2023), the DfE has also committed to: 'consider how the proposal to strengthen the mandatory training requirement is implemented' (DfE/DoHSC, 2023: 57–58).

Recent doctoral research, outlined below, highlights the importance of high-quality training, understanding of the SENCO role in schools and the developing professional identity of the SENCO:

Case Study – An Exploration of How Newly Qualified SENCO Understand Their Professional Identity and Implications for the Ongoing Development of the Professional Role

Liz Harby

In my recent doctoral research study I used Interpretative Phenomenological Analysis as a theoretical framework and research approach to explore newly qualified SENCOs experiences of their developing professional identity. Through personal understanding of the challenges of the role, I sought to gain an insight into current factors that aid or impede those new to role in developing a secure professional identity to support them in the context of changing education policy and the ongoing challenges of supporting children and young people with SEND (DfE/DoHSC, 2022).

Seven participants from primary, secondary and independent settings were interviewed within their first year of completing the National Award for SEN Coordination and then again about 10 months later.

Five key themes emerged:

- Their experience of relationships
- Their experience of sharing
- Their identification of their attributes as a SENCO
- The importance of knowledge
- Their experience of policy and guidance in relation to professional identity.

Relationships

Within their experience of relationships, participants described the importance of all stakeholders, within and beyond school, understanding what the role of SENCO entailed. Many had themselves been surprised by the breadth and depth of the role. Further enhancing this were their experiences of being trusted and supported by colleagues, parents/carers and pupils. For some, feelings of isolation affected their confidence and ability to develop a secure professional identity, which was in part related to their context and, for most, these feelings had dwindled by the second interview having sought support from other SENCOs in their area. Other tensions included some feeling that it was a 'thankless' job or that practices within other agencies were affecting their ability to support pupils and their families.

Sharing

The experience of sharing contributed to participants positivity and confidence which in turn supported the development of their professional identity. Notably, the experiences of sharing responsibility, shared interest or focus and sharing of identity and experiences were most important. Participants gave examples of working with colleagues, developing shared responsibility in school and developing collegiate working with other SENCOs, local authority teams, health colleagues to support children and young people with SEND.

Attributes as a SENCO

Initially it was challenging for participants to think beyond the jobs they do, which for some was compounded by 'wearing many hats'. However, with further discussion and careful analysis, they shared that the most important attributes that were supporting the development of their professional identity included: strategic leaderships skills; emotional intelligence; communication skills; operational skills; their demeanour and their beliefs and values. For some, it was evident that these were innate skills or those that they had developed through previous roles, whilst others had either enhanced these skills 'on the job' or had sought opportunities to develop these through other means such as a leadership secondment. A surprising finding was that those who already held senior leadership roles had been most challenged by the emotional aspect of the role. Where the attributes were strongest, the newly qualified SENCOs presented with greater confidence to respond to the everyday challenges of the role.

Knowledge

This linked closely with participants perceptions of the importance of knowledge, gained through experience, induction and training and their desire to further enhance specific knowledge and skills. All acknowledged the importance of teaching experience to be able to understand children and young people and the strategies that can be used to support them in the classroom. Some felt nervous about having time away from the classroom and indicated the need to maintain some teaching to ensure their own skills and understanding did not diminish. Six of the seven participants had not specifically chosen the career path of becoming a SENCO but had been appointed following a request by their headteacher. Consequently, several had no induction into the role, but some participants described shadowing colleagues prior to taking on the role or having access to an experienced SENCO for support. This was expounded as highly valuable. For those who had been unable to attend training beyond the National Award for SEN Coordination (NASENCO) Award, there was concern that their skills and knowledge would not be as fully developed and may impede their ability to support pupils and colleagues effectively.

Policy and guidance

When discussing whether any policies impacted upon their professional identity, the SEN and Disability Code of Practice (DfE/DoH, 2015) was readily mentioned, as was the schools' own SEND policy. For some, this was highly positive as they felt that it clearly defined their role and there had been schoolwide training when the national policy was updated. This was further enhanced where local authorities provided clear guidance and transparent processes in relation to SEND to be used by all settings. However, barriers affecting those new to role included changing policy or pedagogy such as grading systems, funding, practices of wider agencies and importantly, how policy changes are communicated. This relates back to the concepts of relationship and sharing, with those having the most positive experiences, working in a collegiate manner to develop policies within or beyond school and ensuring that any changes are clearly shared with all involved.

The research clearly identified key knowledge, skills and characteristics required for the role. The emotional aspect of the role should not be underestimated, and the participants acknowledged the importance of having support to manage this aspect of the role, either within the setting or through formal supervision. Lack of formal induction and planned CPD for SENCOs was evident. Through better understanding and preparedness for the role and support identified through line management processes, recruitment and retention to the role is likely to be enhanced. Furthermore, the importance of small, local networks was deemed invaluable to some, and this may be used to enhance local authority meetings, which to some were overwhelming.

Planning for practice

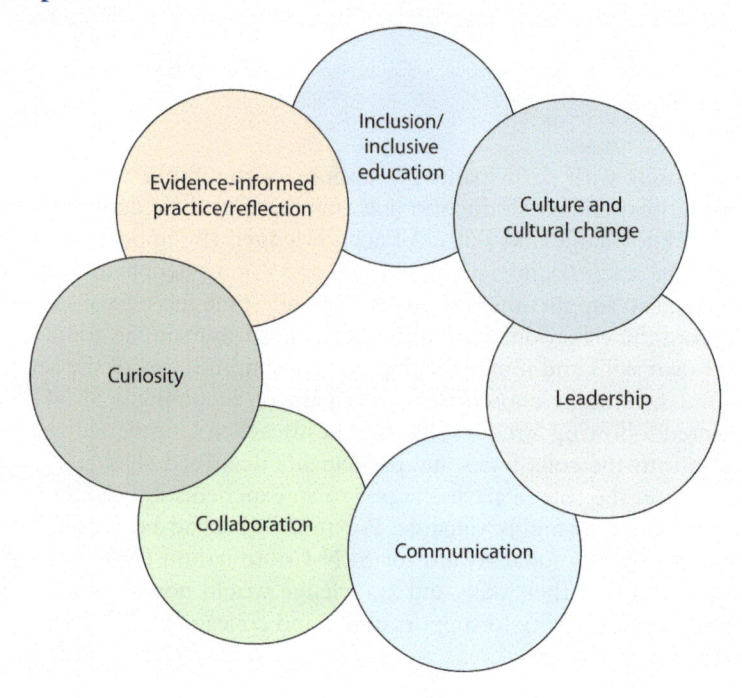

Figure 4.1 Key principles model

To develop outstanding leadership of SEND in schools requires a focus on *inclusion, leadership, communication* and *collaborative practices*. At times it may involve *cultural change* and this needs to be well-managed and planned, based on *professional curiosity* and a desire to always reflect on the changing needs of pupil cohorts and whether existing practices and attitudes continue to be fit for purpose, with a continued commitment to exploring *evidence-bases* to continually develop and improve practices.

Underpinning everything is the need to focus on relationships, respect and the emotional impact of the work that is undertaken in schools.

Understanding leadership

The starting point to ensuring effective SEND leadership is to develop a deeper understanding of the key principles of effective leadership and strategic leadership:

Reflective Activity

- Review your current school leadership in relation to the seven strong claims (Leithwood et al., 2008) earlier in the chapter, and also in relation to the four key ways that leaders achieved their leadership tasks

- Which of the claims and key areas of focus are already well embedded and effective within your school setting?

  How has this been achieved?
  What works well?

- Are there any areas that still need to be developed?

  How can this happen?
  Who needs to be involved?

- How are these key principles also understood and enacted in relation to the leadership of SEND in your school setting?

Reflective Activity

Think of an effective leader that you have worked with, or have heard of. Think also about a time when a change was well-led and managed. Use those examples to reflect on the key questions below to consider in more detail the factors that were central to that leader, or the leadership of that change, being successful:

- What key areas of focus, skills or attributes would you identify with effective strategic leaders?
- Why?
- What impact did those skills, attributes or practices have – on practice and on others in the organisation?
- Are there any skills, qualities of practices that you would identify as NOT being aligned to effective strategic leadership?

Strategic leaders

Have a look at the characteristics of effective strategic leaders identified by Cheminais (2015) below:

- Challenge and question – they are dissatisfied and restless with the status quo
- Prioritise their own strategic thinking and learning
- Display strategic wisdom based on a clear values system
- Have powerful personal and professional networks
- Possess high quality personal and interpersonal skills.

    – How far do you agree with these aspects?
    – How are they evidenced in practice in your own school setting?

Fullan's Framework for Leadership (Fullan, 2020: 9), also provides a useful framework for thinking about the different aspects of effective school and SEND leadership. This framework identifies the central principles underpinning the work of leaders:

- Moral purpose
- Nuance: understanding change
- Relationships, relationships, relationships
- Knowledge building and deep learning
- Coherence making

These central principles are all embedded within Enthusiasm, Hope and Energy.

This then leads to commitment by members (both external and internal); which in turn results in a positive impact/outcome – 'more good things happen; fewer bad things happen' (Fullan, 2020: 9).

Reflective Activity

Reflect on Fullan's Framework for Leadership (Fullan, 2020: 9).

- In your school setting, which aspects are already deeply embedded?
- How has this been achieved?
- Are there any areas to develop further?

Effective leadership, however, is not just about the practices, qualities and attitudes of the leader. Determining how effective the leadership is requires a focus on the impact in practice. Fullan (2020) cites the longitudinal study completed by Google into team performance, which identified five key aspects central to effective practice:

- Psychological safety: team members feel safe to take risks and be vulnerable in front of each other
- Dependability: team members get things done on time and meet Google's high bar for excellence
- Structure and clarity: team members have clear roles, plans and goals
- Meaning: work is personally important to team members
- Impact: team members think their work matters and creates change (Google, 2019: 6).

(Fullan, 2020: 34–35)

These five aspects are clearly directly influenced by the practices, qualities and attitudes enacted by the leader and therefore it is essential to review the impact that leadership has on practice.

> **Reflective Activity**
>
> - How far do you think that the qualities outlined above are evident and embedded in the working practices that you have in your school setting?
> - What is working well?
> - Why/how is that?
> - What has been done to achieve that success or effective way of working?
> - Are there any areas that still need to be developed further?
> - How could this be achieved?

Leadership of change

> **Reflective Activity**
>
> Write a list of recent changes that you have experienced or led in your school setting over the past three years.
>
> - Reflect on the levels of planning that were put in place for each of them – were they part of structured change and development planning processes, or reactive/responsive changes?
>
> Write a list of words or phrases that you would associate with the term 'change'.
>
> - Review your list – do the words on your list have largely negative or positive connotations?
> - What does this tell you about your own personal approach to change?
> - Do you know how others in your school setting feel about the term and concept of change?
> - How do you know?
>
> Complete the activity as a staff group and reflect on the words that are shared.
>
> - What might this suggest about how staff in your school as a whole may perceive change?
> - What are the implications of this for practice?

As we have identified, change can be a difficult thing to effect – particularly in large organisations. We therefore need to have a really well-embedded understanding of principles and tools to support effective change processes to be able to move forward effectively in our settings.

58 *Outstanding leadership of SEND*

The model in Table 4.1, based on the work of Martin and Holt (2002), is a helpful tool to support deeper understanding of the key principles that need to be considered and planned for to enable change processes to be effective:

Table 4.1 The effective change process

Vision	+ Skills	+ Incentives	+ Resources	+ Action Plan	= **Change**
	Skills	+ Incentives	+ Resources	+ Action Pan	= **Confusion**
Vision		+ Incentives	+ Resources	+ Action Plan	= **Anxiety**
Vision	+ Skills		+ Resources	+ Action Plan	= **Resistance/gradual change**
Vision	+ Skills	+ Incentives		+ Action Plan	= **Frustration**
Vision	+ Skills	+ Incentives	+ Resources		= **False Starts**

Source: Martin and Holt (2002).

Reflective Activity

Use Table 4.1 to reflect on any changes that have recently been implemented in your school setting.

- Do you feel that you had all five key aspects (Vision, Skills, Incentives, Resources and Action Plan) in place to support the change?
- What was the impact of that?
- Are there any changes that have been implemented that have not had all of those five key aspects in place?
- What has been the impact of that?

Think about any changes in practice that you are planning to implement:

- How will you be able to use this understanding to ensure that the change process is more successful?

Other tools that can be helpful in supporting effective change processes within the school setting include:

- **SWOT Analyses** – identifying, preferably as a group to engage collective understanding and ownership of the planned change, the Strengths; Weaknesses; Opportunities and Threats relating to the planned change. This will lead to deeper understanding of any areas that need to be considered further ahead of the implementation of the planned change
- **Forcefield Analyses** – identifying, as above, as a group where possible, the Driving Forces (those which will bring positive energy and commitment to the change) and the Restraining Forces (any barriers which will impact on the success of the planned change)
- **Coaching/Mentoring** – providing coaching and mentoring opportunities to support individual members of staff to be able to engage positively in change processes
- **Use of the EEF Putting Evidence to Work – A School's Guide to Implementation Guidance Report** (EEF, 2019) to support thinking about the Change and Implementation processes (see Figures 4.2 and 4.3) – see also further discussions in Chapter 13.

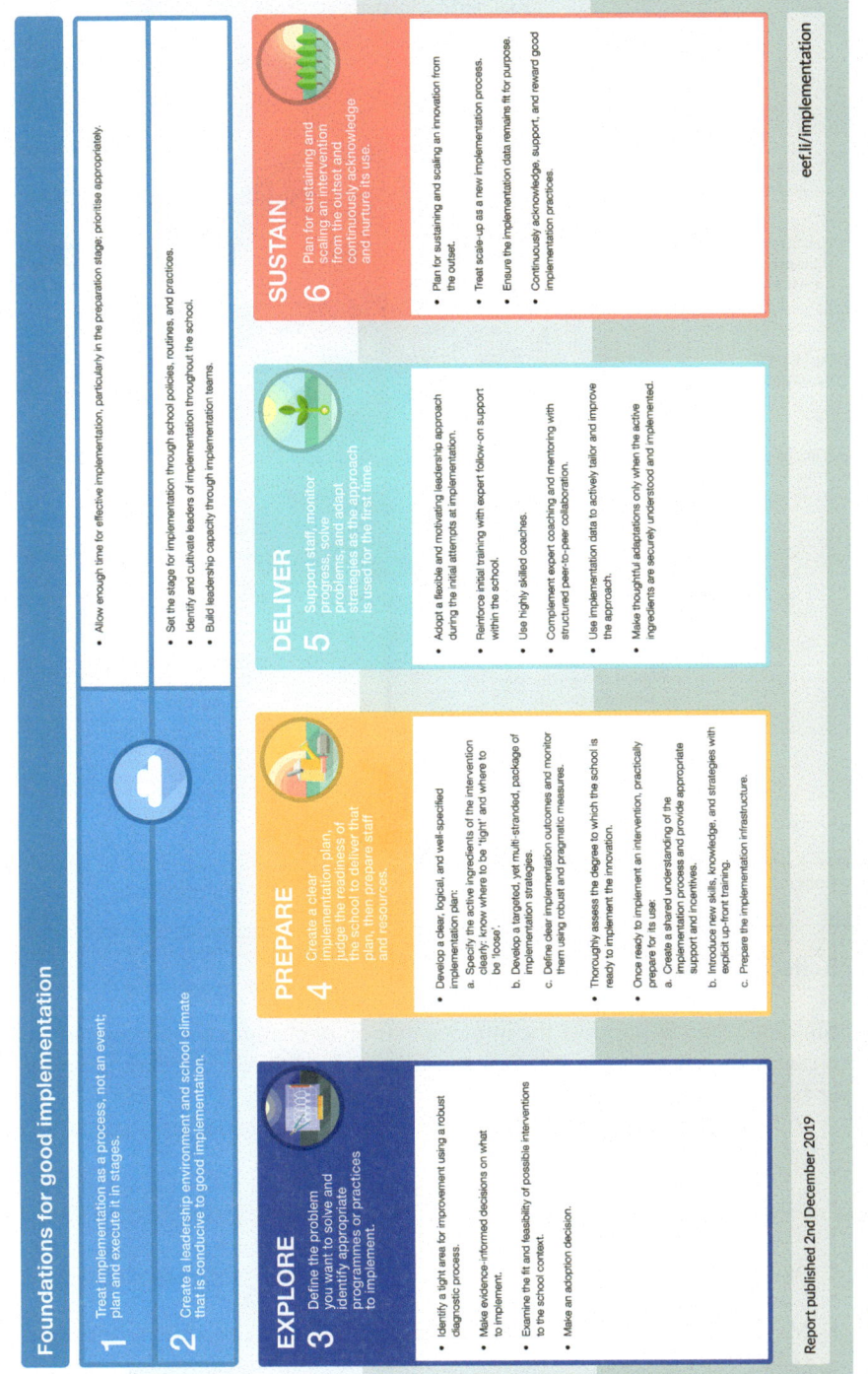

Figure 4.2 EEF – Schools' guide to implementation diagram

PUTTING EVIDENCE TO WORK: A SCHOOL'S GUIDE TO IMPLEMENTATION
Summary of recommendations

Education Endowment Foundation

Foundations for good implementation

1. Treat implementation as a process, not an event; plan and execute it in stages.
   - Allow enough time for effective implementation, particularly in the preparation stage; prioritise appropriately.

2. Create a leadership environment and school climate that is conducive to good implementation.
   - Set the stage for implementation through school policies, routines, and practices.
   - Identify and cultivate leaders of implementation throughout the school.
   - Build leadership capacity through implementation teams.

EXPLORE
3. Define the problem you want to solve and identify appropriate programmes or practices to implement.
- Identify a tight area for improvement using a robust diagnostic process.
- Make evidence-informed decisions on what to implement.
- Examine the fit and feasibility of possible interventions to the school context.
- Make an adoption decision.

PREPARE
4. Create a clear implementation plan, judge the readiness of the school to deliver that plan, then prepare staff and resources.
- Develop a clear, logical, and well-specified implementation plan:
  a. Specify the active ingredients of the intervention clearly: know where to be 'tight' and where to be 'loose'.
  b. Develop a targeted, yet multi-stranded, package of implementation strategies.
  c. Define clear implementation outcomes and monitor them using robust and pragmatic measures.
- Thoroughly assess the degree to which the school is ready to implement the innovation.
- Once ready to implement an intervention, practically prepare for its use:
  a. Create a shared understanding of the implementation process and provide appropriate support and incentives.
  b. Introduce new skills, knowledge, and strategies with explicit up-front training.
  c. Prepare the implementation infrastructure.

DELIVER
5. Support staff, monitor progress, solve problems, and adapt strategies as the approach is used for the first time.
- Adopt a flexible and motivating leadership approach during the initial attempts at implementation.
- Reinforce initial training with expert follow-on support within the school.
- Use highly skilled coaches.
- Complement expert coaching and mentoring with structured peer-to-peer collaboration.
- Use implementation data to actively tailor and improve the approach.
- Make thoughtful adaptations only when the active ingredients are securely understood and implemented.

SUSTAIN
6. Plan for sustaining and scaling an intervention from the outset and continuously acknowledge and nurture its use.
- Plan for sustaining and scaling an innovation from the outset.
- Treat scale-up as a new implementation process.
- Ensure the implementation data remains fit for purpose.
- Continuously acknowledge, support, and reward good implementation practices.

Report published 2nd December 2019

eef.li/implementation

60 *Outstanding leadership of SEND*

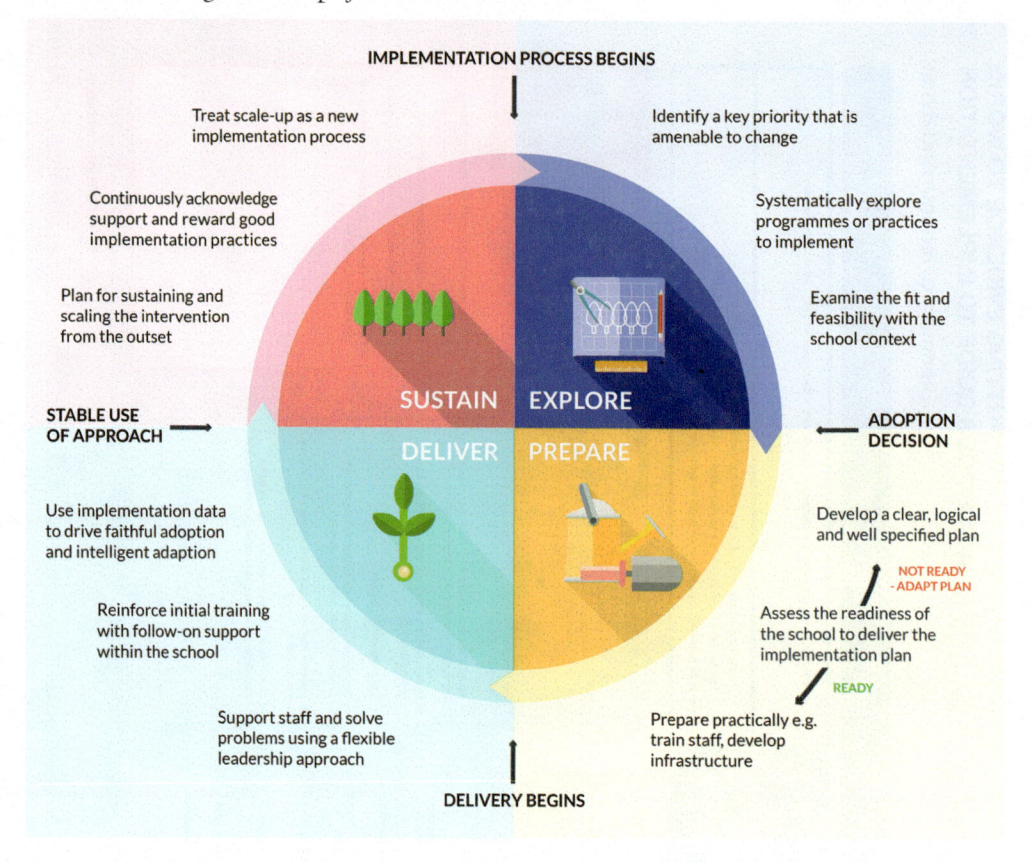

Figure 4.3 EEF – implementation process diagram

Source: EEF (2019: 5) – https://d2tic4wvo1iusb.cloudfront.net/eef-guidance-reports/implementation/EEF_Implementation_Guidance_Report_2019.pdf?v=1684757981 (accessed 21.5.2023)

Reflective Activity

Building teams to support the implementation of changes within your school setting is essential, and the makeup of each team may be different depending on the change or task needing to be completed.

Reflect on the skills that may be needed within the team – this may include, for example:

- Vision setting
- Analysis of data
- Review of evidence-bases
- Action-planning
- Communication
- Managing expectations and encouraging buy-in from others outside the team (EEF, 2019)
- Monitoring and evaluation.

Are there any other key skills that you would need to plan for?
How could you develop a team to include people with those different skills?

The development of the SENCO as a strategic leader

As we have seen, leading SEND effectively within the school setting cannot rely on the SENCO alone – it has to be a whole-school approach and commitment to understanding and meeting the needs of all pupils, including those with SEND.

Yet – the development of the SENCO within this is essential – moving the SENCO into a more strategic leadership role than the traditional coordinator role that the SENCO used to hold.

Reflective Activity

- How far is the SENCO seen as a strategic leader in your school setting?
- Are they on the senior leadership team currently, and what is the impact of that?
- If not – how are they able to influence the strategic direction of practices in the school to ensure that they are fully inclusive and support the needs of all pupils with SEND?

Reflective Activity

To be able to develop practices effectively, we need to stop and reflect on what is already in place and the effectiveness of those. We need to introduce 'principled interruptions' (Ainscow et al., 2006) which enable us to 'make the familiar unfamiliar' (Delamont & Atkinson, 1995) and engage in a critical review of the effectiveness of what is already in place to then stop systems, processes and practices that are not effective and identify more effective or efficient practices to embed moving forward.

To help to reflect on the role of the SENCO within your own setting, complete a work diary to record all of the tasks and activities that the SENCO engages with in their SENCO time in one week.

Bearing in mind that no week is 'typical' and fully representative of the daily and ongoing workload of the SENCO, review the work diary that has been collated.

- What are your initial thoughts when you review it?
- Is there anything that surprises you?

Now, consider the activities again and try to categorise them into the following activity types:

- Strategic
- Enabling/empowering others – developing the skills/confidence of others in the school setting
- Administrative
- Reactive
- Working directly with pupils with SEND

- What proportion of time is given to Strategic and Enabling/Empowering Others within your school setting?
- What does this tell you about the current role of the SENCO and how effective it may be?

To be able to develop effective practices, it is also essential that others, particularly senior leaders in your school setting have a really good understanding of the role and responsibilities of the SENCO.

Often, the breadth and range of strategic responsibilities that are now linked to the role of the SENCO is something of a surprise to colleagues, as, the role is now significantly different to the traditional 'coordinator' role that it once was.

To help everyone have understanding of the extent of the strategic leadership aspects of the role of the SENCO, it may be helpful to share with colleagues the current 49 SENCO Learning Outcomes set out as part of the statutory National Award for SEN Coordination (NCTL, 2014).

Whilst these were never intended to be used as a job description, they do currently set out the different aspects of the role that SENCOs now have to evidence that they are meeting in their role to achieve the mandatory SENCO qualification.

Although this will change in the years to come with the move away from the current National Award for SEN Coordination into the new NPQ for SENCOs, training providers and other stakeholders are working hard with the government to ensure that the quality of the statutory qualification is retained, and that there is effective support for SENCOs to develop all aspects of their role.

Consider the Case Study presented below, which provides a good example of the strategic leadership role of an effective SENCO who has gone beyond individual actions into planning for strategic approaches which enable, involve and empower the whole school community in relation to an aspect of practice and need that had been identified:

Case Study – Empowering Teaching Staff to Support the Present Needs of Our Four-Form Entry Mainstream Infant School

Carol Holah

In my school there was a noticeable increase in need in the category of Social, Emotional, and Mental Health (SEMH) within pupils identified with SEND (DfE/DoH, 2015). This was both for pupils with co-occurring and complex needs; such as Cognition and Learning needs and challenging behaviour, that were impacting on their progress, attendance and well-being. As SENCO, the data I analysed highlighted this. A further exploration commenced. This reflects the importance of going beyond the data; a 'spiral of inquiry' strategic approach (Halbert & Kaser, 2013). Anecdotal teacher feedback was considered. They were 'unable' or 'not confident' in supporting the pupils within lessons in an equitable way. The pupils were withdrawing, unable to articulate their feelings and presenting with behaviour of anger or disrupting their own or other's learning. Senior leaders were frequently called upon to manage and support both the teaching staff and pupils, impacting on workload, well-being and self-confidence for teaching staff but most importantly, the pupils with SEMH needs were not making progress.

Fundamental understanding of the SEMH needs was required. Initially a Boxall Profile assessment was carried out on each of the pupils. This would provide evidence of concerns and early identification of which pupils required support (Nurture UK, 2023). The results of the assessments were then categorised into three groups – first pupils who would benefit from attending a Nurture Group; these were pupils who had missed early nurturing experiences. Second, pupils who required more specialist, bespoke support such as accessing play therapy or sessions with our Emotional Literacy Support Assistant (ELSA) after experiencing trauma (past or present) and those who would benefit from their time in class when learning being supported with nurturing principles. As a result, clear pathways were established in how best to support our pupils with SEMH needs. Brief summaries of pupils were created in collaboration with parents/carers, staff who had past involvement such as previous teachers, the school's family support worker and current staff. Information about their early development, early experiences of play, relationships with parents/carers and what barriers were present in their lives at that time, as well as any information from outside agencies such as paediatricians or speech and language therapists was included. This entire process related to the second recommendation within the EEF (2020) SEND in Mainstream Schools Guidance Report; 'Build an ongoing, holistic understanding of your pupils and their needs' as it is an example of the school understanding individual pupil's learning needs using the Graduated Approach of the 'assess, plan, do, review' approach (EEF, 2020: 1).

Specialist training was sought, and The Nurture Programme was attended by two key members of staff who gained the qualification of Nurture Practitioners. A Nurture Group was set up. The analysis of the Boxall ensured close and specific identification of need and the staff training with its accompanying resources provided appropriate targets and activities to develop resilience and their capacity to deal more confidently with any trials or tribulations of their lives (Nurture UK, 2023).

Advice was sought from local specialist provision outreach services. Wider CPD was organised as a priority in the areas of attachment and trauma informed approaches. This was facilitated alongside safeguarding training so that links could be explicitly made around staff responsibility. As SENCO I ensured that all staff received this training, so line managers cascaded their CPD to their teams – lunch time leaders, office staff and breakfast/after-school care workers. The benefit was that all staff had more understanding and empathy as the CPD had thoroughly explained theory of different presentations of attachment styles. The evaluation proformas I analysed post the training detailed this. The attachment friendly and trauma informed approach of the staff started to develop and enabled suitable reasonable adjustments to be implemented. Planning and the classroom environments were adjusted accordingly. Therefore, there was 'buy in' to setting up a Nurture Group and releasing support staff to facilitate it.

To ensure a strategic and 'spiral' approach would be regularly reviewed and acted upon a number of steps were carried out. Regular triangulation between Nurture Practitioners, myself as SENCO, the family support worker and teaching staff ensured that any updates within the wider family picture, any essential background information and behaviour challenges present within class were shared. Learning Walks carried out as SENCO were an opportunity to review how the CPD was being embedded and provided an opportunity to observe the pupils within all three of the identified pathways. The pathways were interchangeable for pupils, as a clear identification process was now embedded. I started to see staff referring pupils for the different pathways but only after an exhaustion of the quality first teaching adaptations. During Pupil Progress Review Meetings, the class provision maps were updated, utilising the results of the most recent Boxall Profile results. This ensured up to date record keeping of who attended which provision but also provided information about the impacts. One tension identified was that some pupils attending the provision were missing out on some key subjects such as Science. Therefore, that triangulation process evolved to leading not only sharing key information but also adapting curriculum opportunities within the nurturing setting and within class. I monitored how teachers were adapting their teaching and timetables so that the pupils with SEMH needs had access to their skills. The quality of teachers' planning and of their delivery of teaching and learning has a major impact on every pupil's development and any intervention is purely there to supplement it, not replace it (EEF, 2020).

Over time, less calls were made to SLT to support as teachers were equipped with skills in including these pupils. There was a significant reduction in negative behaviour incidents, particularly around pupils who had similar needs. This ensured that immediate 'repair' and restorative approaches could be implemented. Staff rapidly began to see the impact. Pupils were more engaged and made progress within lessons. To ensure longevity of the journey our school had encountered, this approach was eventually built into all key policies such as behaviour and SEND as well as featuring as a priority within the school improvement plan. Nurture featured regularly within school and class assemblies, newsletters and expectations in how staff spoke to and addressed pupils. When all put into action, the school is giving these most vulnerable pupils the social and emotional skills to do as well at school as their peers.

Reflective Activity

Reflect on the Case Study provided above.

- What are the key strategic leadership aspects that the SENCO has taken in this example?
- How has the SENCO ensured a whole-school responsibility for this area of focus?
- Are there aspects of practice, or the approaches taken, in this Case Study that would benefit your current setting and role?
- In what ways?
- How could you plan to take this forward?

Being an effective and outstanding leader of SEND today, within the challenging context for SEND nationally, the SENCO needs to draw on a number of key leadership qualities to mediate the concerns and frustrations experienced by everyone – parents/carers navigating adversarial systems and processes which are not fit for purpose, and the workload concerns raised by staff as a result both of the rising complexity of what are now seen as 'predictable' needs and the impact of the cost of living crisis on staffing levels in schools.

Within this storm of emotional experiences, frustrations and concerns, most importantly, the SENCO therefore needs to retain a strong moral purpose and be the advocate of those pupils, and their families, who may be considered to have the most challenging and complex needs.

In this, we see the SENCO's role to be multi-faceted, but to certainly include the following key aspects:

- **Advocate** – 'Champion of Children'
- **Enabler** – of all. To enable pupils, staff and parents/carers to be able to access information and opportunities in the most effective ways
- **Strategic development** – having a direct impact on Quality of Education
- **Coach** – embedding Solutions-focused approaches (see also Chapter 6)
- **Translator/interpreter** – of statutory responsibilities and guidance and SEND 'jargon' for all – staff colleagues, parents/carers and pupils.

Above all, the SENCO must imbue positivity and a can-do approach and attitude to, at times, meeting the needs of the most complex pupils in our education system. They need to be able to inspire others through their positivity, enthusiasm and passion for meeting the needs of all pupils. Through modelling and positive communications, the SENCO should gently and positively challenge any embedded assumptions and deficit approaches to understanding needs and support colleagues to understand difference and needs in more inclusive ways.

Central to this, as we will see throughout the book, is the need for effective communication systems and real visibility of the SENCO.

One of our key mantras is to acknowledge the fact that people 'don't know what they don't know'. When people don't know or understand something fully, this can lead to an increase in negative emotional responses – including fear, anxiety, defensiveness, lack of confidence and self-efficacy.

The role of the SENCO, therefore, needs to firmly be positioned around ensuring ease of access to information to help all staff to know what they need to know and be able to apply it in practice. As we demonstrate throughout the chapters of this book, simple tools and formats which provide key information linked to Red Amber Green (RAG) rating scales or simple, concise strategic overviews can therefore be really effective in giving staff access to the key information that they need to know.

Reflective Activity

Reflect on the key qualities of the effective SENCO identified above.

- How far are those key qualities reflected in your work, or the work of the SENCO?
- What practices currently work well to support this?
- Is there anything that could be developed further?

Concluding comments and reflections

Outstanding leadership of SEND in schools is a complex and dynamic process, deeply embedded in a clear moral purpose, built on inclusive values and effective communication and relationship skills. Outstanding leadership of SEND, however, is not something that one person can take forward alone. For SEND leadership to be effective in our schools, it must be something that involves everyone – that everyone is committed to and sees as their responsibility.

To be able to achieve this requires a focus on the culture and leadership practices of the school as a whole, and a deep, shared understanding both of SEND statutory responsibilities (and the moral purpose embedded in inclusive practices) and the role and responsibilities of the SENCO. To be effective, the SENCO must be supported and enabled to develop their strategic leadership skills and have the time to be able to support others in the school setting to be able to fulfil their statutory responsibilities for SEND.

Individual Reflection

- What new information/learning have you gained from this chapter?
- What are your key reflections?
- What are your next steps/actions as a result?

References

Bourke, J. and Titus, A. (2020) *The key to inclusive leadership*. Harvard Business Review. https://hbr.org/2020/03/the-key-to-inclusive-leadership (accessed 29.4.2023).

DCSF (2008) *Education (Special Educational Needs Coordinators) (England) regulations 2008: Explanatory note for governing bodies*. London: DCSF.

DfE/DoHSC (2023) *Special Educational Needs and Disabilities (SEND) and Alternative Provision Improvement Plan – Right support, right place, right time*. London: HMSO.

EEF (2019) *Putting evidence to work: A school's guide to implementation*. London: EEF.

EEF (2020) *SEN in mainstream schools*. London: EEF.

Ekins, A. (2017) *Reconsidering inclusion – Sustaining and building inclusive practices in schools*. Abingdon: Routledge.

Fullan, M. (2020) *Leading in a culture of change* (2nd Edition). Hoboken, NJ: Jossey-Bass.

Leithwood, K., Harris, A. and Hopkins, D. (2008) 'Seven strong claims about successful school leadership'. *School Leadership and Management* 28(1), 27–42.

Martin, J. and Holt, A. (2002) *Joined up governance*. Ely: Adamson Books.

NCTL (2014) *National award for SEN coordination learning outcomes*. London: NCTL.

Ottesen, E. (2013) 'Inclusion: A critique of selected national policy frameworks'. In: Ruairc, G., Ottesen, E. and Precey, R. eds. *Leadership for inclusive education: Values, vision and voices*. The Netherlands: Sense Publishers.

Passy, R., Georgeson, J., Schaefer, N. and Kaimi, I. (2017) *Evaluation of the Impact and effectiveness of the National Award for Special Educational Needs Coordination*. https://pearl.plymouth.ac.uk/bitstream/handle/10026.1/10077/SENCo report_final_18.08.2017+Appendices.pdf?sequence=1&&isAllowed=y (accessed 31.5.23).

Precey, R. and Mazurkiewicz, G. (2013) 'Leadership for inclusion an overview'. In: Ruairc, G., Ottesen, E. and Precey, R. eds. *Leadership for inclusive education: Values, vision and voices*. The Netherlands: Sense Publishers.

Ruairc, G., Ottesen, E. and Precey, R. eds. (2013) *Leadership for inclusive education: Values, vision and voices*. The Netherlands: Sense Publishers.

5 Whole-school approaches to SEND

> In this chapter, we critically examine and explore the following key aspects:
>
> - Inclusive school cultures
> - Teacher and staff self-efficacy and confidence levels
> - Training in SEND
> - Whole-school inclusive pedagogy
> - High-quality teaching
> - Inclusion by design
> - Scaffolding and adaptation

Key issues

Understanding and meeting the needs of all pupils with Special Educational Needs and Disability (SEND) needs to be a commitment enacted at all levels within the school setting. It is not and should not be seen as the sole responsibility of the Special Educational Needs Coordinator (SENCO), although the SENCO will have the responsibility to coordinate and lead the development of effective practices to enable and empower all staff to understand and meet their statutory responsibilities in relation to SEND.

We have long heard the mantra of 'All teachers are teachers of SEN'– first mooted in the National Curriculum Inclusion Statement (DfEE/QCA, 1999) and subsequently consistently referenced in the various versions of the Special Educational Needs (SEN) Code of Practice (DfES, 2001; DfE/DoH, 2014, 2015) and in the various versions of the Teacher Standards (DfE, 2021).

Yet, whilst we agree with this statement, we believe that the issue should be about more than 'all teachers being teachers of SEN' – it should be about deep-rooted and full understanding of and commitment to SEND at all levels within the school context. This starts with the development of an inclusive culture which understands and prioritises planning for the needs of pupils with SEND as the central core around which all other planning develops from.

Key issues central to the effective embodiment of whole-school approaches to SEND therefore include a focus and attention on:

1. The importance of inclusive school cultures
2. The implications and impact of teacher and staff self-efficacy and understanding of statutory responsibilities for SEND
3. Developing a whole-school inclusive pedagogy.

DOI: 10.4324/9781003033554-5

Current policy/research context

Inclusive school cultures

Within schools, the responsibility for SEND must be seen as a whole-school shared responsibility, and the culture and practices within the school must reflect this focus and commitment to meeting the needs of all pupils with SEND at all levels, and in all ways.

Schools need to adopt an inclusive culture, one that positions inclusivity for all pupils, including those with SEND, at the heart of thinking and practice.

Much has been written both nationally and internationally about the importance and concept of inclusion and inclusive school cultures (Booth & Ainscow, 2000, 2002, 2011, 2016; Ekins, 2017) and this is now also emphasised in the EEF (2020) SEN Mainstream Schools Guidance Report which identifies that

> In an inclusive school, pupils with SEND are not just *in* the school, they are *part* of the school – they have the same opportunities as their peers to benefit from the highest quality teaching the school can provide.
>
> (EEF, 2020: 12)

As the EEF (2020: 10) note: 'Creating an inclusive environment is the most important thing a school can do. An inclusive culture is a prerequisite for an effective school: it brings happiness, a feeling of safety and being part of the community, and, of course, it impacts positively on learning, both in the classroom and beyond. It is our job to prepare pupils to flourish and feel truly included in society'.

The importance of inclusion and inclusive school cultures is also emphasised in the SEND and Alternative Provision Improvement Plan (DfE/DoHSC, 2023), with the government expressing that their 'vision is to create a more inclusive society that celebrates and enables success in all forms, with the cultures, attitudes and environments to offer every child and young person the support that they need to participate fully, thrive and fulfil their potential. We want the process of identifying needs and accessing support to be early, dignified and affirmative, focusing on a child or young person's achievements, talents, and strengths' (DfE/DoHSC, 2023: 7).

The DfE/DoHSC (2023: 22) are committed to 'significant societal change' to provide an inclusive system where everyone can 'thrive and feel a strong sense of belonging' (DfE/DoHSC, 2023: 22–23).

Key to inclusion and the sense of being part of the school community is therefore the concept of BELONGING. As the DfE/DoHSC (2023: 23) note, 'a whole-setting inclusive ethos improves the sense of belonging for those with SEND and has been found to increase acceptance of difference amongst peers'.

To be able to achieve an inclusive culture, requires more than one person dedicated to inclusive values or championing the needs of specific vulnerable groups, for example SEND. The approach instead needs to be embedded across the whole school, in the values and practices of all members of the community. Thus, 'adopting inclusive practice requires distributed responsibility for SEND' (EEF, 2020: 12) (see also discussions in Chapter 4).

A fully distributed approach, where everyone understands and is committed to meeting the needs of all pupils, including those with SEND can be difficult to achieve and, as we will see in the Planning for Practice section of this chapter, will require ongoing prioritisation and enactment of those inclusive values to ensure that they filter into every aspect of whole-school planning and development, from policy, to curriculum planning, to environment, to relationships and communication.

Teacher and staff self-efficacy and understanding of statutory responsibilities for SEND

Understanding and meeting the needs of pupils with SEND can, at times, be challenging and this can impact on the confidence of the teacher (Ekins et al., 2016). Looking at teacher and staff levels of self-efficacy is therefore an important factor in supporting the development of increasingly effective inclusive and SEND practices. Self-efficacy relates both to confidence levels and beliefs/feelings (Ekins et al., 2016) and is directly connected to the support that they have been provided with, or perceive that they have received as well as their general attitudes towards inclusive education.

Unfortunately, despite years of reports identifying that teachers generally do not receive enough training, and therefore do not feel confident or have the levels of self-efficacy around understanding SEND and knowing how to meet the needs of pupils with SEND within their classrooms (House of Commons Select Committee, 2006; OFSTED, 2010; Ekins et al., 2016; DfE, 2017), we still face a situation where it is noted that teachers do not receive enough training to help them to feel confident in this area:

- 'Typically, teachers, especially secondary school teachers, receive minimal information on SEND as part of their initial teacher training. This knowledge is often something that comes informally, piecemeal and from experience' (DfE, 2017: 14)
- Respondents 'also made reference to the impact that lack of training has on their ability to support learners with SEN/ALN/ASN. For instance:

Neither me nor my TA have received specialised training to support SEN children who each year have very different needs' (NASUWT, 2018: 7)

- 'We were told by the National Development Team for Inclusion (NDTI) that there was a "lack of confidence in schools to include children and young people with more complex SEND which has led to a deskilling of competencies regarding a graduated response"' (House of Commons Education Committee, 2019: 45).

Fortunately, this is therefore something that the DfE/DoHSC (2023) have acknowledged and committed to address in the SEND and Alternative Provision Improvement Plan (DfE/DoHSC, 2023):

- 'Our programmes and policies will build confidence and expertise at every level of the workforce, from teachers and classroom staff through to specialists, and to leaders who set the overall direction and culture of their settings' (DfE/DoHSC, 2023: 53)
- 'We need to go further if we are going to achieve the aim of improving mainstream provision so that it is more inclusive of children and young people with SEND. Respondents consistently highlighted the need for ongoing teacher training – and when children and young people who are in alternative provision were asked what would have helped them stay in their mainstream school, the most common answer was teacher training in SEND' (DfE/DoHSC, 2023: 54).

A dedicated focus on effective training about SEND, therefore, is seen to be essential to supporting teachers to be able to understand and feel confident in meeting the needs of pupils with SEND. Thus, as the SEN and Disability Code of Practice (DfE/DoH, 2015: 93) identifies:

> The quality of teaching for pupils with SEN, and the progress made by pupils should be a core part of the school's performance management arrangements and its approach to professional development for all teaching and support staff.

Training about SEND and the different areas of need (see Chapters 6, 8 and 9) is therefore vital, yet it is not without its challenges and complexities.

Whilst teachers do need to know about and understand different 'types' of SEND, we still need to recognise that every child, and every child with SEND, is individual and that therefore their needs, differences and individual strengths will be very different – personal to them and impacted by the individual contexts and circumstances that they live in. Thus, as the DfE (2017: 15) identify,

> it is not normally useful to assume that "all" those with a particular need will require the same type of support. Mitchell (2014) suggests rather that:

> my strong advice to you is that you should develop a repertoire of such strategies nested within your own philosophy ... professional wisdom, and above all knowledge of the characteristics and needs of your students.

That deep knowledge of the child as an individual, and supporting teachers to understand and be able to use this, is paramount and is focused on further in Chapters 6 and 10.

Whilst training and knowledge can therefore be helpful, effective teaching and learning for pupils with SEND is about more than that – research cited by the EEF (2020) by Rix et al. (2009) identified the importance of 'positive attitudes towards the inclusion of children with SEND' and that teachers who held those positive attitudes then engaged in better quality interactions with pupils, as the teachers 'saw themselves as responsible for the learning of all pupils and had longer interactions with pupils with SEN, using time to ensure they fully participated in the class' (EEF, 2020: 11). Teachers' position and values therefore are influential determining factors in providing an inclusive environment. Forlin et al. (2011: 51) explored teachers' Sentiments, Attitudes and Concerns about Inclusive Education (SACIE) and identified:

> Understanding pre-service teachers' beliefs about inclusion is important as positive attitudes towards inclusion are amongst the strongest predictors of the success of the inclusion reforms (Avramidis & Norwich, 2002; Forlin, 2010a). Effective inclusionary practices have been found to depend to a noticeable extent on the sentiments of teachers – about the nature of disability and their perceived roles in supporting students with special education needs (Jordan, Schwartz & McGhie-Richmond, 2009).

The issue is therefore seen to be more about positive attitudes towards SEND and 'requires positive relationships and interactions between teachers and pupils' (EEF, 2020: 11).

Developing a whole-school inclusive pedagogy

Whilst 'SEND' and meeting the needs of pupils with SEND continues to be seen by many as a daunting or overwhelming task, one that many teachers still do not feel adequately equipped to be successful at, yet, as the EEF (2020) identifies:

> The evidence review for this guidance report found strong evidence that high quality teaching for pupils is firmly based on strategies that will already be in the repertoire of every mainstream teacher or can be relatively easily added to it.
>
> (EEF, 2020: 20)

This needs to be our starting point to support the development of more inclusive and effective learning environments to meet the needs of all pupils – what we are focusing on here is the development of effective teaching strategies and skills – ones that can then be applied and used to support the needs of all pupils, rather than it all being about completely different and separate strategies for pupils with SEND. Indeed, as the DfE/DoHSC (2023: 54) note:

> Teacher quality is one of the most important in-school determinants of pupil outcomes, reducing the risk that children fall behind due to missed opportunities or lack of appropriate support. High-quality, evidence-based teaching is critical in ensuring that the special educational needs of pupils are not mis-identified when their difficulties may be due to poor classroom provision, as well as ensuring that the needs of those with SEN are met effectively.

There is, therefore, widespread recognition of the importance of a rigorous focus on high-quality teaching although, as the House of Commons Education Committee (2019) identify unfortunately it is again one of those concepts that is discussed as if it is a given, without clear definition of what is actually meant. Thus, the House of Commons Education Committee (2019: 45) 'received conflicting evidence on this point. Information about "quality first teaching" included that schools are struggling to deliver it, schools are delivering it well and that it was listed in an EHCP as an educational intervention. It appeared that there may be challenges around schools being able to provide quality teaching to all its pupils, or that pupils with SEND are left to the postcode lottery of the quality of teaching in their schools'.

The focus, therefore, should be on developing the quality of teaching and curriculum delivery, including adaptive teaching to ensure that it meets the needs of all pupils. Addressing misconceptions and providing additional support should be planned as part of the daily whole class teaching rather than being left to be addressed through withdrawn intervention at the end of a taught topic.

Moving forward, this will hopefully be addressed through the new National Standards and the SEND and alternative provision practice guides which will provide consistent evidence-informed information about expectations for practice (DfE/DoHSC, 2023: 28), and which will enable 'every leader [to] be bought into a shared vision for how needs should be identified and supported, whether at the universal, targeted, or specialist level'.

Alongside the new recommendations of the DfE/DoHSC (2023) SEND and Alternative Provision Improvement Plan, the EEF (2020) SEN in Mainstream Schools Guidance Report, provides a clear structure and evidence-informed recommendations for developing practices to support effective whole-school approaches to SEND.

The five recommendations (see Figure 5.1) therefore provide a clear framework for thinking and the development of practice.

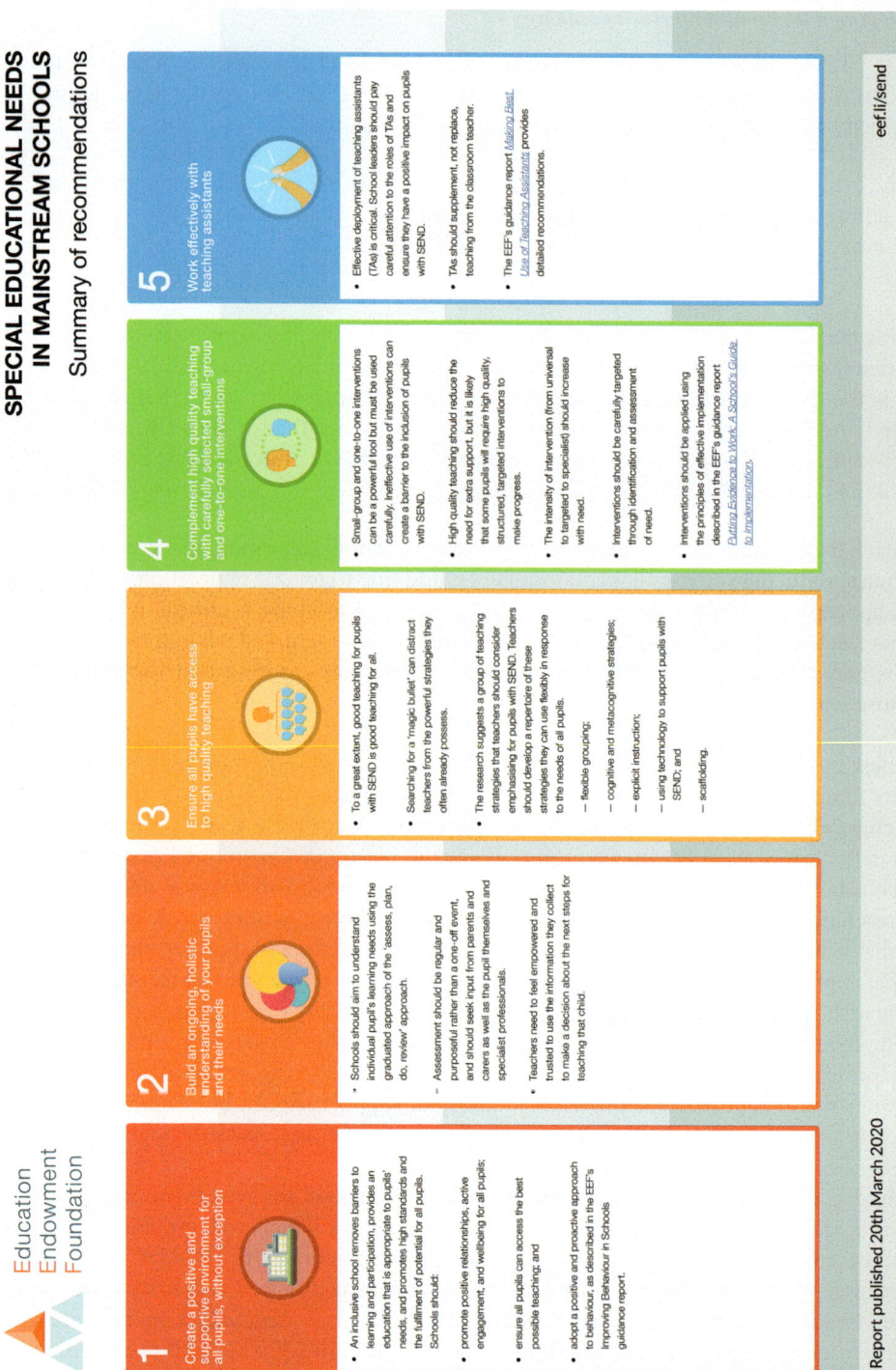

72 *Whole-school approaches to SEND*

Figure 5.1 EEF SEND recommendations

Source: https://d2tic4wvo1iusb.cloudfront.net/eef-guidance-reports/send/EEF_Special_Educational_Needs_in_Mainstream_Schools_Recommendations_Poster.pdf?v=1685459753 (accessed 1.5.2023)

Built within the first key recommendation is the concept of 'Inclusion by design' – as the EEF (2020: 10) identify – 'An inclusive environment does not come by accident, it is achieved through design. Furthermore, it is imperative that leaders embed this culture proactively'.

In this, there is a proactive prioritisation to ensure that thinking and planning to ensure that all pupils can be positively included and that barriers to participation and access are removed from the start – at the design stage – rather than considered once aspects of practice have already been planned – as an after-thought.

Inclusion by design also refers to purposeful planning and design of all aspects of the school – not just learning activities. In this, attention is positively paid, at the design stage, to not only the curriculum and learning activities, but also social and physical activities and environments, the general environment and ethos (including the structure and timings of the school day), the communication systems that are used, the food and drink options that are available, and ways that they are available.

Inclusion by design therefore positively refers to all aspects of the school environment and experience for all pupils and provides a useful framework for further thinking and exploration of ways to achieve inclusive school settings. The planning for all of these aspects is then firmly *built in* to planning and design for the curriculum and environment for all from the start – rather than being *bolt on* to existing models of practice that do not accommodate the needs of all pupils.

Planning for practice

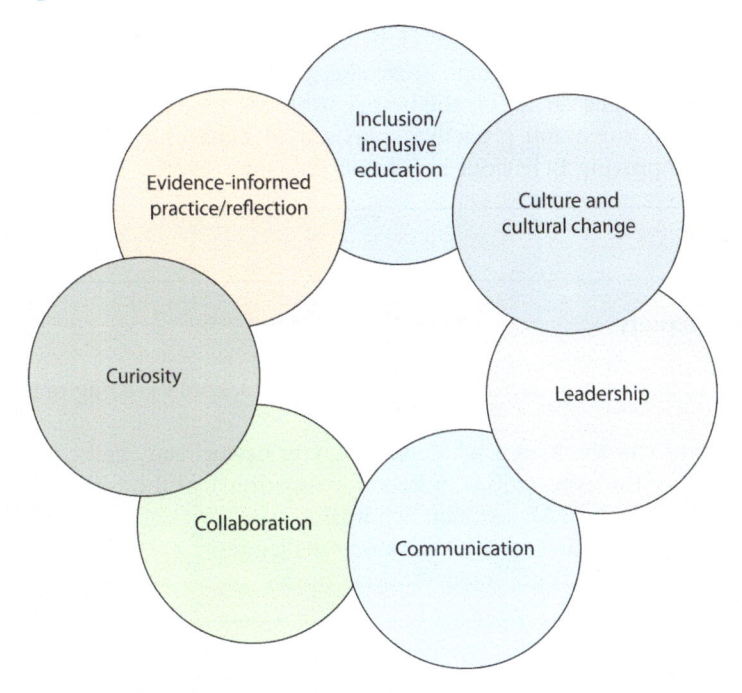

Figure 5.2 Key principles model

As we identified in Chapter 1, our statutory responsibilities for SEND need to start with a principled approach to recognising the importance of accepting diversity and the rights of the child to a quality education – one that is able to meet their individual needs (EEF, 2020).

Doing this requires a clear commitment to all of our key principles: ***Inclusive values***, ***Cultural Change***, ***Leadership*** approaches which reflect and are built on inclusive values, effective ***Communication*** with and the ***Collaboration*** of everyone within the school context, opportunities for professional ***Curiosity*** to consider and reconsider practices and different ways of working and thinking/understanding and an engagement with and development of ***Evidence-Informed Practices*** and ***Reflection***.

Inclusive school cultures

Recommendation 1 from the EEF (2020) Special Educational Needs in Mainstream Schools Guidance Report is crucial in ensuring principled approaches to guarantee that the school as a whole is committed to understanding and meeting their statutory responsibilities for SEND:

EEF (2020): Special Educational Needs in Mainstream Schools

Recommendation 1: Create a positive and supportive environment for all pupils without exception

- An inclusive school removes barriers to learning and participation, provides an education that is appropriate to pupils' needs, and promotes high standards and the fulfilment of potential for all pupils. Schools should:
    - Promote positive relationships, active engagement, and well-being for all pupils
    - Ensure all pupils can access the best possible teaching and
    - Adopt a positive and proactive approach to behaviour, as described in the EEF's Improving Behaviour in Schools guidance report.

Reflective Activity

Using the audit tool in Table 5.1 start to audit your school's existing practices.

- How far do you think, as a whole school, you have already embedded practices to meet all of the expectations in Recommendation 1 of the EEF (2020) Special Educational Needs in Mainstream Schools?
- What are the remaining areas to work on/challenges?
- How will you plan to continue to address those?

Table 5.1 Audit tool for schools to explore the EEF (2020) Special Educational Needs in Mainstream School

Recommendation – the school:	RAG* rating	What is already in place? How do you know? What evidence do you have?	What more needs to be developed? How will you do this?
Understands, recognises and removes barriers to learning and participation			
Places support for pupils with SEND at the heart of school priorities – *being inclusive by design*			
Ensures that planning and understanding of the needs of pupils with SEND is reinforced in the language, activities, routines and strategies across the whole school setting as well as the classroom context			
Provides an education that is appropriate to pupils' needs			
Promotes high standards and the fulfilment of potential for all pupils.			
Promotes positive relationships, active engagement, and well-being for all pupils			
Ensures that teachers see themselves as responsible for the learning of pupils with SEND and have longer interactions with pupils with SEND to ensure that they are able to fully participate in the lesson			
Creates an environment that is genuinely positive and supportive for all pupils, without exception			
Ensures all pupils can access the best possible teaching			
Adopts a positive and proactive approach to behaviour, as described in the EEF's Improving Behaviour in Schools guidance report			

* R = Not yet in place; A = In place but not yet embedded; G = Fully embedded

Reflective Activity

- What are the starting points for your staff in relation to their understanding of Inclusion and key concepts relating to the development of inclusive practices in school?
- How do you know this?
- Review the Case Study next and consider any actions that you may take to develop shared understandings further
    - What will you plan do to?
    - Who will you involve in this?

> **Case Study – Developing Shared Understandings of Inclusion and Key Concepts Relating to the Development of Inclusive Practices**
>
> **A range of primary and secondary schools**
>
> In response to a focused piece of work around developing everyone's understanding of statutory SEND responsibilities, the SENCOs in each school led a Professional Learning session with a range of activities designed to gather initial understandings.
>
> The session began with quick fire post-it note activities to gauge individual understanding of Inclusion
>
> - What does the term inclusion mean to you?
>
> Staff were given one minute to record their immediate response to this question, and the anonymous post-it notes were then collected and, after the session, collated to produce a document that could be reviewed by all staff to review their collective understandings of inclusion.
>
> This simple, one-minute activity was then able to provide a really clear definition of inclusion for the school setting – that came from and was owned by the staff members, rather than imposed upon them.
>
> During the Professional Learning session, staff also worked in phase or subject groups to work together to start to consider and define the following key concepts central to the development of inclusive practices and the implementation of statutory SEND responsibilities:
>
> - Inclusion by design
> - Removing barriers to participation and access
> - Graduated approach.
>
> Staff were given time to talk through their shared understandings of each phrase and ways that they embedded those concepts in practice, recording their responses on large sheets of flip-chart paper.
>
> This was followed by brief feedback altogether and information to all staff about the actual meanings of the terms and where they have stemmed from (e.g. Booth & Ainscow, 2002; DfE/DoH, 2014, 2015; EEF, 2020), after which the staff phase or subject area groups had time to review their own responses and add on anything else that they wished in terms of capturing their current practices and also in terms of identifying next steps and things that they collectively wanted to focus on to develop further.
>
> Finally, staff were given time to walk around and look at each other's responses to support the furthering of a collective understanding of those terms in practice within their school setting.
>
> The impact of this approach to Professional Learning and the development of a shared understanding of these central concepts in practice, rather than a 'lecture-style' delivered continuing professional development (CPD) session to staff was that they engaged actively in the processes of meaning-making and planning for next steps. The definitions that were produced were owned by the staff themselves, rather than imposed from outside, meaning that there is now a greater understanding and collective buy-in to and engagement with the concepts in practice.

Teacher self-efficacy and understanding of statutory responsibilities for SEND

In order to support and enhance teacher and staff self-efficacy and confidence levels in relation to being able to meet the needs of all pupils, including those with SEND, it is essential that there is a clear and explicit approach to providing key information. Emotional responses towards understanding and meeting the needs of pupils with SEND are heightened when staff perceive that they are faced with something that they do not know about or understand. Key to increasing confidence levels and reducing stress and anxieties is therefore about the systems that you have in place to share information in accessible ways which encourage staff to engage directly and meaningfully with it (see also the discussions in Chapter 5 about different ways to provide meaningful staff CPD, and the discussions in Chapters 6 and 7 about effective systems and processes for sharing information).

Ultimately, the key information about our statutory responsibilities for meeting the needs of pupils with SEND is set out in the SEN and Disability Code of Practice (DfE/DoH, 2015), which is built upon the previous SEN Code of Practices (DfE, 1994; DfES, 2001). It is therefore this to which we must continue to refer and adhere to in terms of ensuring that practices and statutory responsibilities within the school setting are effective and legally meet the needs of pupils with SEND (see also discussions in Chapter 3 relating to SEND law).

Reflective Activity

- What do you already know about the statutory responsibilities for schools for SEND?
- How do you know this?
- How recently have you revisited this information to check that your understanding of them is complete and up to date?
- How fully do you think all colleagues in your school setting are aware of and understand the statutory responsibilities?

Ensuring that everyone in the school context is familiar with the statutory responsibilities for SEND as set out in the SEN and Disability Code of Practice (DfE/DoH, 2015) and the new SEND & Alternative Provision Improvement Plan (DfE/DoHSC, 2023) is crucial in ensuring an embedded culture of practice where SEND is a shared responsibility and not simply delegated to the SENCO.

Chapter 6 of the SEN & Disability Code of Practice (DfE/DoH, 2015: 91–110) sets out the information about statutory responsibilities for SEND in schools and it is therefore really important that not only the SENCO knows and understands this information, but that all staff in the school setting are aware about it.

Case Study – Using the SEN and Disability Code of Practice to Ensure Staff Understanding of the Statutory Responsibilities for SEND

This case study comes from practices developed in a number of different school settings.

Key issue

SEND was a priority area of focus for the schools and the SENCO had identified that underpinning the challenges with being able to move forward practices, was the fact that staff did not have a shared understanding of the statutory responsibilities for SEND. Too often SEND was seen as something that could just be 'passed on' to the SENCO, and often staff were making inappropriate recommendations to parents/carers about provision or the need for statutory assessment, without understanding what was already available, in place or the thresholds for statutory assessment.

The SENCO therefore needed to find ways for staff to be more aware of their statutory responsibilities, and also the processes that would be followed by the SENCO once a child had been identified as having SEND.

The SENCO had already developed a comprehensive SEND policy and had shared this with staff in a staff CPD session at the start of the year, but was concerned by the lack of active engagement with this and the lack of application of the knowledge/information following the session.

Implementation

To encourage more active engagement with the information, the SENCO therefore then planned a different approach, using Chapter 6 from the SEN and Disability Code of Practice (DfE/DoH, 2015).

Staff worked in pairs and were provided with one page from the Chapter 6 of the SEN and Disability Code of Practice.

Each pair of staff read their page and highlighted any key information that they felt was particularly important for all staff to be aware of, and any key questions that they had about how that may be implemented in practice in their school setting.

Each pair then joined other pairs so that each larger group was formed of pairs who had all read different pages from Chapter 6.

The pairs took it in turns to share with each other the key information that they had highlighted and the key questions that it had generated for them.

As a group, the staff members then summarised their top three key learning points from everything that they had read and discussed, and their top three questions about how to implement it in practice.

The staff group came back together again as a whole and shared their top three learning points and top three questions.

As a whole staff group, they then agreed their whole-school top three learning points and critical questions that they would explore and develop/implement through the year.

Impact

As a result of this more active CPD session, all staff members engaged directly with Chapter 6 of the SEN and Disability Code of Practice (DfE/DoH, 2015) in a way that many had not ever done before.

It generated meaningful discussion and reflection, and stimulated key questions that were then a shared area of focus for the staff as a whole.

> All staff had a deeper understanding and knowledge of the statutory responsibilities for SEND, and their individual accountabilities, and the questions that had been generated and answered helped them to see how those would be met within the school setting.
>
> Teachers were more confident in responding to questions from parents/carers and also in using the Graduated Approach (see Chapter 7) to themselves know when further identification of SEND was needed, and had more understanding of the systems and processes that needed to be followed.

To successfully embed a whole-school culture and commitment to SEND and inclusive practices, requires that everyone involved, not just the SENCO, has the needs of pupils with SEND at the heart of all decision making and planning.

This is embodied in our current OFSTED Inspection Framework, where SEND sits within Quality of Education and is a central focus for discussions and learning walks with subject leads and teachers through the deep dives.

It is, therefore, imperative that senior and middle/subject leaders know about the current profile of SEND within the school, and the implications of this for planning and the ongoing development of the curriculum and other areas of development in the school. It is also essential that this knowledge and understanding is used to inform the prioritisation of new initiatives and developments, to ensure that the school as a whole really is embodying the concept of 'Inclusion by design' (EEF, 2020) – that practices are developed with inclusive values at the heart.

> **Reflective Activity**
>
> Use the audit tool (see Table 5.2) to help subject leaders to start to audit their existing knowledge about SEND within the school setting.
>
> - How far do you think, as a whole school, subject leaders are already fully aware of and using information about SEND to inform their planning and developments in their curriculum areas?
> - What are the remaining areas to work on/challenges?
> - How will you plan to continue to address those?
>
> Once Senior and Middle/Subject leaders have worked with the SENCO and are familiar and confident with the information about SEND that they need to know to lead developments in their areas, the audit tool could also be shared with all staff to support the development of their knowledge and understanding about current trends and profiles of SEND within the school.
>
> The more that this is done, shared and reflected on altogether, the deeper and more effective the shared understanding of SEND and inclusive policies within the school setting will be.

Table 5.2 Knowing, understanding and meeting the needs of children with SEND through effective curriculum planning and review

Key Prompts for Subject Leaders			
Key Question:	How do I know? What information do I have already?		What more do I need to do/know? How will I do that?
Knowledge of SEND profile and current strategies			
How many pupils/students are there in the school with EHCP's? And on a pathway towards statutory assessment?			
What are the key need types for pupils/students with EHCP's?			
And for pupils/students with SEND overall?			
Do staff access and use adaptations and strategies from the SEN Support Plans/EHCP Provision Plans consistently? How do they do this, and how is this checked from a subject perspective?			
How much training have you and colleagues in your department had to support your knowledge of the high incidence needs?			
How confident do you and your colleagues feel about meeting the needs of all students with SEND?			
Curriculum planning and delivery			
What are the implications of the profile of high incidence needs in the school for curriculum planning and delivery in your subject area?			
What support/provision/adaptation is in place currently to meet the needs of pupils/students with SEND?			
Give specific examples of curriculum adaptation and how that has been achieved to meet the needs of pupils/students with EHCP's. What has the impact been?			
What impact have the needs of children with SEND had on the development and delivery of the curriculum?			
Curriculum review			
What is the overall strategic approach for curriculum planning for SEND?			
How often is the curriculum reviewed to take into account changing cohort SEND needs?			
Give specific examples of things that you have done to reflect your review and understanding of changing SEND needs. What impact has this had?			

(Continued)

Table 5.2 (Continued)

Key Prompts for Subject Leaders		
Key Question:	How do I know? What information do I have already?	What more do I need to do/know? How will I do that?
How has the SENCO/SEND team been involved with you in reviewing cohort needs and the curriculum? Give specific examples.		
Is the curriculum adapted well enough for pupils/students with SEND? How do you know?		
Do pupils/students with SEND make good progress in your subject area? How do you know? What progress do pupils/students with adaptations to their curriculum make?		
How effectively do you embed the Graduated Approach (Assess, Plan, Do, Review) to your review of your curriculum and provision for pupils/students with SEND in your curriculum area?		
Does the curriculum prepare children with SEND for their next phase of education? How? Give specific examples.		
Lesson planning and delivery		
How is the child's learning linked to the class composite goal and adapted to the individual level of the child?		
Are there systems in place to identify starting points and adaptation to the curriculum for individual pupils/students with SEND?		
Is the curriculum broken down into smaller steps of learning for pupils/students with SEND? Do teachers know what they need to provide to enable pupils/students to secure the knowledge?		
Does the learning for pupils/students with SEND match the ambition for all students, or are expectations lowered? How do you ensure an ambitious curriculum for all?		
How have you ensured that pupils/students with SEND have opportunities to work independently? How is independent work evidenced?		
What is the best possible outcome for the individual pupil/student with SEND in your subject area. How do you know? Is this achieved? – give specific examples.		

82 Whole-school approaches to SEND

Developing a whole-school inclusive pedagogy

The pedagogical approaches that are embedded within the school – the high quality, universal teaching strategies that are consistently emphasised and implemented, and the approaches that are used to ensure that the curriculum and practices are inclusive by design (EEF, 2020) need to come from a deep understanding of the changing needs of the cohort as a whole and individuals within it (see Chapter 6).

In this, the need for ***evidence-informed practice***, which uses up-to-date knowledge and research about practices that are effective in support learning for all pupils, including those with SEND, is essential. The importance of building a shared understanding of what those key pedagogical approaches and practices are, why and how they are important and support effective learning, and then the consistent application of them is key to the development of effective practice.

For all pupils, most particularly for pupils with SEND, the most important aspect will be consistency so that there are consistent approaches that are regularly reinforced. In this way many of the barriers to learning (anxiety, stress, unfamiliarity with what is being asked/required) will be removed, which will then enable more effective and quicker learning to take place.

Reflective Activity

- What is the embedded pedagogy, or pedagogical practices (e.g. key high-quality teaching approaches and strategies that are prioritised) in your school setting?
- How do you know?
- Do you think that this is a shared pedagogy?
- Is it an inclusive pedagogy?
- Would all colleagues be able to identify the same key elements of a whole-school pedagogy?
- Would the children also be able to identify those same key elements?
- Are key pedagogical practices consistent across the school?
- What impact does this have on the pupils and their ability to be successful learners? What impact does it have on pupils with SEND?
- How do you know?
- Are there any challenges to overcome? How could these be addressed?

Look at the EEF's (2020) 'Five a Day' High Quality teaching tool (see Figure 5.3), which is based on evidence-informed approaches, and consider whether, and how, these key practices are already embedded in the pedagogical practices in your school setting, and ways that this could be used to enhance existing practices.

In addition to whole class pedagogical practices, in recent years, the concepts of scaffolding and adaptation have entered into educational language in schools. The Teachers' Standards (DfE, 2021: 11) includes the term 'Adapt teaching to respond to the strengths and needs of all pupils'. The Initial Teacher Training (ITT) Core Common Framework which underpins all ITT courses in England includes the term 'adaptive teaching' throughout (DfE, 2019).

High quality teaching benefits pupils with SEND
The 'Five-a-day' principle

The research underpinning the EEF's guidance report 'Special Educational Needs in Mainstream Schools' indicates that supporting high quality teaching improves outcomes for pupils with SEND. Five specific approaches—the 'Five-a-day' indicated below—are particularly well-evidenced as having a positive impact. Teachers should develop a repertoire of these strategies, which they can use daily and flexibly in response to individual needs, using them as the starting point for classroom teaching for all pupils, including those with SEND.

1 Explicit instruction — Teacher-led approaches with a focus on clear explanations, modelling and frequent checks for understanding. This is then followed by guided practice, before independent practice.

2 Cognitive and metacognitive strategies — Managing cognitive load is crucial if new content is to be transferred into students' long-term memory. Provide opportunities for students to plan, monitor and evaluate their own learning.

3 Scaffolding — When students are working on a written task, provide a supportive tool or resource such as a writing frame or a partially completed example. Aim to provide less support of this nature throughout the course of the lesson, week or term.

4 Flexible grouping — Allocate groups temporarily, based on current level of mastery. This could, for example, be a group that comes together to get some additional spelling instruction based on current need, before re-joining the main class.

5 Using technology — Technology can be used by a teacher to model worked examples; it can be used by a student to help them to learn, to practice and to record their learning. For instance, you might use a class visualiser to share students' work or to jointly rework an incorrect model.

More information about finding better ways to support pupils with SEND, including these five principles and more specialist interventions, can be found in the EEF's guidance report '*Special Educational Needs in Mainstream Schools*'.

Education Endowment Foundation

Figure 5.3 EEF – Five a day principle

Source: EEF (2020), https://d2tic4wvo1iusb.cloudfront.net/eef-guidance-reports/send/Five-a-day-poster_1.1.pdf?v=1667220820 (accessed 1.11.2022)

The term scaffolding is now used in place of differentiation, and refers to the need to 'scaffold' learning for pupils. This includes when a new concept is introduced, where scaffolding will be provided for all/most pupils to help them to understand the concept, and also prolonged scaffolding to enable pupils with SEND to be able to access learning and make progress.

The EEF (2020) therefore describe scaffolding as:

> "Scaffolding" is a metaphor for temporary support that is removed when it is no longer required. Initially, a teacher would provide enough support so that pupils can successfully complete tasks that they could not do independently. This requires effective assessment to gain a precise understanding of the pupil's current capabilities. Support could be visual, verbal, or written. The teacher will gradually remove the support (the scaffold) as the pupil becomes able to complete the task independently. If the teacher is supporting a pupil with SEND, that scaffold may be in place for longer to promote confidence and competence that can be sustained once the scaffold is removed.
>
> (EEF, 2020: 26)

As has been seen above, scaffolding is one of the five key 'Five a Day' principles for effective teaching and learning and is therefore something that needs to be understood and developed in practice in all schools to enable pupils at all ages and stages to be able to access learning and make progress.

For some pupils with SEND, particularly those with EHCPs and more complex learning needs, adaptation to the curriculum will be needed.

For those pupils, often working many years below the expected level for their peers, the teacher, with support from the SENCO, will need to be able to identify their individual starting level, and the curriculum components relevant to them and then provide an adapted curriculum so that they can access learning at a level appropriate to their needs, but that is matched to the general topic and area of focus of the learning for the rest of the class. Adaptations are therefore very individualised and require deep understanding of the level of functioning and ability of the individual child. Adaptations should also ensure a focus on supporting and promoting the child's independent learning skills – so should provide opportunities for the child to consolidate and reinforce prior learning to build independent learning and study skills, rather than just be about task completion.

Reflective Activity

- How well embedded and understood are the principles and practices of scaffolding and adaptation in your school setting?
- How do you know?
- What good examples do you have of curriculum adaptation for individual pupils, and how could those examples be used to build further understanding and effective practice across your school setting?
- Are there any challenges, and how could these be overcome?

Take a look at the scaffolding and adaptation 'ladders' provided in Figures 5.4 and 5.5.

Often, quite a superficial understanding and implementation of scaffolding and adaptation is embedded in schools, where resources and learning may be scaffolded – but it is scaffolded for everyone and not in response to individual learning needs – both for pupils with SEND and for pupils who are of higher ability and either do not require the scaffolded resource, or could benefit from a scaffolded resource/activity to deepen their understanding and learning.

The 'ladders' in Figures 5.4 and 5.5 therefore aim to help to deepen understanding of how to use scaffolding and adaptation, with the simplest form of scaffolding and adaptation at the bottom of the ladder, and more complex examples provided as you move up the ladder.

Whilst the statements on each ladder are not intended to be purely linear, so it is possible to identify some embedded practices on higher rungs and identify areas still to be developed/embedded on lower rungs, generally the most straightforward and common types of scaffolding and adaptation practices are positioned at the bottom of each 'ladder'.

- Where would you position current practice in your school setting on the 'ladders' at the moment?
- Are there any other aspects that you would want to add on to reflect the pedagogy, curriculum and practices central to your school setting?
- How could you use these 'ladders' in collaboration with others to deepen understanding and practice?

Is scaffolding used to support homework tasks and independent learning activities?
Is there individualised scaffolding in books- including different ways to record information (not all copying from the presentation) and feedback/ annotations to highlight the scaffolding that has been provided (where appropriate/ needed)? Is there evidence of scaffolds being removed over time?
Is there evidence of the use of scaffolded interactions (see EEF Scaffolded Interactions model) to support the development of students' independent access and engagement with learning?
Is scaffolding evidenced for students in the sixth form, and what does this look like? How does this support the development of their independent learning and study skills?
Can you see ways that SEN Support Plans and EHCP Provision Plan strategies, and key inclusive SEND strategies have been used to ensure that the scaffolds are appropriate and effective?
Is there evidence of individualised scaffolding that breaks learning down or extends learning in response to individual needs- eg: – Lowest 20%/ SEND; EAL; PP; Top 20%; Students with a low Reading Age?
Can you see examples where students prompt each other, or are prompted by the teacher to access available scaffolding resources to support their learning?
Are there generic scaffolding resources available to support wider literacy/ numeracy skills which the students can access as needed to support their learning- eg number squares/ High Frequency Words/ Time-lines/ voice-notes etc?
Is scaffolding available for the whole class when teaching a new concept- eg writing frames/ keyword lists/ formula sheets etc, and does the teacher identify who will need which scaffolds?
What is already in place, and what still needs to be developed?

Figure 5.4 Review of scaffolding

86 Whole-school approaches to SEND

Is homework appropriately adapted to ensure that the student is able to complete learning tasks independently to reinforce and consolidate their learning?
Is the adapted curriculum planned for the student suitably ambitious, ensuring that expectations are not lowered? How do you know?
With the adaptations that have been provided, is there evidence that the student is making progress from their starting point and that they can show a level of independence in being able to complete appropriate learning tasks?
Are the adaptations that have been provided for the student clear to see in the student's exercise book- eg annotations of support provided/ adapted resources that link to the composite goal being taught?
Is there evidence of teacher-led planning for appropriate curriculum adaptations, linking developmentally appropriate adaptations to the composite goal being accessed by the rest of the class? Is information from the child's EHCP and Provision Plans used effectively to ensure that the planning is relevant and linked to the individual child's SEN?
Does the teacher have a clear understanding of the current level of functioning of students who require adaptations to the curriculum (ie how many years below their age group are they currently functioning/ which year group curriculum content is appropriate for them?)
Does the teacher have a clear understanding of which students (with EHCP's or complex learning needs) require adaptations to the curriculum?
What is already in place, and what still needs to be developed?

Figure 5.5 Review of adaptation

Once this focus on effective whole-class teaching strategies and pedagogy is firmly established and embedded, it will then be possible to add on the more specialist approaches or resources that are needed for some pupils with SEND (EEF, 2020) – more information about this is provided in Chapters 8 (Planning effective intervention) and 12 (Working effectively with other professionals).

Concluding comments and reflections

Ensuring that everyone in the school setting is fully aware of the statutory responsibilities for SEND and how to implement those through a shared, collective responsibility and a commitment to an inclusive culture is essential to be able to ensure that the needs of all pupils with SEND are met.

Yet, despite the SEND statutory responsibilities being embedded in policy for years (DfE, 1994; DfES, 2001; DfE/DoH, 2014, 2015) there remains a lack of full understanding of and commitment to those statutory responsibilities at all levels in the school setting. More therefore needs to be done to increase staff awareness of and confidence in understanding and meeting the needs of pupils with SEND, to continue to ensure that SEND is not seen as the priority and responsibility of the SENCO alone.

> **Individual Reflection**
>
> - What new information/learning have you gained from this chapter?
> - What are your key reflections?
> - What are your next steps/actions as a result?

References

Booth, T. and Ainscow, M. (2000, 2002, 2011, 2016) *Index for inclusion: Developing learning and participation in schools.* Bristol: Centre for Studies on Inclusion in Education.

DES (1999) *The National Curriculum key stage 1 and 2.* London: DES.

DfE (1994) *Special Educational Needs Code of Practice.* London: DES.

DfES (2001) *SEN Code of Practice.* London: DfES.

DfE/DoH (2014) *SEN and Disability Code of Practice.* London: DfE.

DfE/DoH (2015) *SEN and Disability Code of Practice.* London: Crown Copyright.

DfE (2017) *SEN support: A rapid evidence assessment research report.* Coventry: Coventry University.

DfE (2019) *Initial Teacher Training (ITT) Core Common Framework.* Available from https://www.gov.uk/government/publications/initial-teacher-training-itt-core-content-framework (accessed 31.5.23).

DfE (2021) *Teachers' Standards.* Available from https://www.gov.uk/government/publications/teachers-standards (accessed 31.5.23).

DfE/DoHSC (2023) *SEND and Alternative Provision Improvement Plan.* London: HMSO.

DfEE/QCA (1999) National Curriculum: Handbook for Secondary Teachers in England. London: DfEE/QCA

EEF (2020) *SEN in Mainstream Schools.* London, EEF.

Ekins, A., Savolainen, H. and Engelbrecht, P. (2016) 'An analysis of English teachers' self-efficacy in relation to SEN and disability and its implications in a changing SEN policy context'. *European Journal of Special Needs Education* 31(2), 236–249.

Ekins, A. (2017) *Reconsidering inclusion – sustaining and building inclusive practices in schools.* Abingdon: Routledge.

Forlin, C., Earle, C., Loreman, T. and Sharma, U. (2011) 'The sentiments, attitudes and concerns about inclusive education revised (SACIE-r) scale for measuring teachers' perceptions about inclusion'. *Exceptionality Education International* 21(3), 50–65.

House of Commons Select Committee (2006) *Special educational needs: Third report of session 2005–2006.* London: TSO.

House of Commons Education Committee (2019) *Special Educational Needs and Disabilities.* London: House of Commons.

Mitchell, D. (2014) *What really works in special and inclusive education.* Oxford: Routledge.

NASUWT (2018) Special Educational Needs (SEN), *Additional Learning Needs (ALN) and Additional Support Needs (ASN).* England: NASUWT.

OFSTED (2010) *The special educational needs and disability review: A statement is not enough.* Manchester: Crown Copyright. Reference no: 090221.

Rix, J., Hall, K., Nind, M., Sheehy, K. and Wearmouth, J. (2009) 'What pedagogical approaches can effectively include children with special educational needs in mainstream classrooms? A systematic literature review'. *Support for Learning* 24 (2). https://doi.org/10.1111/j.1467-9604.2009.01404.x

6 Identifying difference and needs

In this chapter, we critically examine and explore the following key aspects:

- The challenges of identification
- Inclusive approaches to identifying needs
- Screening assessments
- Solution-focused approaches
- Communication systems – Class Profile of Needs
- Identifying SEND
- SEND Register
- SEND referral systems

Key issues

Whilst it is important that we recognise and identify needs and then ensure that support is provided to meet those needs, this in itself is a challenging task, and staff in school therefore need to be supported to understand and explore the complexity inherent in this.

At a basic level, it is not always easy to identify the underlying cause underpinning needs, and too often the focus of attention is on the presenting behaviour, rather than the underlying cause or need that provokes the behavioural response that is seen. There are also fundamental challenges with systems that seek to label children and needs, as labels can often be reductionist and do not adequately reflect the child as a whole.

The key issues explored in this chapter, therefore focus on:

- The challenges of identification
- Inclusive approaches to understanding and identifying needs
- Identifying SEND.

This chapter supports an approach to implementing practices which focus on understanding the needs of the individual, as an individual rather than as part of a homogenous group. It is about recognising that all children/people may need support at any time, and that a focus on recognising learning differences and support needs, rather than one based on narrow labels and diagnoses is the most effective to take.

The chapter also seeks to support practitioners to have a more critical understanding and approach to the concept and practice of 'labelling' needs – recognising that at times

DOI: 10.4324/9781003033554-6

this is necessary and helpful, but that fundamentally such practices are reductionist and may lead to practices which do not support the individual and their needs as experienced within the context of their whole development and the wide range of factors impacting on that. It is this that leads to the 'Identification dilemma' and the notion of 'Dilemmas of difference' (Norwich, 2007, 2009).

Diagnoses and 'labelling' needs/pupils can therefore be less effective than developing systems and processes to ensure a deeper understanding of the holistic experience of the child within the school setting, and any barriers that they may experience impacting on their ability to successfully access and participate in all aspects of school life.

Current policy and research

The challenges of identification

Before moving on to consider and develop existing systems for identifying needs, we need to first start by challenging why this continues to be an established and needed practice in our education systems today.

Fundamentally, why is there a need to 'label' pupils – as having SEND, as having Pupil Premium (PP) or English as an Additional Language (EAL), etc? Is this helpful? Does it lead to positive actions and support or does it simply lead to the perpetuation of assumptions about individuals or cohorts of pupils? What does this say about the education system within which we work, one that may be predicated on the 'inability of general education to accommodate and include the full diversity of learners (Reindal, 2010: 2)' (Ekins, 2015).

The challenge, or 'dilemma' (Minow, 1990; Norwich, 2007, 2009) is that any approach to labelling, suggests that there is a 'norm' that 'we' belong to, and that there are therefore 'others' who are 'different' to the 'norm' and as such require 'labelling' (Florian, 2007; Norwich, 2007, 2009 2015). Thus, as Florian (2007: 11) identified: 'There are two interdependent problems facing the field of special education. The first is the concept of normal and good, and the second is the dilemma of difference'.

Such concepts of 'normal' and 'different' are both complex and uncomfortable when we step back to really think about it.

The research completed by Norwich (2008: 215) concluded that there was 'some evidence to suggest that the tensions inherent in the identification dilemma could be resolved by finding alternative ways of providing additional provision. This was seen as a way of reducing the extent of special education identification. This might involve improving general education, either by preventing difficulties through more adaptive provision and/or by additional provision organised through more general and less separate systems. However, where identification for special education was still required, efforts would be focused on going beyond negative labeling, changing attitude to SEN/disabilities and enhancing communication between professionals, parents and children/students'.

Inclusive approaches to identifying needs

To address some of the issues identified in the identification dilemma (Norwich, 2008) outlined above, a more holistic approach to understanding needs and the range of factors which may impact on and influence/affect a child's development must be developed.

90 *Identifying difference and needs*

This is recognised in the EEF (2020) SEN in Mainstream Schools Guidance Report, which has, as the second key recommendation:

- Build an ongoing, holistic understanding of your pupils and their needs.

'Better understanding of a pupil's experience of school can provide information about their individual needs that can inform the next steps for teaching' (EEF, 2020: 15).

The Bronfenbrenner model shared in the EEF (2020: 6) SEN in Mainstream Schools Guidance Report, see Figure 6.1, is a useful model to use to develop this understanding of the need to look beyond simplistic labels and deficit identification models. This model therefore usefully recognises that the development of an individual is constantly influenced by the 'interaction of "what happens in the class every day" with their personal characteristics, wider environmental influences, and time' (EEF, 2020: 5):

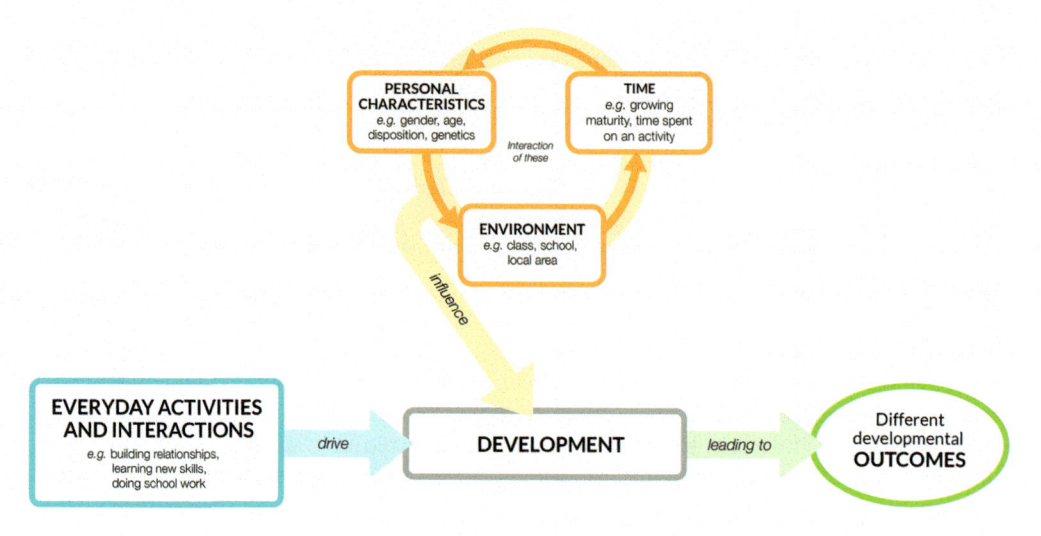

Figure 6.1 EEF (2020) Bronfenbrenner model

By using understanding of this model, practitioners are able to ensure that when considering the identification of needs for individual pupils, it is considered holistically. It is not just about what happens during the lesson. A pupil's development and experience will also be impacted by the interactions, relationships and experiences that they have across the day as a whole, to include those they had before school (at home as well as on the journey to school); whilst at school (during unstructured times at the start of the day, breaktimes, lunchtimes, transitions between lessons) as well as in the different lessons (including with different teachers or class groups, particularly for secondary age pupils, and different subject lessons). All of these things will have an impact on the child in different ways, and it may be the anxiety caused during any one of those different times which may result in the withdrawn or oppositional behaviours that are then seen at another time.

The DfE (2017a) Rapid Evidence Assessment Research Report also supported this concept of looking for a holistic assessment of pupil needs to support planning and provision:

> Our rapid evidence assessment focused on support, rather than identification or assessment. However, a recurrent theme across the literature is that the most effective support relies on a full and recent assessment of a child or young person's individual

strengths and weaknesses. A wide range of underlying difficulties can cause certain symptoms or behaviours. For example, difficulty in following classroom instructions could indicate hearing difficulties, language difficulties, attention difficulties, short-term memory difficulties or frustration at other, seemingly unrelated situations such as friendships or home life. A child often seeming worried or anxious could have learning difficulties, sensory processing issues, worries from outside of school and so on. Until these different options have been explored and a full picture of a child or young person's strengths and weaknesses, in terms of cognitive skills, relevant medical issues such as hearing and vision, and family support, motivation and engagement is considered, support is likely to be sub-optimal.

This assessment does not need to be lengthy in most cases. Discussion with the parents is likely to provide much useful background information. Observation of how the child behaves in the classroom, small groups and individually can also provide a guide on what aspects of the learning environment a child finds most difficult. Hearing and sight tests can be carried out at the GP or the opticians at the request of the parents. This can usefully supplement information from academic tasks completed in school time.

(DfE, 2017a: 14)

The importance throughout is about challenging any embedded assumptions that we may have, and ensuring effective systems and processes for actually talking to and gathering feedback from the child themselves about the cause of any difficulties or barriers that they experience (see also Chapter 10).

Identifying SEND

Building on from the discussions about developing consistent understandings about what SEND is in Chapter 2, here we need to scrutinise existing practices and confidence levels in identifying SEND as part of a whole-school approach to identifying needs.

Thus, against the background and understanding of the inclusive approaches to understanding and identifying needs outlined above, we are still living and working in an education system where there is an embedded requirement to identify and 'label' SEN. Whilst we recognise the arguments shared in Chapter 2 and above relating to the impact of 'labelling' and the understanding of SEND as a complex, abstract and subjective concept, rather than an absolute concept that can easily be applied, and note the arguments of those who argue against the simplistic framework of identifying SEND and those pupils who do not fit 'normal' expectations for performance and engagement, looking instead for a broader, and arguably more inclusive understanding, of needs upon a continuum (House of Commons Select Committee, 2006; Norwich, 2008), the current context means that we have to address ways of identifying SEND.

The DfE (2017b) survey of schools in relation to SEN Support identified a number of key themes and information relating to the identification of SEN. In this survey 33.8% of staff said that they 'did not have responsibility for identifying SEN' (DfE, 2017b: 8). The NASUWT report (2018) identified that 'fifty-nine percent (59%) of respondents said that they are made aware of the specific needs of each learner with SEN/ALN/ASN that they teach. However, almost one-third of teachers (31%) said that they were only made aware of the specific needs of some learners. Alarmingly, one in ten respondents said that they were not made aware of learners' specific needs' (NASUWT, 2018: 5).

92 *Identifying difference and needs*

It is clear, therefore, that more needs to be done to develop consistent approaches and understanding of a shared responsibility for identifying and knowing about SEND and ways to be part of this (see also discussions about collective, statutory responsibilities for SEND in Chapters 3 and 5).

Individual local authorities also have a duty to provide localised interpretations of national guidance around SEND, and will therefore also provide additional guidance about the identification of SEND to support schools with their understanding of this in practice.

As has been explored in Chapter 2, the current concerns about lack of understanding and consistency or provision for SEND have been acknowledged by the DfE/DoHSC (2023) and it is hoped that the new National Standards which will be developed will provide clarity to support understanding about identifying SEND and consistent expectations for levels of provision.

Planning for practice

Figure 6.2 Key principles model

A number of key practices underpin the effective development of systems and processes to identify needs within the school context. These include:

- The need for inclusive approaches to identification
- Whole school approaches and understandings of the impact of identification and labelling
- Knowledge of how to use effective screening tools to support the ongoing assessment and diagnosis of specific SEND
- Strategic approaches to using information about identification of needs to inform the effective development of practice.

Underpinning all of the approaches is the need to recognise that pupil's needs will change over time, that they are not static and fixed and that they are an interaction between the pupil's personal characteristics and the environment that they are in, and the interactions and relationships that they experience within it (EEF, 2020).

Therefore, the key principles underpinning the effective development of practice in this area include: ***inclusive approaches***, which ensure that inclusive approaches to identification are used; ***curiosity and reflective practices***, to ensure that assumptions about pupil's needs are challenged and do not become fixed, that we embed approaches that seek to add understanding of the unique experience of the individual; and ***communication***, to ensure that there are robust and effective practices and processes in place to ensure that information about needs are shared in accessible ways and then used effectively by all staff to inform the approaches that are used to support the child.

The challenges of identification

Reflective Activity

- What do you think is meant by the notion of an 'identification dilemma'?
- What is the dilemma?
- How is this understood and experienced in your own school setting?
- How is 'difference' understood in your school setting?
- Are differences celebrated as being strengths or is there a more deficit-based approach to difference?
- What are the current practices for identifying needs in your school setting?
- Do those practices enable a deep understanding of needs that an individual may experience, relating to the wide range of factors which impact upon them? Or do your current practices of identification reduce understanding and perpetuate unsubstantiated assumptions about individuals or cohorts of children?
- How do you know?
- How could you find out more?

The identification dilemma remains a real dilemma which needs to be critically challenged in our schools today. In this, embedded assumptions relating to difference, particularly deficit-based approaches to understanding difference and ways to value and respect or highlight and negatively expose those differences, need to be explored.

What is the impact of this on staff within your school? But also, what is the impact on pupils and families? Are differences between pupils and families highlighted or accepted, within a broader culture of inclusive values and practices?

To help to explore this further, use the reflection tool Table 6.1 individually and then part as a whole-staff activity to help to start some conversations and deeper thinking about difference and the identification dilemma. The same activity, or an adapted version of it, may also be really useful to complete with pupils to start to encourage them to also be thinking in critical ways about deeply embedded notions of difference and identification labels. In this, we recognise that to support deeper societal changes towards more inclusive practices and understandings in the future, we have a responsibility now to do all we can to support our pupils to examine and understand those challenging concepts and existing practices.

94 Identifying difference and needs

Table 6.1 Dilemmas of difference reflection tool

Statement	Initial reflections	Examples from current practice	What could be done to develop understanding of this further?
'When does treating people differently emphasise their differences and stigmatise or hinders them on that basis?' (Minow, 1990: 20)			
'When does treating people the same become insensitive to their differences and likely to stigmatise or hinder them on that basis?' (Minow, 1990: 20)			
'Difference is linked to stigma or deviance and sameness is a pre-requisite for equality. Perhaps these assumptions must be identified and assessed if we are to escape or transcend dilemma of difference.' (Minow, 1990: 50)			
Dyson (2001: 25) identified 'an intention to treat all learners as essentially the same and an equal and opposite intention to treat them as different'			
Was the intention to rid ourselves of limiting labels by bringing all categories under the umbrella of special educational needs futile? 'simultaneously ... make them the same as and different from the rest. Clearly this was an impossible task.' (Warnock et al., 2010: 125)			

Inclusive approaches to understanding and identifying needs

As has been discussed, it is essential that we are able to effectively understand and identify underlying needs that cause the behaviours that may be presented or experienced by the pupil. It is only by understanding and addressing the underlying cause that progress will be able to be made to remove barriers to learning and participation and enable the child to more effectively access and make progress in the education system.

Reflective Activity

- How do you currently find out about a pupil's experience of school?
- What systems and processes, strategies or approaches, do you already use to build this understanding and information about ways that individual pupils experience school?
- Are the same systems and processes, strategies or approaches used for every child?
- What may be the implications of this?

For more information about ways to engage pupils in meaningful reflection and sharing of their experience of school, see Chapter 10.

Whilst formal assessment and diagnosis pathways across the country are known to be over-stretched and with extremely lengthy waiting lists for assessment, there are things that the school can do to build as full a picture as possible of the underlying needs of the child. This will include:

1 *Discussions with parents/carers:*
   - What does this tell you about the child's developmental history; contextual factors which may impact on them and have an impact on their learning and/or behaviours?
2 *Discussions with the child:*
   - As we will explore in more detail in Chapter 10, the child themselves will have a unique understanding of their own needs and factors that impact on them. Rather than starting with assumptions about what are the causes of any difficulties presented, practitioners need to start with ***curiosity***, asking questions to find out more so that strategies and approaches can be individualised and effective.
3 *Screening assessment:*
   - As the EEF (2020: 15) identifies, 'There is a strong consensus across America and England that a structured process of formative assessment is a sound logic model for identifying, and then addressing, learning needs. The process needs to be repeated regularly as pupils' development is not linear and pupil's needs will vary in patterns of development over time'. A range of screening assessments are commonly available and regularly used in schools to help staff to get a better understanding of underlying difficulties (see also discussions below with information from the DfE (2017b) about key screening assessment tools that can be used).

Case Study – Identifying Children's Needs Within a Primary School Context

Sophie Matthews

School context – a one form entry primary school with a specialist resource provision for autistic children.

The EEF (2020) offers five recommendations for supporting children with SEND in schools. The first recommendation is to ensure that the school is a positive environment for all children – and means that ensuring high-quality, inclusive teaching must be a priority for school leaders. However, the second recommendation from the EEF states that schools should 'build an ongoing, holistic understanding of your pupils and their needs' (EEF, 2020: 1). Where a child has difficulties in many areas, it may initially be challenging to identify their difficulties.

Within our school setting, we initially consider whether a child might have language difficulties. Research from AFASIC shows that 7.5% of children have developmental language disorder and language difficulties might present as difficulties with learning, behaviour or wellbeing. Using Language Link, an online assessment tool, helps us to assess a child's receptive language skills and provide targeted support as needed. The online screening tool assesses children's receptive language skills in the areas of concepts, verb tenses, negatives, instructions, pronouns, narrative skills, questions, verbal reasoning, vocabulary skills, complex sentences, narrative inferences and more. The assessment provides an overall standardised score and recommendations and also indicates any areas of specific weakness with a pass/fail indicator. We look at the overall score and recommendations, but also at individual areas of strength and need.

Any reports are shared with a child's class teacher, alongside any supportive strategies pertinent to that child. Teachers within our school make use of the Kent Mainstream Core Standards as part of their daily practice and can refer to presenting needs and relevant strategies. We have weekly meetings with a focus on inclusion and the school Special Educational Needs Coordinator (SENCO) works closely with class teachers to scaffold and adapt learning so that children with language needs can access it alongside peers. All staff have accessed training on Colourful Semantics, the use of Widgit and inclusive questioning.

Where children are identified as benefitting from intervention, school staff deliver language interventions from Language Link or using other resources such as Black Sheep Press programmes. Support staff leading these interventions work closely with the speech and language therapy team and have received training in Colourful Semantics, narrative, the use of communication books and boards and more. The SENCO regularly observes these interventions and monitors children's progress towards their small step targets.

If receptive language difficulties were not indicated in the Language Link assessment, we would use other tools to further investigate the child's learning needs. These might include using the Renfrew Action Picture test to evaluate expressive language skills, the Bristol Picture Vocabulary Scale, or the GL Dyslexia Screener. Within these assessments, we would likewise be looking at a child's overall standardised score and areas of strength and need, as well as considering any 'spikes' within their profile. This information would then be used to influence the quality first teaching within the classroom, for example by providing a task board for a child with identified difficulties processing information or supporting children with writing speed difficulties to use a voice-to-text function on an iPad to record their ideas.

We also use the Boxall Profile to consider the child's social, emotional or wellbeing needs. The reports from this tool identify a child's needs within two elements – diagnostic and developmental. School staff identify key strands of focus and incorporate this within the classroom and discrete interventions, as necessary.

- **Solution-focused approaches**

To support with deeper understanding and planning for individual and cohort needs, it is useful to consider the use of solution-focused approaches.

This approach, rather than approaching the understanding and planning of support for individuals from a deficit 'in-child' problem position, takes a different approach by starting with a question and then enabling the proactive and inclusive sharing of ideas and 'solutions' to how to answer the question. This approach immediately turns the discussion away from an approach which can focus on perpetuating assumptions about 'in-child' difficulties, into an approach which is more creative, positive and productive – focused on finding innovative solutions, using everyone's expertise and differing perspectives.

As a starting point, the following structure can be used, and then this can be developed further to suit the school environment and particular situation and context for the individual child:

Case Study – The Solution-Focused Approach

Jill Ansell

A solution focused approach works best within a multi-layered approach. The principles behind this method are about listening, selecting, providing and recognising solutions that are doable and goal-orientated rather than focusing on just the immediate problem. The main principle of the approach is supporting people in making a move from the concern being a problem and moving that to the focus of the concern being a solution focused outcome (DfES, 2005; Corcoran & Pillai, 2009).

This approach is used regularly with school staff seeking advice to support pupils in accessing education successfully. The solution focused approach is not about solving the problems it is about recognising what can be done to support the needs of that pupil identified and moving that forward with positive outcomes.

Key aspects of this approach

- You do not need to fully understand the problem before you can find a solution
- Everyone supporting this approach has skills to offer
- Having a clear question helps everyone in the group to have a focus to concentrate on
- Finding out what is working and what change could look like for the child
- There will be some aspects that are already working which can be expanded on
- We may not be able to change what has already happened to cause the problem so we must focus on the future
- An approach that sits within a multi-agency partnership that offers a safe open environment to provide advice and support to those that seek to move problems into solutions
- Questions are the key part of a solution focused approach and should be encouraged from all professionals within the group.

Example of how the solution focused approach works in practice

Within our multi-agency meeting a child's information was brought by the school seeking advice. With this approach the person presenting gives a question to the group on what they would like to solve for the child, the question should not be about the adults the emphasis should always be on the child. The question is helpful in supporting the group to focus on what questions they may want to ask the presenter, and to help focus on providing solutions.

The child was in Key stage 1 and was struggling to access any of the curriculum with her peers, her behaviour had escalated with her hitting out and hurting her others. There were two questions to be considered: (1) How can the pupil play safely with her peers? (2) How can the pupil engage in the curriculum to access learning? This approach can be done within a timed framework, or it can be free flow depending on the length of time available to the group.

When the case is presented professionals around the table can ask questions before solutions are drawn together. With this group of professionals, we had a Speech and Language therapist, an Education Psychologist, Specialist Teachers and primary

SENCOs. The questions can be quite in depth, but it is again useful to concentrate on what solutions are practical, there is no point providing a suggestion or solution unless the school staff can take that idea or strategy and implement it.

The solutions in response to this case were to look at the pupil's developmental stage rather than her chronological age. To then consider the portage checklist to look at recommendations for a child in that developmental stage. The speech and language therapist was able to offer some significant advice around language assessment and support. The Education Psychologist gave advice on learning assessments and strategies to put in place to help that child access appropriate learning in the classroom. The specialist teachers offered outreach support to come to the school and observe the child and meet with the class teacher, as well as offering training around adapting the curriculum. The presenter went away with several strategies and support mechanisms to hopefully provide a more positive educational outcome for the pupil.

The benefits of using a solution focused approach is therefore about drawing together solutions that are achievable and using the guidance and advice from the professionals within that environment.

- **Understanding and planning for cohort needs – communication systems**

One of the most important things that we need to implement in schools to ensure that all staff have the information that they need to be able to provide high-quality teaching and learning experiences for all pupils, is a clear and accessible overview of what the differing needs of all of the children in the class actually are.

Schools are data and information-rich places, and too often there is just so much information available that it then ends up not being used at all.

Developing simple and effective systems to summarise key information so that teachers can easily assess it to aid their planning for their class or cohort, and to aid strategic analysis and evaluation of cohort (class, year group, Key Stage, whole school) trends and the implications of this for staff deployment, staff training and development and the purchasing of key resources/equipment is therefore critical.

One system that has effectively been in use for many years is the Class Profile system (see Table 6.2) (Ekins & Grimes, 2009; Ekins, 2012; Ekins, 2015).

This is a simple tool that in essence uses a full class list produced in a 'register' format on one page of A4, against which a range of crucial information relating to pupils' individual characteristics, needs and key strategies can be recorded:

The benefit of having a holistic system for recording all needs in one easy to access and use format, means that we can ensure that staff do have all of the information that they need in one place, and there is not the danger of schools developing more and more separate 'additional needs' registers.

Whilst this should then be used by the class teacher to support the day to day planning for the needs of the class that they are teaching (ensuring that all teaching and learning approaches are individualised and adapted to respond to the profile of needs of the class as a whole and individuals or groups of pupils within it) it is also an important tool to aid strategic planning and review.

Class Profiles should therefore also be used by the SENCO in ***collaboration*** with other senior leaders to review and analyse trends and patterns in need types – across the whole school; across different year groups so that changing patterns of needs can be identified and then positively and proactively addressed in the planning for whole-school developments.

Identifying difference and needs 99

Table 6.2 Register of pupils' individual characteristics, needs and key strategies

Pupil name	Pupil characteristics	Description of need	Useful strategies
Ajay	EAL	Punjabi	
Ben	SEN Support – C&L	Literacy difficulties	Writing frames and key word lists to support all writing
Claire	ChiC		
Daniel	PP		
Escovijk	EAL	Bulgarian	
Fin	SEN Support – C&I; PP	ASD	
Gerta			
Hassan	Health	Epilepsy	See Individual Health Care Plan
Isla	EHCP – C&I; C&L; Health; PP	ASD; Dyslexia; Asthma	
Jon			
Kieran			
Lev	EAL	Greek	
Michael			
Noa			
Olive			
Pasha	EAL	Turkish	
Ravi			
Steven	EHCP – SEMH; C&L	ADHD, Dyslexia	
Teresa			
Una			
Vernon	ChiC; PP		
William			
Yessica			
Zara			

Identifying SEND

Reflective Activity

- What support and guidance do you receive from your local authority to support with localised interpretations about SEND?
- How can you use this to ensure that practices in your school setting are consistent with others in local schools?
- What measures/processes are in place to moderate the localised interpretations so that you can be confident that the identification of SEND in your local area is the same as in other local authorities?
- Why is this important?
- What is the implication of this for individual children with SEND and their families?

The DfE Research Report (DfE, 2017b) provides some useful information, based on feedback received from schools, about the processes for Identifying SEND:

> **Identifying SEN: DfE (2017b) SEN Support: A Survey of Schools and Colleges. Research Report, pp. 18–23**
>
> 'SENCOs in all types of settings used a range of methods to identify pupils who may have SEN, which are divided here into three categories: referrals, assessment and documentation:
>
> **Referrals**
>
> Across all types of setting, SENCOs said they received referrals from a variety of sources. These sources included parents, teachers or tutors and outside professionals such as Speech and Language Therapists or medical professionals. Within secondary schools, and particularly in colleges, it was also highlighted that students could refer themselves for support if they felt it was required. In all settings the importance of referral information from students' previous settings during the transition process was considered useful.
>
> **Assessments**
>
> SENCOs indicated that a range of assessments were used to identify students who may have SEN, including standardised assessments to measure skills. The most common assessments mentioned by SENCOs in primary schools were "The Ravens Progressive Matrices Test", "British Picture Vocabulary Scale" (BPVS) and "Neale Analysis of Reading Ability" (NARA). In secondary settings, the "Cognitive Abilities Test" (CAT), "York Assessment of Reading for Comprehension" (YARC) and "Comprehensive Test of Phonological Processing" (CTOPP) were most commonly used. Within a small number of secondary and college settings, there were "screening tools" used – often a battery of different tests – when students transferred to the setting to gain insight into any difficulties they may experience.
>
> Tests to assess social and emotional needs such as the Boxall Profile Test and Emotional Literacy Test were also described by SENCOs in primary schools, and the "Strengths and Difficulties Questionnaire" and "Pupil Attitudes to Self and School" in secondary schools.
>
> **Documentation**
>
> A range of documentation was used across the different settings. The main method reported by SENCOs in primary and secondary schools was the analysis of on-going assessment data which could highlight if a pupil was not making expected progress. While much of the focus was on academic progress, a minority of settings (one primary and two secondary) reported using behaviour logs or records to support the identification process. Within college settings, data which indicated a student had received exam concessions in their previous school was used by SENCOs, as well as information gained through the application process' (DfE, 2017a: 18–19).

Classroom information

'Members of staff said they used the information they would gather as part of their everyday assessment procedures to identify if students were not working at expected levels to support the identification of SEN. In primary and secondary settings, it was also suggested that getting to know students was important to understand how they performed across different areas of learning and their social and emotional needs' (DfE, 2017a: 21).

'SENCOs in all settings said that once they had been approached about a child who may have SEN, they would take the information provided and, if necessary, gather further evidence. This could involve discussion with parents and/or gaining more detailed information from a class teacher or previous settings. It could also involve the SENCO conducting further assessments or arranging for assessment from other professionals such as Educational Psychologists, Speech and Language Therapists or Occupational Therapists' (DfE, 2017a: 22).

'Once further information had been gathered, SENCOs in all settings described how they would provide additional support for students. This could involve supporting class teachers with additional teaching strategies, through the setting of targets, the provision of interventions and additional staff input' (DfE, 2017a: 23).

Reflective Activity

- How many of these processes are already embedded in practice in your own school setting?
- How effective are they?
- Are there any other areas/aspects that still need to be developed?
- How can this be achieved?

Whilst the Class Profile system (discussed earlier) helps to ensure that there is one record of all the identified needs for pupils in the school setting, listed by class group, it is essential to also have a separate SEND Register. This should record all pupils who have been identified and are placed on the school's SEND Register, and should have clear information about the level of SEND that they are receiving (SEN Support or an Education, Health & Care Plan), and should provide details about the areas of need and the specific SEN that the child has been identified with. The template in Table 6.3 is a useful one for ensuring that all key information that is required on a SEND Register is recorded in as simple a format as possible.

With no absolute concrete framework for identifying SEND and needs, the practice remains very subjective. The issue for the SENCO and school, therefore, is now to build knowledge across the staff group about how needs should be identified, and how to ensure that this is consistent with local and national practices.

Clear referral processes within the school to ensure that concerns about a child can be raised in a strategic and proactive way – but which resist systems where other staff simply 'pass responsibility' for a child if they feel that there is a need – need to be developed. The referral process should therefore ensure that the teacher has already taken actions to find out more about the child's presenting needs, such as the discussions with parents/carers and the child as outlined earlier; and in larger school contexts, particularly secondary school contexts, that discussions have happened with other colleagues to support the development of understanding and planning for meeting needs (e.g. Head of Year to find out about wider pastoral factors which may impact; Head of Departments to review curriculum planning and strategies that can be used).

Table 6.3 A template for the SEND Register

Name	Year group	SEN level	SEN areas of need	Census labels	Description of Need
		(e.g. SEN Support or EHCP)	(e.g. C&L; C&I; SEMH; P/S – just use the broad 4 Areas of SEN here)	(e.g. MLD; SpLD; SLCN, etc. – as the Census requires different labels of SEN to be recorded, it is useful to clarify this here)	(e.g. details of the specific areas of needs, including any diagnoses and when they were given)
Anna	6	SEN Support	C&L; SEMH	MLD; SEMH	Literacy difficulties; ADHD (diagnosed by Dr …; 9.9.2021)
Ben	6	EHCP	P/S	PD	Cerebral Palsy
Callum	6	EHCP	C&I; C&L	ASD; SpLD	ASD (diagnosed by Dr …; 7.4.2018); Dyslexia (diagnosed by … 5.1.2019)
Danesh	6	SEN Support	SEMH; C&I	SEMH; SLCN	Anxiety; social communication difficulties

Reflective Activity

- What do you already have in place in your school setting?
- How do staff raise concerns about a pupil?
- How does this then lead to positive action?
- Is the process that is currently used effective and strategic?
- How do you know?
- Is there anything that could be developed further?

Once a concern has been raised, it is then important to ensure that this leads to clear communication of needs – whether as a result of the concern, further assessment, observation, (including discussion with parents/carers) has identified that there is an underlying special educational needs, and the child therefore needs to be added to the SEND Register; or that the needs that the child displays are not to the extent that placement on an SEND Register is not necessary.

With this latter option, it is important to ensure that this is clearly communicated back to staff involved, that there is support put in place to provide additional information and potentially modelling, of inclusive teaching approaches that can be used to more effectively meet the child's needs.

Only the needs of children who have been identified through this process (see also discussions about the Assess, Plan, Do, Review Graduated Approach in Chapter 7) as having an underlying SEND requiring SEN support should be recorded as 'SEND' on the Class Profile and SEND Register.

To further support strategic approaches to identifying SEND, bearing in mind the challenges that we have already identified in relation to understanding 'SEND' as an absolute concept (Chapter 2), it can be helpful to consider ways to embed moderation practices within localities and across schools so that there can be some discussion and moderation of the identification SEND to moderate judgements and decisions so that there is some consistency and so that the identification of needs is not completely swayed by individual school interpretations or contexts.

Concluding comments and reflections

Establishing and embedding effective systems and processes in the school setting to ensure that there are consistent and well-understood/accessed ways to share information about the identification of needs is essential.

Yet, within that approach needs to be a deep understanding of the problems/dilemmas (Norwich, 2007) of the very approach that we are aiming to embed, and ways that the labelling of pupils can lead to a reductionist approach which focused on the perpetuation of stereotyped 'assumptions' about the needs of individuals or cohorts.

Individual Reflection

- What new information/learning have you gained from this chapter?
- What are your key reflections?
- What are your next steps/actions as a result?

References

Corcoran, J. and Pillai, V. (2009) 'A review of the research on solution-focused therapy'. *British Journal of Social Work* 39(2), 234–242.

DfE (2017a) *SEN Support: A rapid evidence assessment research report*. Coventry: DfE.

DfE (2017b) *SEN Support: A survey of schools and colleges*. Coventry: DfE.

DfE/DoHSC (2023) *Special Educational Needs and Disabilities (SEND) and Alternative Provision Improvement Plan – Right support, right place, right time*. London: HMSO.

DfES (2005) *Primary National Strategies: Focusing on solutions – A positive approach to improving behaviour*. London: DfES.

Dyson, A. (2001) 'Special needs in the twenty-first century: Where we've been and where we're going'. *British Journal of Special Education* 28(1), 12–52.

EEF (2020) *SEN in mainstream schools*. London: EEF.

Ekins, A. (2012) *The Changing Face of Special Educational Needs: Impact and implications for SENCOs, teachers and their schools*. Abingdon: Routledge.

Ekins, A. (2015) *The Changing Face of Special Educational Needs: Impact and implications for SENCOs, teachers and their schools* (2nd Edition). Abingdon: Routledge

Ekins, A. and Grimes, P. (2009) *Inclusion: Developing an effective whole school approach*. Maidenhead: Open University Press.

Florian, L. (2007) 'Reimagining special education'. In: Florian, L. ed. *The SAGE handbook of special education*. London: SAGE Publications.

House of Commons Select Committee (2006) *Special Educational Needs: Third report of session 2005–2006*. London: TSO.

Minow (1990) *Making all the difference: Inclusion, exclusion and American law*. Ithaca, NY: Cornell University Press.

NASUWT (2018) *Special Educational Needs (SEN), Additional Learning Needs (ALN) and Additional Support Needs (ASN)*. England: NASUWT.

Norwich, B. (2007) *Dilemmas of difference, inclusion and disability: International perspectives and future directions*. Oxon: Routledge.

Norwich, B. (2008) Dilemmas of difference, inclusion and disability: International perspectives on placement. *European Journal of Special Needs Education* 23(4), 287–304. https://doi.org/10.1080/08856250802387166

Norwich, B. (2009) 'Dilemmas of difference and the identification of special educational needs/disability: International perspectives'. *British Educational Research Journal* 35(3), 447–467.

Warnock, M., Norwich, B. and Terzi, L. (2010) *Special educational needs: A new look*. London: Continuum International Publishing Group.

7 Co-ordinating provision effectively

> In this chapter, we critically examine and explore the following key aspects:
>
> - Effective, accessible systems
> - Models to support the coordination of provision
> - The Graduated Approach
> - Tiered approaches to planning provision
> - Provision Mapping
> - Individual Class Inclusion Maps
> - Evaluating provisions

Key issues

The need to implement effective systems for the coordination of provision is not new as this has been embedded in policy and practice for decades (OFSTED, 2004, 2011; DCSF, 2007, 2008; DfE, 2011; DfE/DoH, 2014, 2015). But yet, this remains an area that schools typically still find really challenging to embed effectively.

Here, the focus is on the electronic/paper-based systems and processes used by schools to identify needs, plan support and intervention and monitor and evaluate the impact of those systems. This will include systems and processes such as:

- Provision Mapping
- Intervention monitoring logs and records
- Individual Special Educational Needs (SEND) outcomes, targets and plans (SEN Support Plans; EHCP Provision Plans).

and will link in with the systems and processes discussed in previous chapters to effectively identify needs:

- SEND Register
- Class Profiles
- Identification or SEND Concern forms.

DOI: 10.4324/9781003033554-7

The key issues explored in this chapter, therefore focus on:

1. The need for effective, accessible systems and processes which are used to inform and direct practice
2. Developing understanding of the Graduated Approach
3. Tiered approaches to planning provision.

Current policy and research

Over recent years, concerns have risen about the quality of support and provision that pupils with SEND are able to access, both in terms of quality teaching and learning provision within the school setting (including access to effective education in classes with their peers, rather than separated in withdrawn intervention groups) and in terms of access to the specialist support and provision that some pupils with more complex SEND require. In research undertaken by NASUWT (2018: 6), teachers considered whether learners in their school received appropriate support to meet their needs:

- 39% said that learners mostly receive the support to which they are entitled
- 37% said that they sometimes receive the support to which they are entitled
- 7% said that learners always received the support to which they are entitled
- 18% said that learners rarely or never received the support to which they are entitled.

Many respondents noted that there is now a 'lack of specialist knowledge of the needs of learners' (NASUWT, 2018: 6) and that this therefore impacts on support and provision. Whilst there is a need to review the training that all staff have to be able to understand and meet needs (see discussions in Chapter 5), there is also a need to review the systems and processes for sharing information to ensure that they are effective. The Special Educational Needs and Disabilities (SEND) and Alternative Provision Improvement Plan (DfE/DoHSC, 2023) refers to the challenge of addressing appropriate training and resources for school, and propose:

> Our programmes and policies will build confidence and expertise at every level of the workforce, from teachers and classroom staff through to specialists, and to leaders who set the overall direction and culture of their settings. We want ordinarily available provision and high quality teaching to meet children and young people's needs wherever possible, and specialist support to complement the skills and expertise of the wider workforce.
>
> (DfE/DoHSC, 2023: 53)

There is, therefore, a real need to review the systems and processes that we use in schools to ensure that they are providing effective information and are easily accessible to support all staff to better understand what provision is in place for pupils with SEND, and the strategies and approaches that need to be consistently embedded to support them to be able to engage and participate fully in the whole curriculum.

Effective, accessible systems to inform practice

Systems and processes to coordinate provision are often time-consuming, and, too often are separated and seen as separate to practice – so Provision Maps or SEN Support Plans will be completed, but perhaps by the Special Educational Needs Coordinator

(SENCO) separate from the class teacher, or, at best, by the class teacher – but then not used to directly impact on the planning of practice on a day to day basis. Too often, these really important SEND plans and planning tools, systems and processes are simply filed (electronically and/or in hard copy) and not used as working documents to directly impact on day to day planning and practice for meeting the needs of pupils in the classroom. What is needed instead is a more dynamic system and process which understands and responds to the need for the systems and processes to be working documents that underpin the planning for provision and practice in linked ways, as illustrated in the Inclusion in Action model (Ekins & Grimes, 2009) (see Figure 7.1):

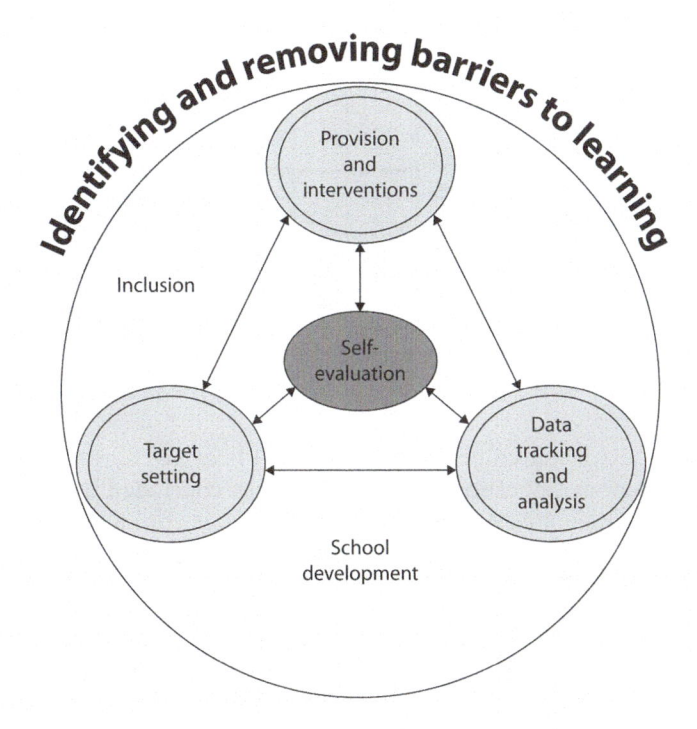

Figure 7.1 A model for 'Inclusion in Action' Ekins and Grimes (2009)

Developing understanding of the Graduated Approach

The need to effectively plan for and coordinate the support and provision needs of pupils with SEND is now firmly embedded in the Graduated Approach (DfE/DoH, 2014, 2015) (see Figure 7.2). All schools are required to have a Graduated Approach, which sets out the four key stages of the cycle – Assess, Plan, Do, Review:

> This SEN support should take the form of a four-part cycle through which earlier decisions and actions are revisited, refined and revised with a growing understanding of the pupil's needs and of what supports the pupil in making good progress and securing good outcomes. This is known as the Graduated Approach.
> (DfE/DoH, 2015: 100)

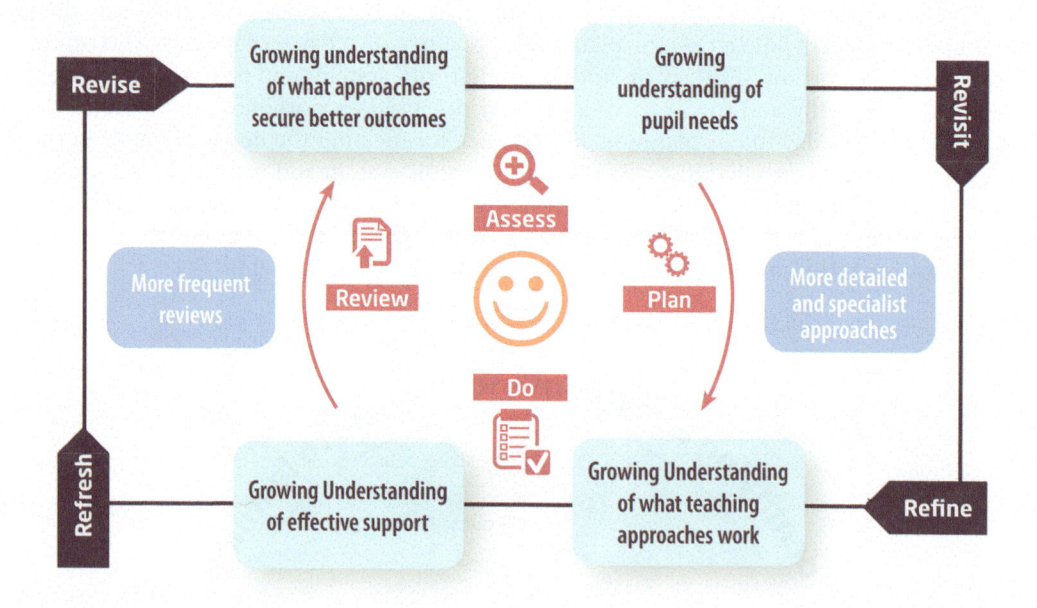

Figure 7.2 The Graduated Approach: The Assess, Plan, Do, Review model

Source: https://www.kelsi.org.uk/__data/assets/pdf_file/0004/117256/Special-educational-needs-mainstream-core-standards.pdf (accessed 14.5.2023)

Despite this model being embedded into the 2014 SEND Reforms, disappointingly, the House of Commons Education Committee Report concluded that 'there has been a lack of focus on the Graduated Approach and what good practice looks like for pupils with SEN Support' (House of Commons Education Committee, 2019: 44) as a result of the focus on embedding EHCPs. Below is an overview of the four stages of the Graduated Approach:

- *Assess* – Assessment is crucial to identifying the needs and starting points, as well as strengths of the individual and using this to plan, and then implement, effective intervention and provision. Teachers are fundamental to gaining a clear overview of the pupil's needs alongside any screening, school testing and specialist assessments that might have taken place.

  The Assess stage is more complex and complicated now though, since the removal of consistent attainment levels against which to measure and track pupil progress. The current expected, below, above/greater depth terms that are used are much more difficult to measure small steps progress against, and therefore schools have needed to develop their own approaches to ensuring that small step progress is able to be tracked. This will include the use of additional assessment and screening tools, as outlined in Chapter 6, as well as small step progress trackers.
- *Plan* – Based on the information gathered as part of the assess stage, very clear plans can be set with or by teachers regarding the evidence-based interventions or adjustments that need to be made for the pupil. This needs to involve the parents/carers so that all are able to contribute towards successful outcomes.
- *Do* – Teachers develop their understanding of what works as they implement or review the strategies they are introducing, or the interventions taking place in class. The

formative assessment taking place, is really valuable information which will feed into the review stage where decisions might be made on what approaches need to continue, be adapted or stopped based on the individual pupil and the overall impact of what have been put into place.

- *Review* – The review stage enables teachers to share their understanding of what strategies have been useful to support the pupil, help them make progress and meet identified outcomes. It is also useful at this evaluative stage to identify what is not working and why. 'Teachers continually review pupils' progress, formally and informally, and this should be no different for pupils with SEN' (Nasen, 2014: 13).

A key responsibility of the SENCO is to advise 'on the Graduated Approach to providing SEN support' (DfE/DoH, 2015: 108). As outlined above, it is the teacher who is really at the centre of planning, assessing and reviewing the impact of the planned approach taken for the pupil. DfE/DoH (2014: 53) highlight that: 'Teacher quality is one of the most important in-school determinants of pupil outcomes, reducing the risk that children fall behind due to missed opportunities or lack of appropriate support'. Therefore the SENCO needs to ensure the teaching staff are very clear on the Graduated Approach and how this is realised in school.

The Graduated Approach starts at whole-school level. Teachers are continually assessing, planning, implementing and reviewing their approach to teaching all children. However, where a potential special educational needs has been identified, this cyclical process becomes increasingly personalised.

(Nasen, 2014: 2)

Whilst the Graduated Approach has been embedded in policy for some time, and does link to typical school practices, there is still a need to ensure that all staff are familiar with the terminology of the Graduated Approach and ways that the Graduated Approach is embedded in practice within their school setting. The school's process related to the Graduated Approach must also be published in the school SEN Information Report in relation to 'arrangements for assessing and reviewing children and young people's progress towards outcomes' (DfE/DoH, 2015: 106). Using visuals such as Figure 7.2 to illustrate the process in school may provide clarity for parents/carers, but could also be used as a way to share clear information with staff on the process and how this is undertaken in school. Ways to encourage real understanding and a collective responsibility for the implementation of the Graduated Approach is therefore key to ensuring a distributed approach to fulfilling statutory responsibilities for all pupils with SEND.

Tiered approaches to planning provision

As a way to plan for different needs within a structured approach, the National Strategies (1997–2011) introduced the Waves of Intervention (DfES, 2002, 2003) (see Figure 7.3).

Whilst the language of Waves of Intervention was removed by the coalition government (2010 onwards), the principles behind the model continue to be used and are effective in ensuring that, rather than only focusing on additional intervention, a strategic approach to evaluating the impact and implications of a tiered approach to meeting needs is embedded within the school setting.

Models which carefully review and plan for provision at a Universal, Targeted and Specialist level are therefore essential in ensuring that there is a structured approach, and that

110 *Co-ordinating provision effectively*

there is appropriate focus on developing the Universal teaching approaches, strategies and pedagogy to ensure that the model of practice in the school setting does not become overloaded, and overly reliant on additional, separate interventions.

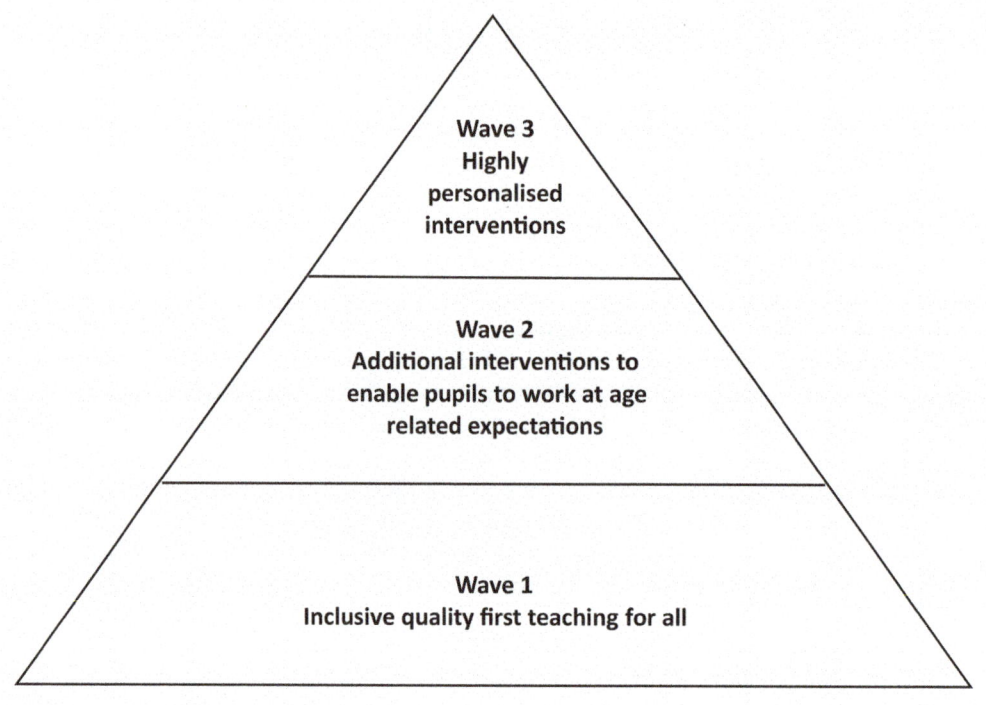

Figure 7.3 Waves of Intervention (DfES, 2002, 2003)

A similar approach has been taken to more appropriately support children with access to Alternative Provision (DfE/DoHSC, 2023). The model in Figure 7.4 outlines how this same tiered approach enables children to be supported at the relevant stage dependent upon their needs:

A three-tier model for alternative provision

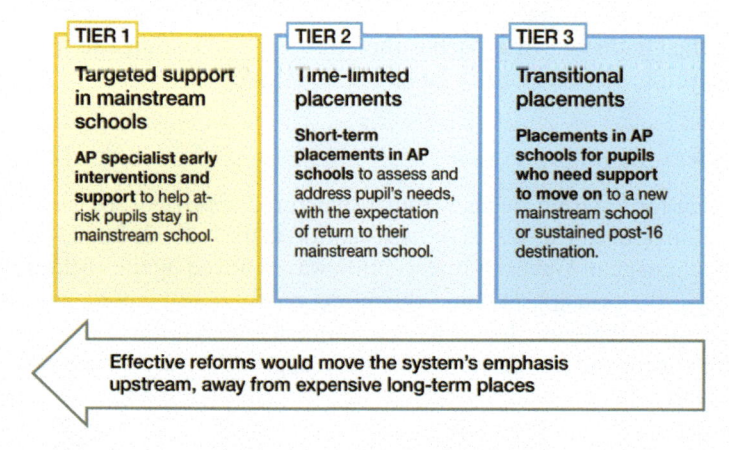

TIER 1	TIER 2	TIER 3
Targeted support in mainstream schools	**Time-limited placements**	**Transitional placements**
AP specialist early interventions and support to help at-risk pupils stay in mainstream school.	Short-term placements in AP schools to assess and address pupil's needs, with the expectation of return to their mainstream school.	Placements in AP schools for pupils who need support to move on to a new mainstream school or sustained post-16 destination.

Effective reforms would move the system's emphasis upstream, away from expensive long-term places

Figure 7.4 DfE/DoHSC – Three-tier model for alternative provision
Source: SEND and alternative provision improvement plan – GOV.UK (www.gov.uk) (accessed 14.5.2023)

In this way, reflection on the balance of the Universal, Targeted and Specialist model in operation is essential in helping schools to review where to focus their development to ensure that the needs of all pupils can be met.

Within the current OFSTED Inspection Framework (2019), there is a significant emphasis on all pupils having access to high-quality teaching opportunities alongside their peers – with a move away from the previous traditional model of large numbers of separate withdrawn intervention groups to meet the needs of pupils working at different levels of ability and pace.

Now, the focus is not to reduce access to the curriculum, so finding ways to ensure that all pupils have access to the full curriculum, and are taught alongside their peers, whilst also having any specific SEND needs met through targeted and effective specialist interventions as needed is more complex and requires careful consideration within the school setting.

It is for this reason that ensuring that the focus for support and development is put in to developing the quality of the Universal, Quality First Teaching, approaches is essential. By ensuring that the Universal teaching approaches and pedagogy underpinning the school and class setting is effective and will meet the needs of the children within the class/school, needs will be more effectively met and there will be less need for separate withdrawn intervention groups. As identified by the DfE/DoHSC:

> High-quality, evidence-based teaching is critical in ensuring that the special educational needs of pupils are not mis-identified when their difficulties may be due to poor classroom provision, as well as ensuring that the needs of those with SEN are met effectively.
> (DfE/DoHSC, 2023: 54)

Where there is a need for more targeted or specialist interventions, they need to be evidence-informed and of the highest quality possible, delivered by someone with the training and knowledge to be able to understand the intervention and deliver it effectively to meet the needs of the pupils that they are working with. The interventions need to be time-limited and with clear start and end data and expected outcomes to ensure that the intervention is as focused and successful as possible.

Planning for practice

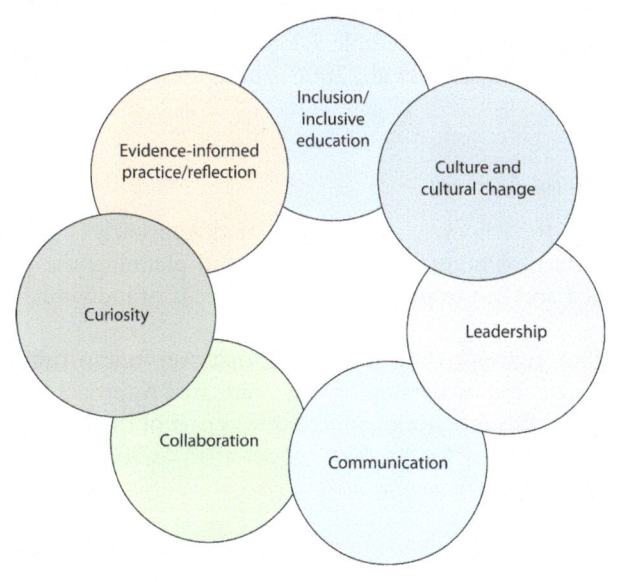

Figure 7.5 Key principles model

112 *Co-ordinating provision effectively*

Whilst developing the paper-based and electronic systems and processes to enable effective coordination and planning for provision for pupils with SEND continues to remain a complex issue for many schools, following a principled approach to this, which embeds the key principles and values of ***inclusion, communication, collaboration, curiosity and evidence-informed practice*** will ensure that the systems and processes can be as effective as possible. In particular, it essential that the following aspects are understood and embedded:

- Ensuring that all of the systems and processes work within the context of whole-school systems and processes for tracking and recording progress, target setting and planning for intervention and support so that they are as ***inclusive*** as possible and are not seen as something that is separate from the day-to-day practice of teaching and learning, and therefore the embedded responsibility of everyone in the school setting
- Ensuring that the systems and processes do not become 'tick box exercises' to be completed and filed – that instead they are regularly used, accessible, talked about, shared across the school community – between staff and, as appropriate, with parents/carers and the pupils themselves
- Ensuring that a ***curious*** approach is taken to reviewing data when monitoring and evaluating the impact and outcomes of provision that has been planned and put in place. Ensuring that this curious approach drives decisions about what works and why, instead of simplistic decisions being taken without fully understanding the data that has been shared
- Ensuring that the whole school community are engaged directly in reviewing and reflecting on ***evidence-bases*** and current research about what works, and that there are processes in place to be able to check whether that research and evidence will fit the context within which you are working and be effective for the pupils and whole school community.

Effective, accessible systems to inform practice

The starting point for planning practice must be a review of the systems and processes that are currently in place and being used in the school setting, to reflect on how effective and accessible. The questions in Table 7.1 prompts may be useful in supporting that 'principled interruption' (Ainscow et al., 2006) and critical review of the systems that are used currently.

Embedding the Graduated Approach

The Assess, Plan, Do, Review cycle of the Graduated Approach (DfE/DoH, 2015) provides some helpful starting points for identifying and planning the provisions that will need to be prioritised and put in place to meet the needs of individual pupils or groups/cohorts of pupils.

As discussed earlier, central to this is ensuring that everyone within the school setting has an understanding of, and ownership of, the Graduated Approach so that there is a collective responsibility for this functioning effectively as part of the whole-school approaches and systems, and expectations for practice, rather than as something that is only done separately by the SENCO.

Table 7.1 Reviewing existing processes for coordinating provision

Key question	RAG rate existing practice	Actions to develop practice further
What are the systems and processes that you have in place currently to coordinate provision?		
How effective and accessible are they in practice? – do all staff members have access to them and use them directly to inform their day to day practices with pupils with SEND? – How do you know?		
Are the systems that you have in place inclusive systems and processes– do they encourage and support an inclusive approach to meeting the needs of all pupils, or are they unintentionally highlighting and emphasising differences? – How do you know?		
Do the systems and processes that you use retain a strong focus on monitoring and evaluating the impact and effectiveness of the approaches and interventions that are used?		
Is the knowledge and understanding from the monitoring and evaluation information used to directly impact on decisions about whether interventions need to be retained/developed further/or stopped? – How effective is this? – How do you know?		
How robust and effective/meaningful are the systems that you have in place to embed robust and reliable ways to make judgements about the progress that a pupil makes within a policy context that has moved away from discrete 'levels' of attainment into an approach which focuses instead on much broader statements about whether a pupil is Expected/Below Expected/Exceeding, or Developing, Fluency, Accuracy or Mastery?		
How is small step progress and the effectiveness/impact of teaching approaches and interventions measured and recorded? – How effective is this? – How do you know?		

* Red = Not evident in practice; Amber = some aspects evident in practice; Green = Fully evident in practice.

Reflective Activity

- How well is the Graduated Approach embedded in your school setting?
    - Think about how the SENCO uses it to inform their work and processes
    - Think about how well other staff, teaching and support staff, are aware of and are part of the Graduated Approach and embed and contribute directly to the Assess, Plan, Do, Review cycle.
- Are all staff confident with the terminology and concept of the Graduated Approach and understand that this is linked to the SEN and Disability Code of Practice (DfE/DoH, 2015)?
- What further support do you think may be needed to ensure that this model is fully understood and embedded by everyone in your school setting?

The Case Study below provides information about how one SENCO, working within a three-form entry primary school worked closely with class teachers to embed this shared understanding of and commitment to the Graduated Approach:

Case Study – Collaborative Working Relationship Between SENCO and Class Teacher

Maria Macnab

This case study is based within a three-form entry mainstream primary school, focussing on one class in lower Key Stage 2 with 30% of pupils with diagnosed and undiagnosed SEND, many with ADHD, ASC, or a mix of both. Earlier teachers had struggled with this class and as part of the SENCO team we thought it imperative that their new teacher who was to have them at the start of a new academic year, had a clear picture of their needs as individuals and as a class, and not just subjective opinions of others.

Although necessary, I had previously found, when informing class teachers of objectives and strategies to accommodate or deliver within their class, it could make the teacher feel overwhelmed with yet more demands on their planning, delivery, and expectations and could result in an unconstructive SENCO–Teacher relationship.

Therefore, to avoid this negative and reactive relationship, I made the time to sit down and work with the teacher. Whilst complying with the EEF's recommendations on scaffolding, this:

1 informed the teacher
2 formulated a plan which would work well for pupils with SEND, and work well with the class as a whole
3 ensured inclusivity.

This followed a positive SENCO–Teacher relationship as detailed in Figure 7.6, specifically using the 'PLAN' phase of the model.

Nurturing a productive relationship with the teacher, the agenda of the meeting consisted of two main goals:

Understanding of the pupils' diagnoses and needs

This entailed not just stating the label, but what this actual meant for the individual– ASC, for example was presenting very differently in two different pupils in the same class. We also covered the difficulties each pupil faced within the school environment, including the impact on their accessibility to the curriculum, processing, retainment and engagement, in addition to interaction, mood and behaviours. Although the teacher had encountered many of these high incidence needs previously, it was important they understood the individuals and how they coped with this need prior to teaching them.

Core strategies for the pupils

The strategies which were in place for the pupils were explained, with a focus on why they work. (It is difficult to place an importance on something and be

Co-ordinating provision effectively 115

ASSESS:
Teachers should work with the SENCO to carry out a clear analysis of needs. Teachers should use prior assessment and observations of the pupil comparing these to internal and national data, sharing this information with the SENCO.
The SENCO with the teacher will try to identify barriers to learning

PLAN:
Teacher and SENCO should (with the parent and pupils) agree on interventions, adjustments and support to be implemented. Expected outcomes should be set.

Secondary level – more commonly this plan will be designed by the SENCO (with parent and pupil) and shared with the teacher

Assess, Plan, Do, Review Model (DfE/DoH, 2015; 101-102) Focussing on Teacher–SENCO relationship

REVIEW:
The teacher with the SENCO should review the outcomes met and effectiveness of the interventions and support. Decide on any changes required.
To start again at assessment of the next stage of development

DO:
The teacher is responsible for the pupil's teaching and learning.
The SENCO will support the teacher in further assessments and in the implementation of support, ensuring its effectiveness

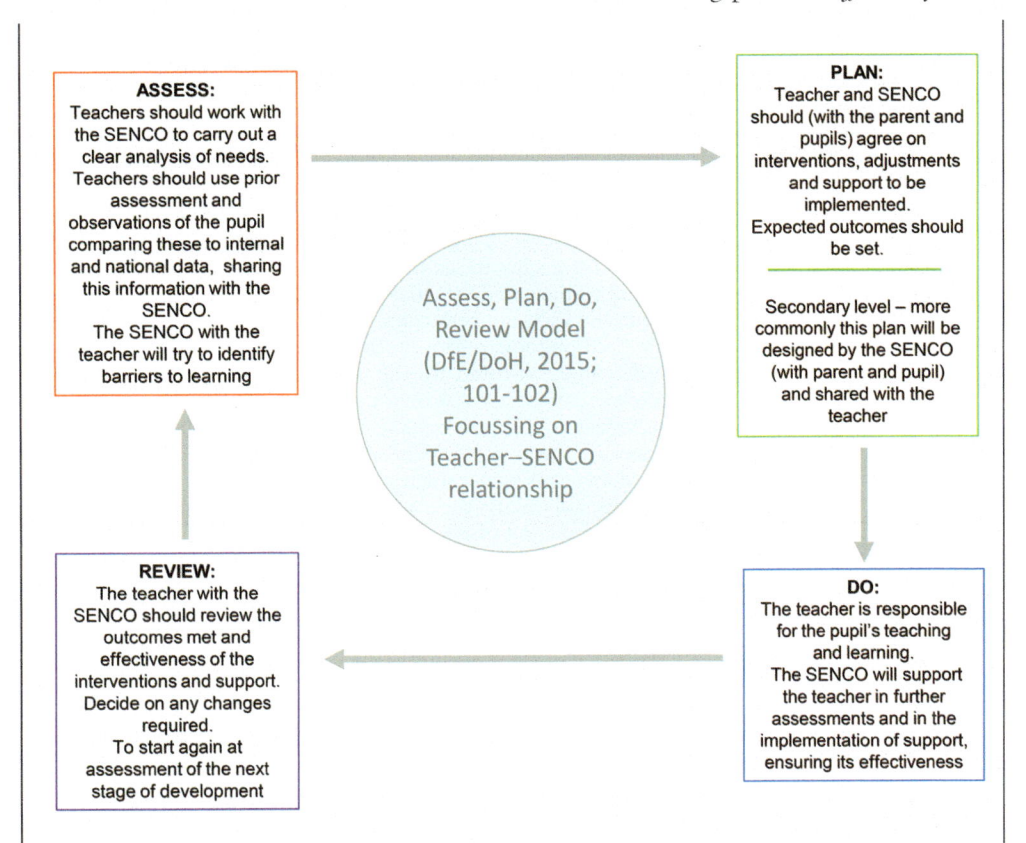

Figure 7.6 Positive SENCO–Teacher relationship

consistent with it if you do not understand why and the implications of not fulfilling it). This also gave an opportunity to discuss with the teacher, their own ideas of embedding the proposed strategies into their class – giving them ownership and enthusiasm.

It was through this discussion when I was explaining the high levels of sensory needs and hyperactivity towards sensory stimuli, that the teacher came up with her ideas of cushions for the floored area, minimal displays and lamps for lighting.

Positive impacts

Having this collaborative working relationship, where I was able to proactively afford time to support the teacher, gave the teacher confidence and knowledge of her class and how to support and teach them effectively and enthusiastically. It reassured her that she was able to embed strategies into her preferred way of working. Also knowing she had the support of the SENCO team made her feel more confident in approaching the senior leadership team to allow her the changes to her classroom which were beneficial to the pupils.

Table 7.2 Table illustrating proactive approach and collaborative working relationship

Key principle of support	Impact
Time with the teacher	Created a collaborative relationship. The teacher not feeling dictated to with additional work.
	Long-term positive relationship, where the teacher would be happy to discuss changes, ideas, and development.
Explaining the strategies and individuals' needs	Allowed the teacher to see the individuals and not a set of labels, adding to their understanding and empathy towards the pupils needs and inclusion strategies.
	Established ongoing positive relationships with all pupils.
Discussion of proposed strategies	Awarded an opportunity for the teacher to add their own ideas to ways that could assist their pupils. Creating ownership and enthusiasm of the strategies to be put in place, in addition to reassessing these.
	Formed an ethos where the teacher felt empowered to make changes and discuss these with the leadership team for proposed sharing of good practice.

This proactive approach resulted in further reaching positive impact than just the initial setting up of the class, as demonstrated in Table 7.2.

The overall impact of this proactive approach and collaborative working relationship had further positive outcomes than those curtailed to the transition within the classroom. As demonstrated in Table 7.2 and Figure 7.7, the enablement of inclusivity and constructive classroom practice has a productive outcome on both the results seen in the classroom and on the SENCO's time and role.

This is in stark contrast to the possible reactive and negative consequences of a poor Teacher–SENCO relationship (Figure 7.8).

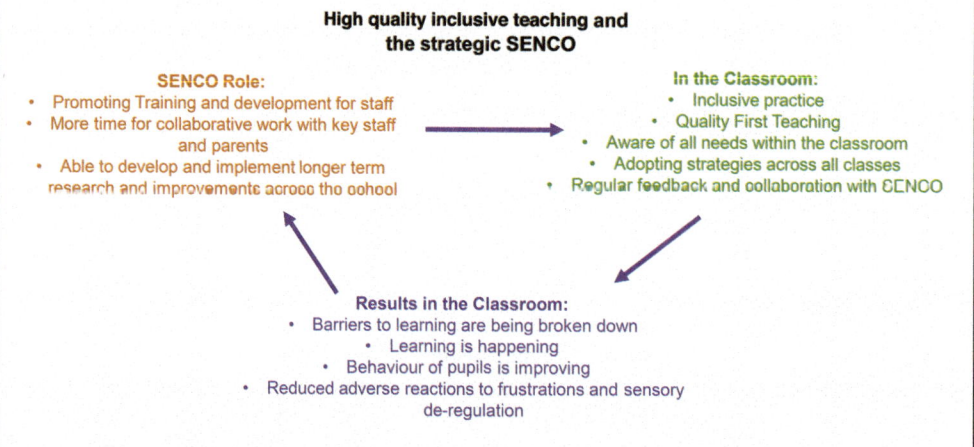

High quality inclusive teaching and the strategic SENCO

SENCO Role:
- Promoting Training and development for staff
- More time for collaborative work with key staff and parents
- Able to develop and implement longer term research and improvements across the school

In the Classroom:
- Inclusive practice
- Quality First Teaching
- Aware of all needs within the classroom
- Adopting strategies across all classes
- Regular feedback and collaboration with SENCO

Results in the Classroom:
- Barriers to learning are being broken down
- Learning is happening
- Behaviour of pupils is improving
- Reduced adverse reactions to frustrations and sensory de-regulation

Figure 7.7 Proactive approach and collaborative working relationship

Inadequate Model:
Teachers and SENCO

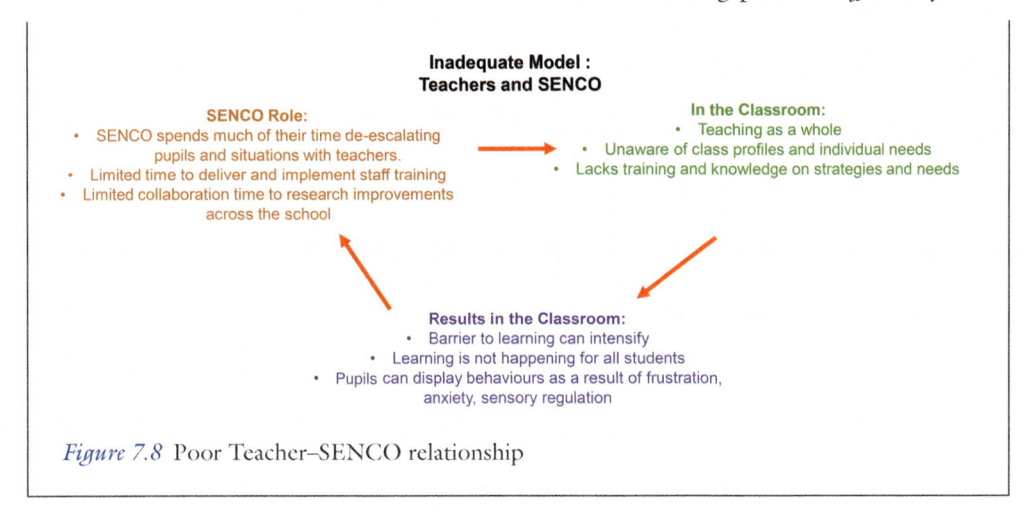

SENCO Role:
- SENCO spends much of their time de-escalating pupils and situations with teachers.
- Limited time to deliver and implement staff training
- Limited collaboration time to research improvements across the school

In the Classroom:
- Teaching as a whole
- Unaware of class profiles and individual needs
- Lacks training and knowledge on strategies and needs

Results in the Classroom:
- Barrier to learning can intensify
- Learning is not happening for all students
- Pupils can display behaviours as a result of frustration, anxiety, sensory regulation

Figure 7.8 Poor Teacher–SENCO relationship

Tiered approaches to planning provision

Identifying the range of provisions that are needed to meet the needs of individuals, cohorts and the whole school is essential to be able to meet the needs of all pupils. The Graduated Approach (Figure 7.2) and the systems and processes introduced in Chapters 2 and 6 linked to identifying needs will all help with this, and having a clear system of mapping that provision (see later discussion on provision mapping) to enable both a day-to-day overview and a strategic overview is essential.

As a stage in-between those two aspects of identifying needs and mapping the provision, developing a model to capture different tiers of support that are available and ways for staff and pupils to be able to access those different tiers of support will help to ensure that planning and implementation of support and provision is strategic and not reactive.

It is important for all staff to have an understanding of the appropriateness of different types of support and provision, and that there will be more cost-effective and embedded interventions that can be put in place initially, before needing to go to some of the more specialist, and perhaps more costly types of support. This can make communication between staff and parents/carers more effective as all staff will have an understanding of the type of provisions that are available and appropriate to meet the needs of an individual child, and ways that that provision can be developed over time as needed by moving into the more specialist tiers of support.

By developing an over-arching tiered model of the whole-school provisions that you currently offer within your school setting can also help with the strategic understanding and review of how effective your provisions and practices will be to meet the needs of current cohort and whole-school needs. It will enable you to easily identify any gaps in provision that you would then be able to plan how to address through staff training, resourcing or pedagogical approaches.

Reflective Activity

- What does the approach to provision and intervention planning look like in your school currently?
- What implications does this have for whole-school development, staffing and the meeting of needs for the individual child?
- Is the model a balanced one, with the greatest level of focus and support placed into planning effective, evidence-informed Universal strategies that directly relate and meet the needs of the cohort that you have in your own school setting (see Figure 7.9)?

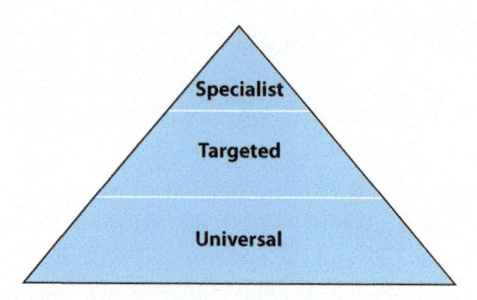

Figure 7.9 Universal, Targeted and Specialist model

Or is the model of practice in your school currently unbalanced, with little thinking and planning about the impact and implications of Universal teaching and support strategies, leading to an imbalance and over-reliance of additional, separate interventions to 'compensate' for the lack of thinking and planning at the Universal level (see Figure 7.10)?

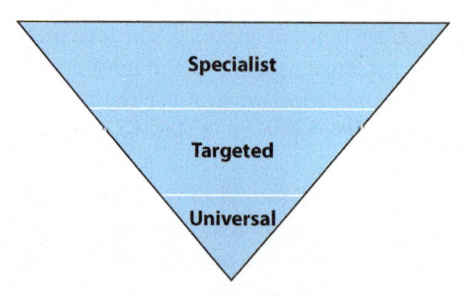

Figure 7.10 Inverted Universal, Targeted and Specialist model

- What are the implications of this for practice?

The Case Study below provides a useful overview of one way that a large mainstream secondary school developed their use of the tiered model of provision – using the SEND Areas of Need as a starting point to capture the range of provisions available for pupils, but using this not just as an exclusive SEND planning tool, but inclusively to capture the range of provisions available for all pupils under the different areas of Cognition and Learning; Communication and Interaction; Social Emotional and Mental Health and Sensory and/or physical needs.

Case Study – Clarifying and Identifying Tiers of Support

The SENCO in a large mixed comprehensive secondary school had identified that whilst the school was implementing a huge amount of different support for pupils, due to the way that the school was structured, in subject departments, an Inclusion pastoral team and a SEND department, with separate whole-school areas of focus on pupils with Pupil Premium and on pupil and Staff Wellbeing, there was not a shared whole-school understanding of what was already in place, how it was being used and how effective that was for supporting and meeting the needs of the pupils.

Instead of adding on more and more new interventions and strategies, the SENCO therefore decided to work with staff to bring together their collective knowledge of the range of approaches and interventions that were already in place.

During a whole-staff CPD session, a collaborative activity was therefore completed to draw together the individual knowledge of all staff and to start to map that into Tiers of Support.

A simple model (see Figure 7.11), based on the previous Waves of Intervention (DfES, 2002, 2003), focused on the 'Universal'; 'Targeted' and 'Specialist' support and provisions that were already available for pupils in the school was used to facilitate the discussions and mapping:

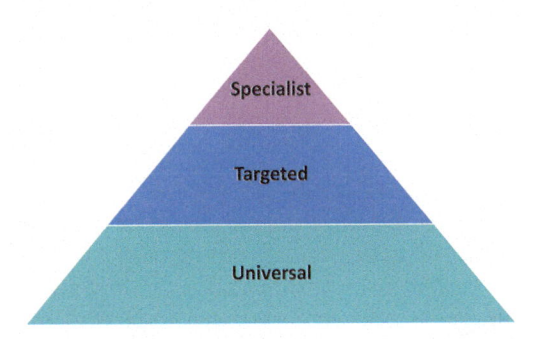

Figure 7.11 Tiered model of planning provision

As the activity was completed as a whole-staff, it effectively brought together knowledge of different approaches and provisions from a wide range of different perspectives and stimulated effective discussions and the sharing of experiences as part of the process. Any embedded assumptions were able to be positively and openly challenged through positive conversations which valued curiosity and the use of open questions to build further understanding.

As a result of the activity, staff in the school are now more aware of the range of approaches that are already in place within the school, and the SENCO has been able to work with key leaders of other areas to develop clear referral processes, including eligibility thresholds so that there is now a more strategic and effective approach to identifying and prioritising support for pupils across the school.

Now that provision has been mapped, it can easily be reviewed and updated, and any gaps in provision can be clearly identified and then addressed.

The mapping of provision in this way has also enabled a more strategic focus on reviewing the evidence-bases for the different provisions used, thereby contributing to an approach which supports the EEF (2020) SEN in Mainstream Schools Guidance Report Recommendation 4 – complement high-quality teaching with carefully selected small-group and one-to-one interventions (see also discussions in Chapter 8).

Reflective Activity

- Do you currently have anything similar in place to clearly set out the provision and support offer available in your school setting?
- How accessible is it?
  - to staff?
  - to parents/carers?
- How effective is this?
  - Is there anything that could be developed further?
- In which ways?

Provision Mapping

The tiered model of identifying the range of provisions that are available to support pupils in your school setting is helpful in providing a whole-school overview, against which you can review current cohort needs to ensure that they can be fully met and to address any gaps in provision. It can also be used to ensure that there is shared understanding by all staff of the range of provisions and interventions that are available within the school setting, and which would be appropriate for which pupils, to ensure that reactive decisions grasping straight for the most specialist resources or provisions are reduced.

From this starting point, it is then important to develop effective systems for mapping the provisions available for key pupils within a given timeframe – using Provision Maps. As the SEND and Disability Code of Practice (DfE/DoH, 2015: 105) identifies, 'Provision maps are an efficient way of showing all the provision that the school makes which is additional to and different from that which is offered through the school's curriculum.

The use of provision maps can help SENCOs to maintain an overview of the programmes and interventions used with different groups of pupils and provide a basis for monitoring the levels of intervention'.

The DfE/DoH (2015) also note the strategic nature of Provision Maps which can contribute to whole school improvement planning, by reviewing and evaluating the range of provisions available and the effectiveness of them for the cohort of pupils currently in the school, class or year group.

We find it most effective to set up Provision Maps three times a year, for each old term: Autumn Term, Spring Term and Summer Term, as this provides enough time to plan and implement the provision, time for the pupils to access the provision and make enough progress through it, and then for it to be reviewed and evaluated ahead of the development of the next Provision Map.

Whilst Provision Maps and Provision Mapping has been a practice embedded in guidance documents for some time now (originally introduced through the National Strategies, 2005–2006), yet it is a practice that many schools still find difficult to embed effectively.

Often, Provision Maps become time-consuming and burdensome – with too much time spent completing them, and not enough time spent using them to impact meaningfully on practice and reviewing them to evaluate the impact of the provisions that are being prioritised and put in place.

Yet, they are essential tools to support knowledge and evaluation of the provisions that are in place for individuals and groups of pupils.

Again, as with all of the approaches discussed in this book, a values and principled-led approach to Provision Mapping needs to be followed to ensure that the practice does become fully effective and that it directly supports the ongoing review and development of practices to meet the needs of all pupils. Provision Maps should, therefore, be both a strategic tool and a day to day working document.

Where Provision Mapping is most effective, the Provision Maps, once completed, are not simply filed until the end of the 10 week intervention period. Instead, they form the basis of the day-to-day planning for the teacher, with all of the additional provision and intervention needs of the pupils in their class clearly planned for, with details about which pupils require which interventions/additional support, what their starting data is, and what the expected outcome of the planned provision/intervention is. Against this, progress should be tracked and monitored through the implementation and delivery of the intervention (see Chapter 8, for examples of ways to monitor and record progress through interventions), and the teacher can make annotations onto the Provision Map to ensure that the Provision Map is as up to date and meaningful as possible. This will include where new pupils are added, or pupils are taken out of planned intervention groups (as a result of further analysis of their starting data and their specific support needs), where the Expected Outcome is amended, if needed, to the needs of the individual or group (for example if the expected outcome is achieved early in the intervention period) it should then be extended further to ensure that the provision time is not wasted.

Ensuring that the Provision Maps effectively and simply record the key information that is needed to support day to day planning and strategic reviews of the impact of existing provisions is essential, and Table 7.3 provides an outline of the key information that should be included in an effective Provision Map.

Table 7.3 An example of a provision map template

Provision	Pupils	When and who	Start data	Expected outcome	End data	Evaluation of impact
Cognition and Learning							
Communication and Interaction							
Social Emotional and Mental Health							
Sensory and/or physical needs							

To help with the strategic review of provisions, although the Provision Maps that we use are not solely SEND-focused, we have found it helpful to capture provisions using the SEND Areas of Need – Cognition and Learning; Communication and Interaction; Social Emotional and Mental Health; Sensory and/or physical needs.

This provides a useful framework for evaluating, alongside the whole-school tiered models introduced in the case study, whether there are any gaps in provision linked to review of the current profile of needs for a particular cohort or for the whole school.

We find that the four areas of need helpfully encompass the range of wider provisions and interventions that we would plan for within the school context, and the Provision Map is then used, as much as possible, to record all the additional provisions and interventions that need to be planned and implemented for all pupils within a particular class or year group – to include specific SEND provisions for pupils on the SEND Register as well as other targeted or specialist interventions that pupils who are not on the SEND Register may need to access for a time-limited amount of time.

Whilst there are different models of Provision Mapping, the headings above will help school staff to record the key information that is required to enable the Provision Map to be as effective and strategic as possible. SENCOs and school leaders should, however, beware of and guard against trying to add too much additional information to the Provision Maps. At times, Provision Maps become so overly complicated with too many different columns, or too individualised focusing just on detailing individual provisions, rather than providing the strategic overview of which provisions have been prioritised for which groups of pupils, that they lose their purpose and the impact that they can have for day to day and strategic use.

Reflective Activity

- Review the Provision Mapping format and processes that you have in your school setting.
    - How effective are they?
    - What works well?
    - Are there any aspects that need to be developed further?
    - How could this be achieved?

Completing Provision Maps

There are now a range of online Provision Mapping products available to support the busy SENCO to ensure that the paperwork and administrative side of the role does not become too overwhelming, as well as a number of different formats for Provision Maps used in different local authorities and school settings.

When reviewing and implementing effective processes for Provision Mapping within your school setting, however, always ensure that a principled approach to this is followed, and that the approach that is utilised, be it an online product or a school-developed format, works WITH rather than AGAINST other whole-school systems and processes. The ultimate aim is to enable Provision Mapping, alongside other systems and processes, to become part of the whole-school expectation for practice so that it does not become something separate and different, only completed by the SENCO for pupils with SEND.

Look, therefore, at what systems and processes are already in place within the school setting, and ways that Provision Mapping can align with those processes.

In primary school contexts, Provision Maps are generally completed for each individual class, owned by the class teacher, with support and guidance from the SENCO.

Many schools continue to have regular Pupil Progress Review meetings to review the progress data of pupils and plan any focused support or provision. Ensuring that Provision Mapping is embedded within those very effective meetings enables the Provision Map to become a useful tool to capture the discussions and planning that is already embedded in practice, rather than something to be completed separately, divorced from those really meaningful and innovative review and planning discussions.

Where possible, it is effective if the SENCO, class teacher and a senior leader can come together to complete those Pupil Progress Review meetings, with the SENCO drafting thoughts onto the Provision Map to free the teacher up to be fully part of the collaborative discussions and review and then provide a draft Provision Map for the class teacher to then take away and review and develop further, ensuring full ownership by the class teacher but that none of the creativity and innovation of the Pupil Progress Review meeting discussions is lost.

In secondary school contexts, Provision Mapping often proves more challenging as there are a number of different teachers responsible for the education of the pupils.

Within such contexts, again, the SENCO and school leaders need to consider what is already in place and working in terms of systems and processes for reviewing pupil progress and planning provision and intervention to meet the needs of individuals and groups.

A number of different models could be considered in order to ensure that Provision Mapping is as effective as possible within the secondary school context. Often, year group rather than class-based Provision Maps are implemented within the secondary school context. These could then be developed in a range of different ways:

- Completed by the SENCO to identify the additional targeted and specialist SEND provisions for pupils within each individual year group
- Shared with the year group teams to include further specific targeted and specialist pastoral interventions or provisions in place from the year group team or agencies that they are working with (e.g. Attendance, Behaviour, Counselling, Mentoring) for identified individuals or groups of pupils
- Shared with subject leads/Heads of Department to add on additional information about subject specific interventions and which pupils have been identified to access those.

124 Co-ordinating provision effectively

In addition to the year group Provision Maps which provide a strategic overview of the provision in place for identified individuals or groups of pupils within each year group, it is also helpful to implement a format to enable teachers, particularly secondary teachers who work with a number of different classes each day, to have a clear overview of specific strategies that pupils within each class group that they teach need to have in place.

A simple format for an Individual Class Inclusion Map (see Figure 7.12), to identify which pupils require which targeted and specialist strategies or provisions to be in place for them, will help teachers, particular those in the secondary context, to have more understanding and direct responsibility for understanding and meeting the needs of the wider range of pupils that they teach each day.

Individual Class Inclusion Map

Class group...................... Term .... Whole class focus..

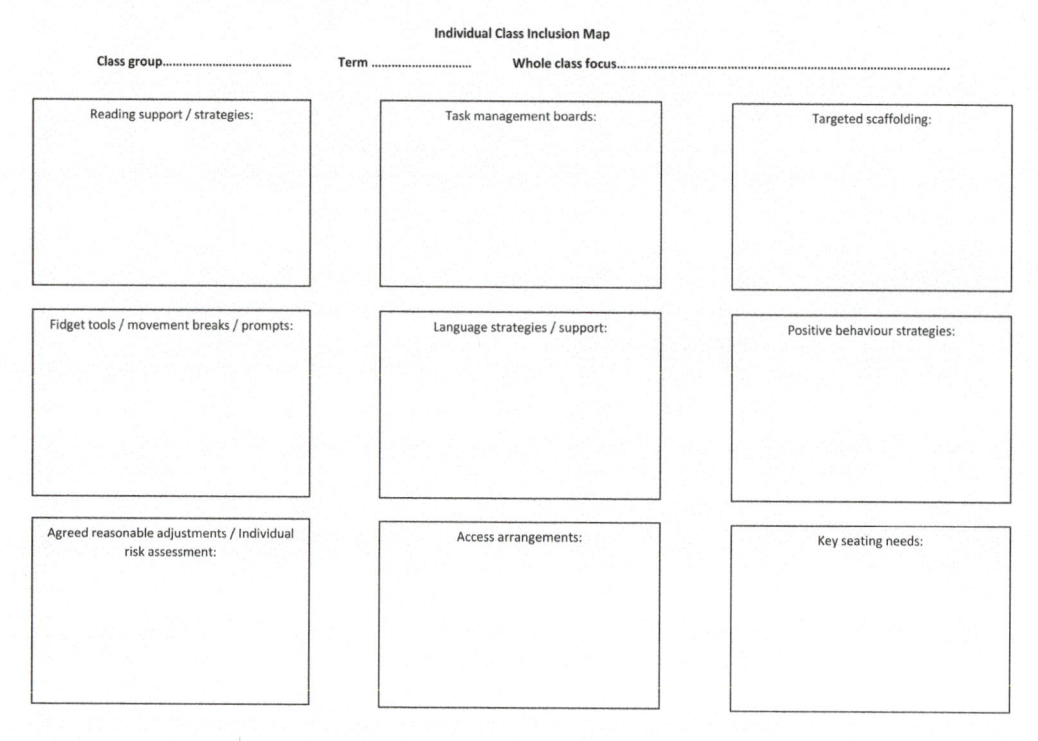

Reading support / strategies:	Task management boards:	Targeted scaffolding:
Fidget tools / movement breaks / prompts:	Language strategies / support:	Positive behaviour strategies:
Agreed reasonable adjustments / Individual risk assessment:	Access arrangements:	Key seating needs:

Figure 7.12 Individual Class Inclusion Map

The boxes on the example above can be amended/adapted to suit the particular needs of the school setting, or class group, although it would be useful to ensure some sort of consistency across the school as a whole.

The whole-class focus identified at the top of the template helps the teacher to identify any whole-class areas of focus, and to then be able to record improvements and progress with how the class as a whole are doing with this – for example moving for a whole class focus on the basics of having the right equipment and behaviour for learning in the Autumn Term, to a whole-class focus on using ambitious vocabulary by the summer term will provide an indication of how the class has settled with the teacher and the key areas that need to be focused on.

Having these Individual Inclusion Maps available so that supply or cover teachers are also able to access and use them, will ensure an effective and consistent approach to applying the key strategies that are required to meet the individual and collective needs within specific class groups.

- **Evaluating Provisions**

To be able to effectively evaluate the impact of provisions, we need to ensure a clear focus on identifying the right data that can be used to measure progress and the impact of the intervention (see also discussions in Chapter 8), at the end of the intervention period (end of each seasonal term, Autumn, Spring and Summer). To enable this, it is essential that there is clear understanding of what the expected outcome was for the intervention, and then the relevant and appropriate data that can be gathered to record the starting point (start data), through the intervention (to check that the intervention is having the impact that it is intended to) and the outcome and impact at the end (end data). For Cognition and Learning interventions, this will largely be levels of learning/Reading Age/scores on phonics/number screening tests, etc.; for Communication and Interaction interventions this may include speech and language screening assessment scores, and also a range of individualised SDQ (Strengths and Difficulties Questionnaires) and rating scale scores relevant to the intervention in place. SEMH interventions will similarly be reliant on identifying appropriate ways to measure progress relevant to the expected outcome of the intervention being delivered. This will include SDQ and individualised rating scores, but may also include attendance or behaviour incident data as a measure of progress and impact. Sensory and/or physical interventions, depending on what the focus is on, may include progress towards a specialised target set by an outside professional, or individualised rating scales, etc. (see also discussions in Chapter 8).

The most important aspect is ensuring that the right way, relevant to the expected outcome that is being focused on, is identified to record progress at the start, through the intervention and at the end of the intervention. Too often data is used that is not directly relevant to the expected outcome that has been identified – e.g. Reading Age or learning data for an SEMH intervention.

At the end of the intervention period, end data will be gathered and added into the End Data column for each pupil in the intervention. Finally, an evaluation of the impact of the intervention itself (not a narrative about how the pupils accessed the intervention) is provided. For this, aim to end up with a % for how many pupils achieved the expected outcome that was originally set – e.g. if there were five pupils in a Reading intervention, and four had achieved the expected outcome, then the overall evaluation of the impact of the intervention would be 80%.

In addition to measuring the outcome of provisions and interventions in terms of progress made against the expected outcomes, it is also helpful to consider which interventions and provisions currently in place in your school setting offer the best value for money. Particularly in the context that we currently find ourselves, with very stretched budgets, it is important to consider the overall cost and value for money versus impact of the interventions and provisions that you have prioritised. This can then help with a strategic review and analysis of the effectiveness of the provisions in your school setting and can help you to identify more clearly which ones to prioritise moving forward and any which are more costly and are perhaps not having the impact that others have.

To do this, once a year (or more as needed), in addition to analysing the overall impact of the provision in terms of what % of pupils achieved the expected outcome, also add on a Cost column to calculate the cost of the provision:

- E.g. Number of minutes per week multiplied 38 weeks (for a yearly cost); divide by 60 to get the number of hours in total

- Multiply by the Staff cost (most local authorities provide general figures for staffing costs: e.g. £15/hour for Teaching Assistant (TAs); £18/hour for Higher Level Teaching Assistant (HLTAs); £43/hour for teachers; £48/hour for SEN teachers)
- Divide by the number of pupils in the intervention group.

E.g. A Reading Intervention which runs for 20 minutes a day, 5 days a week, run by a TA for 6 pupils would cost:

= 100 minutes multiplied 38 = 3,800
3,800 minutes divided by 60 = 63.66 hours × £15 (TA hourly rate)= £950
£950 divided by 6 pupils = **£158 per pupil per year**.

Concluding comments

Coordinating provision effectively within the school setting, whilst not a new concept, remains complex and challenging for many schools to embed in ways that are dynamic and which directly impact positively on the educational experience of the pupils. Fundamentally, principled-led approaches to ensuring that the processes and systems that are used work WITH rather than AGAINST existing whole-school systems and processes, and are therefore inclusive rather than solely SEND systems and processes are essential to ensuring the success and effectiveness of the approaches used.

Systems and processes that are simple to use and which are used on a daily basis to inform the daily planning and delivery of provision for pupils, and which can then be used to strategically to review the effectiveness of the provisions, including the value for money/impact of the provision and whether there are any gaps to fill through additional resourcing or staff training are key to being able to take this forward effectively.

As you reflect on ways to develop or enhance existing systems and processes for planning and coordinating provision for pupils with SEND, it may also be useful to consider the principles set out in the following chapter focused on Planning and Delivering effective intervention, and also the models introduced in Chapter 13, which set out structured approaches to implementing change in effective and evidence-informed ways.

Individual Reflection

- What new information/learning have you gained from this chapter?
- What are your key reflections?
- What are your next steps/actions as a result?

References

Ainscow, M., Booth, T. and Dyson, A. (2006) *Improving schools, developing inclusion*. Abingdon: Routledge.

DCSF (2007) *Primary National Strategy: Pupil progress meetings prompts guidance*. London: TSO.

DCSF (2008) *Education (Special Educational Needs Coordinators) (England) Regulations 2008: Explanatory note for governing bodies*. London: DCSF.

DfE (2011) *Support and Aspiration: A new approach to special educational needs and disability: A consultation.* Norwich: TSO.
DfE/DoH (2014) *SEN and Disability Code of Practice.* London: DfE.
DfE/DoH (2015) *SEN and Disability Code of Practice.* London: Crown Copyright.
DfE/DoHSC (2023) *Special Educational Needs and Disabilities (SEND) and Alternative Provision Improvement Plan – Right support, right place, right time.* London: HMSO.
DfES (2002) *Primary National Strategy in England.* London: DfES.
DfES (2003) *Secondary National Strategy in England.* London: DfES.
EEF (2020) *SEN in mainstream schools guidance report.* London: EEF.
Ekins, A. and Grimes, P. (2009) *Inclusion: Developing an effective whole school approach.* Maidenhead: Open University Press.
House of Commons Education Committee (2019) *Special Educational Needs and Disabilities.* London: House of Commons.
Nasen (2014) *SEN support and the Graduated Approach.* Tamworth: Nasen House.
NASUWT (2018) *Special Educational Needs (SEN), Additional Learning Needs (ALN) and Additional Support Needs (ASN).* England: NASUWT.
OFSTED (2004) *A new relationship with schools.* London: OFSTED.
OFSTED (2011) *Special educational needs and/or disabilities in mainstream schools: A briefing paper for section 5 inspectors.* London: OFSTED.
OFSTED (2019) Education Inspection Framework. Available from: https://www.gov.uk/government/publications/education-inspection-framework (accessed 30.5.23).

8 Planning and delivering effective intervention

In this chapter, we critically examine and explore the following key aspects:

- Key principles underpinning effective provision
- Ways to evaluate the effectiveness and impact of interventions
- Evidence-informed approaches and research relating to interventions
- Digital technology to support interventions
- Interventions based on the SEND areas of need

Key issues

Planning and delivering effective intervention is crucial in meeting the needs of pupils with Special Educational Needs and Disabilities (SEND), and requires very careful thought and planning. Essentially, 'high quality teaching should reduce the need for extra support for all pupils. Nevertheless, it is likely that some pupils will require additional support in the form of high quality, structured interventions to make progress' (EEF, 2020: 28). Challenging questions need to be asked about the nature of 'intervention' and ways that it should and could be implemented effectively to meet the needs of pupils with SEND, whilst still ensuring that they have adequate and effective access to inclusive learning opportunities with their peers, access to the full curriculum and direct access to teaching and learning delivered by the most qualified professionals within the school. This chapter focuses on the following key issues:

1 Key principles underpinning effective provision
2 Evaluating the effectiveness and impact of interventions
3 Developing a critical lens through evidence-informed approaches and research.

Current policy/research context

Key principles underpinning effective provision

Key principles of child-centred practice, inclusive values, high-quality teaching and a Graduated Approach need to be at the heart of what we do. If these key principles are not embedded in practice as a foundation, then interventions will not be effectively applied or

DOI: 10.4324/9781003033554-8

targeted strategically. Historically, intervention has been implemented in response to poor teaching (OFSTED, 2010) which must not happen because it leads to ineffective practice which is also very costly. The ways in which we coordinate provision (as discussed in Chapter 7) alongside very clear plans for evaluating the effectiveness and impact of interventions is essential to ensure positive outcomes for pupils.

Traditionally, since the beginning of the 21st century, there has been a focus on planning and delivering more and more interventions as 'catch up' and 'add on' interventions to meet the needs of children who had gaps in their learning or needed additional support. This traditional approach, however, has been challenged in recent years, with criticisms levelled regarding the 'lifestyle model of intervention' (Ekins & Grimes, 2009: 69). Historically this approach to interventions, that many pupils with SEND experienced, meant an intervention was identified for them, and then that became their norm, with no review or evaluation of the effectiveness of the intervention in actually meeting their needs.

More recently, there have been other criticisms levelled at the nature of 'intervention', with a significant shift away from the practice of thinking about additional 'intervention' that is needed, with instead a focus on really scrutinising the quality of the inclusive educational learning experience that is planned and delivered to all children within the classroom context. There is growing understanding and emphasis on the need for teaching to be carefully planned and prepared to meet the needs of all pupils, and that it should be through carefully differentiated and structured whole class teaching that the needs of all pupils should largely be met. A tiered approach to additional support is needed (see Figure 8.1) to ensure that careful consideration is given to identifying exactly what support is needed and how it can be most effectively provided (EEF, 2020).

Thus, the way that we think about and plan for 'intervention' needs to change to ensure that our planned interventions are responsive to identified needs and not other areas of possible weakness such as poor quality teaching or ineffective lifestyle model interventions. In order to take forward this change, a number of key principles need to be understood and applied to the practice and process of developing effective and evidence-informed interventions to meet the needs of pupils with SEND. Child-centred practice, inclusive

Specialist support. In addition to *'good teaching for pupils with SEN is good teaching for all,'* some pupils will need specialist intervention delivered by a trained professional.

Targeted interventions. If pupils require additional support beyond what can be offered in whole class teaching, a targeted, one-to-one or small-group intervention could provide the intensive focus required for the pupil to make progress. More guidance on effective implementation of targeted interventions is provided below.

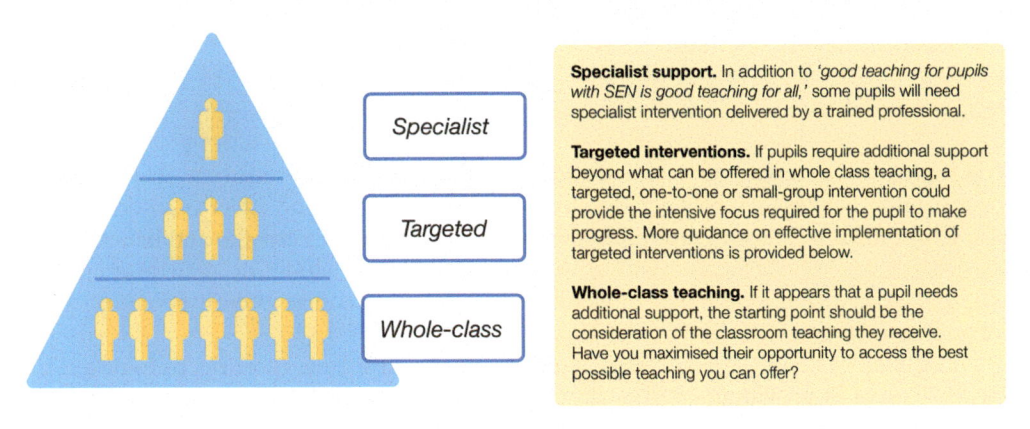

Whole-class teaching. If it appears that a pupil needs additional support, the starting point should be the consideration of the classroom teaching they receive. Have you maximised their opportunity to access the best possible teaching you can offer?

Figure 8.1 EEF (2020) Tiered approach to educational support

Source: EEF (2020: 29). https://d2tic4wvo1iusb.cloudfront.net/eef-guidance-reports/send/EEF_Special_Educational_Needs_in_Mainstream_Schools_Guidance_Report.pdf?v=1667220817 (accessed 1.11.2022)

values, high-quality teaching and a Graduated Approach need to be at the forefront of our practice. These key principles are explored briefly below:

- Child-centred practice:

Intervention needs to be individualised and underpinned by a child-centred ethos (as outlined in Chapter 10). This applies to thinking and planning for the inclusive learning experience of the pupil as a whole, which is supported by the DfE Rapid Review (2017a: 6–7):

> While this review focused on interventions and support strategies, it was clear that detailed assessment of individual children is necessary to select the most appropriate approach, and progress should be monitored when using any intervention to assess whether it is effective for that particular child.

Here, we need to be aware of the totality of the learning experience that the child is given. So that might include how much of their time in school is made up of withdrawn interventions, working by themselves or with a small group. It needs to take account of the time a pupil might be with a Teaching Assistant (TA) rather than with a qualified teacher and the teacher's responsibilities for the child:

> The class or subject teacher should remain responsible for working with the child on a daily basis. Where the interventions involve group or one-to-one teaching away from the main class or subject teacher, they should still retain responsibility for the pupil.
>
> (DfE/DoH, 2015: 101)

With the shift away from the traditional approach to providing multiple withdrawn interventions, teachers now have to really carefully review their knowledge and understanding about how to effectively teach children with SEND, and enable them to make progress, within the context of their own lesson. Fundamental to this will be to ensure that all teachers have a secure and robust understanding of the various needs of pupils within the class that they are teaching.

- Inclusive values:

When planning interventions, we need to pay full attention to ensuring that inclusive values and principles underpin the development of appropriate and effective interventions (see Chapter 5). We need to ensure that pupils with SEND have access to and benefit from the highest quality of teaching within the classroom setting alongside their peers rather than continue with the outdated model of delivering intervention after intervention after intervention.

In addition to considering inclusive high-quality class teaching, there needs to be a clear inclusive focus on providing good quality intervention to meet the needs of any pupil. This needs to be managed in an inclusive way, to address needs as they occur, rather than relying on pupils being placed on a SEND Register before they are able to access and benefit from any support. Pupils with complex needs should benefit from the highest quality teaching input from experienced teachers with high levels of understanding and experience of curriculum, pedagogy and child development.

- High-quality teaching:

In line with the new approach in the OFSTED framework (2019) and current thinking about effective teaching and learning to support the needs of all pupils, it is essential that any review and planning for 'intervention' starts with a full review of the quality of the teaching being provided and the effectiveness of in-class adaptions. Interestingly, in the review of support for children with SEND, the DfE (2017a: 6) found that there was 'good quality research evidence about effective interventions in the areas of Cognition and Learning, Social, Emotional and Mental Health, and Communication and Interaction. However, the evidence about high-quality teaching and adaptations that can support these needs is significantly less extensive'. It may be that further research and focus needs to be placed on classroom practice.

- The Graduated Approach:

As outlined in Chapter 7, the Graduated Approach is a four staged process linked to the Assess, Plan, Do, Review cycle. If high-quality teaching is in place for all learners, then most needs will be met and fewer pupils will require additional targeted or specialist support. It is important to ensure the approach is fully embedded in practice to avoid interventions being put into place when they are not required. Intervention needs to be appropriate and proportionate as supported by the EEF report (2020: 28) Recommendation 4 which notes high-quality teaching needs to be complimented 'with carefully selected small-group and one-to-one interventions'.

Ensuring we follow the Assess, Plan, Do, Review approach will mean the interventions in place are evaluated and therefore supports the next steps and future planning for the learner. It would be an inappropriate use of resources to implement an intensive intervention being run by external specialists without trialling interventions available within school first to see if this is sufficient to support the learner.

Evaluating the effectiveness and impact of intervention

Evaluating the effectiveness of interventions is not only essential to enable us to work strategically, it is now also a requirement of the role of the Special Educational Needs Coordinator (SENCO) 'advising on the deployment of the school's delegated budget and other resources to meet pupils' needs effectively' (DfE/DoH, 2015: 109). We have a duty to ensure that the interventions are appropriate and have positive impact for the pupils as well as ensuring value for money. Clear systems and processes (addressed in Chapter 7) alongside the active and continuing engagement with evidence bases to support our judgements is essential to meet this requirement. The four broad areas of need (DfE/DoH, 2015) will inform the discussion in this section.

Embedded into any effective approach to delivering intervention must be a rigorous approach to evaluating the effectiveness and impact of the intervention that is provided. To be able to do this, staff need to have a really clear understanding of the expected outcome of the provision, and ways that this reflects and meets the needs of the learners accessing the intervention. Staff also need to have a really clear understanding of ways to measure the progress made by pupils through the intervention and the impact that it may have. For some interventions, this may be straightforward – interventions that are focused on narrow improvements in reading or spelling age, for example, will be relatively easy to measure progress from the baseline level at the beginning of the intervention, to the exit reading or spelling age measured at the end of the intervention.

Yet, even with such a seemingly straightforward intervention, there will be complexities and individual variables which will impact on the progress made by individuals. The ways that the reading or spelling age is measured needs to be understood (some reading or spelling scales do not measure the lower levels of ability which will then make it difficult to accurately measure the impact of the intervention delivered). For older pupils, whilst little impact may seem to have been made on a secondary aged reading or spelling age, it may be that the intervention has had a positive impact on the development of wider reading and writing skills, including the development of deeper comprehension or inference skills. The start and end data captured will also be dependent on the child's levels of attention and focus at the time of being assessed – therefore things that have happened to them through the day or distractions at the time of the test may impact on the score achieved. Careful consideration needs to be in place to be aware of the impact of variables such as this, although staff will also need to recognise that it will never be possible to control all variables impacting on the day to day performance of a learner.

Chapter 2 included an overview of the four broad areas of need (DfE/DoH, 2015), which have been included here to consider interventions in practice. However, as discussed in Chapter 2, it is important to recognise children will not neatly fit within these areas of need and the interventions must be responsive to them as individuals rather than being driven by arbitrary and movable categorisation of needs:

- Cognition and Learning

Cognition and Learning is a high incidence need and includes general learning differences as well as specific learning difference, which will require different approaches and/or intervention due to the differences in how this impacts on the pupil:

> General learning difficulties cause problems across the curriculum, while specific learning difficulties refer more to a specific aspect of learning, such as literacy (sometimes known as dyslexia) or numeracy (sometimes known as dyscalculia).
> (DfE, 2017a: 19)

An important aspect to consider is that 'One of the largest areas of need for students on SEN support relates to supporting generalised learning skills, or "thinking skills": attention, working memory and processing differences. Children and young people with moderate learning difficulties are likely to find it difficult to access multiple areas of the curriculum' (DfE, 2017a: 19).

The OFSTED Education Inspection Framework (2019: n.p) has a clear focus on supporting children to know and remember what is being taught, 'over the course of study, teaching is designed to help learners to remember in the long term the content they have been taught and to integrate new knowledge into larger concepts'. This has clear implications for pupils with SEND. Cognition and Learning difficulties may include barriers to an ability to process and consistently remember information from one occasion to another,

Planning and delivering effective intervention 133

and particularly in the ability to then transfer and apply that learning to new situations. This new focus that is becoming embedded in reviewed and renewed school curriculum plans will therefore be really helpful to pupils with SEND and SENCOs leading SEND practice in schools, as ways to focus on memory as a key skill in learning will become part of whole class teaching, rather than something that is done separate to class and subject-based learning. The DfE (2017a) include a range of evidence-informed ways to support 'thinking skills' in the class, some of the key points are included below:

- Reduction of environmental or cognitive load that adds to processing demands
- Provide scaffolding and support. This can be through breaking a task down into component parts or chunks and organising them hierarchically
- Using strategies to help with learning key facts, this could include using resources such as note systems, technology, prompts systems, routines, mnemonics, reinforcement approaches, etc.
- Strengthening memory processes, for example using overlearning, metacognition, active learning, etc.

Dale (1969) developed the Cone of Experience model, which remains useful today in considering ways to embed active and effective learning strategies into the curriculum that we provide to our learners. In this model (see below), Dale (1969) identifies how learners remember:

- 10% of what we read
- 20% of what we hear
- 30% of what we see
- 50% of what we see and hear
- 70% of what we discuss with others
- 80% of what we personally experience
- 95% or what we teach others

- Communication and Interaction

Speech, language and communication differences are a key issue for schools and even more so since the pandemic and the missed opportunities pupils have had to socialise:

> Many providers reported that there are still delays in babies' and children's speech and language development. For example, some have noticed that children have limited vocabulary or lack the confidence to speak. Also, some babies have struggled to respond to basic facial expressions, which may be due to reduced contact and interaction with others during the pandemic.
>
> (OFSTED, 2022, np)

There is an increased need for more universal support for children with language, communication and social skills gaps alongside the need to support those who may have more complex language needs. Norbury et al. (2016) identified that approximately two children in every class demonstrate a significant language difficulty at school entry. Speech and Language UK (2023) includes a range of useful resources based on research. One resource is the Speech, Language and Communication Framework (2023), which is helpful to review the support in place in school at universal, targeted and specialist level. This is available from the following website: The Communication Trust (https://www.slcframework.org.uk/)

- Social, Emotional and Mental Health

Social, Emotional and Mental Health is another area of need which could encompass a range of specific conditions including, depression, anxiety, Oppositional Defiance Disorder (ODD), amongst others. The DfE report (2017a: 50) includes the following definition:

> children and young people who demonstrate difficulties with emotional regulation and/or social interaction and/or are experiencing mental health problems. Children and young people who have difficulties with their emotional and social development may have immature social skills and find it difficult to make and sustain healthy relationships. These difficulties may be displayed through the child or young person becoming withdrawn or isolated, as well as through challenging behaviour.

Social, Emotional and Mental Health has also notably increased since the pandemic:

> Data from February and March 2021 shows that rates of probable mental disorder in children and young people have increased between 2017 and 2021 (rates identified in 2020 were similar to 2021). In 6 to 16 year olds, rates had increased from 11.6% to 17.4%, among 17 to 19 year olds, rates had increased from 10.1% to 17.4%.
>
> (Office for Health and Improvement Disparities, 2022, np)

There are increasing duties on schools with the DfE 'encouraging schools and colleges to identify a senior mental health lead who will have strategic oversight of their setting's whole school or college approach to mental health and wellbeing' (DfE, 2022: n.p).

The most common intervention to support anxiety in both primary and secondary 'was the use of an Emotional Literacy Support Assistant (ELSA). These would be trained members of staff who worked with student to support them to understand and regulate their emotions' (DfE, 2017b: 41).

- Sensory and/or Physical

Sensory and physical includes a number of different physical differences including visual impairment, hearing impairment and physical disabilities. The prevalence of these needs are less common and so schools may have less experience with supporting pupils with this area of need. SENCOs need to be mindful of this because teachers may need more support to feel confident to meet pupils' needs if the need is unfamiliar or they have very little experience of supporting pupils with this need. The interventions may also be quite specialised requiring specific training, e.g. training for personal care or using specialist equipment. Typically specialist teachers would be working with the school to support the pupil:

> specialist teachers with a mandatory qualification for children with hearing and vision impairment, including multi-sensory impairment, and for those with a

physical disability. (Those teaching classes of children with sensory impairment must hold an appropriate qualification approved by the Secretary of State. Teachers working in an advisory role to support such pupils should also hold the appropriate qualification.)

(DfE/DoH, 2015: 103)

Furthermore the proposals (DfE/DoHSC, 2023: 27) may strengthen support with the following claim:

> National Standards will cover the evidence-based approaches to identification and intervention for those with SEN Support and for those with EHCPs. For example, standards will set out how nurseries, schools and colleges must adapt the physical and sensory environment of the setting to enable children and young people with SEND to learn alongside their peers and the role of the local authority in supporting this.

The DfE (2017a: 7) identified the gaps in their evidence base related to this area: 'The research evidence for supporting physical and sensory needs is much less extensive than for the other three areas of need and is often based on small scale case studies'.

Developing a critical lens through evidence-informed approaches and research

As well as drawing on evidence bases to support our judgements, it is important to consider how we might adopt evidence-informed approaches in our practice in light of the increasing drivers for research to be part of the teaching profession.

> Over the past fifteen years, there has been a greatly increased emphasis on using research evidence to guide teaching practice. This has been exemplified in recent years by the work of the Educational Endowment Foundation (EEF).

(DfE, 2017a: 9)

At times, specialised SEND interventions will need to be provided to support the learning needs of pupils with SEND. To ensure that they are fully effective, careful consideration needs to be made of evidence-bases underpinning the interventions that are planned. It can be difficult to take the time or to know where to look to inform our judgements over the interventions we are using. In some cases, we may have little autonomy, dependent upon the school and how they manage purchasing resources. Often, we turn to others as a source of information on what works:

> Staff named other professionals as their most common sources of information about how to support students with SEN, rather than published resources. Over three-quarters of respondents said they used their SENCO frequently as a source of information, and over half frequently used teachers and other staff in their school or college. Similarly, the most common source of information reported by SENCOs was other professionals.

(DfE, 2017b: 10)

As discussed in the chapter on Co-ordinating Provision (Chapter 7), we need to ensure that we move away from 'lifestyle' approaches to intervention. This means making

136 *Planning and delivering effective intervention*

sure that the quality and relevance of interventions that are provided in the school setting is regularly reviewed and evaluated to ensure that the interventions that are offered are up-to-date, that there is evidence of the impact that they can have on pupil progress and that they meet the needs of the current cohort, and are not just based on historic needs and trends.

Schools therefore need to ensure that they are focused on using the available evidence about the quality and effectiveness of interventions, and that they use this information and evidence to make strategic decisions about the interventions that they prioritise and use within the school setting.

Published analyses of the effectiveness of a range of interventions, including the Education Endowment Foundation guidance reports (2023a) and the DfE SEN Support Case Studies (DfE, 2017a, 2017b, 2017c) are all useful documents to refer to support a school-based evaluation of current practice.

Research available in the public domain such as the EEF, for example is useful, but it is also essential to recognise that research conducted in the school (for example lesson study or action research) is also really important to enhance practice (see also discussions in Chapter 13).

Planning for practice

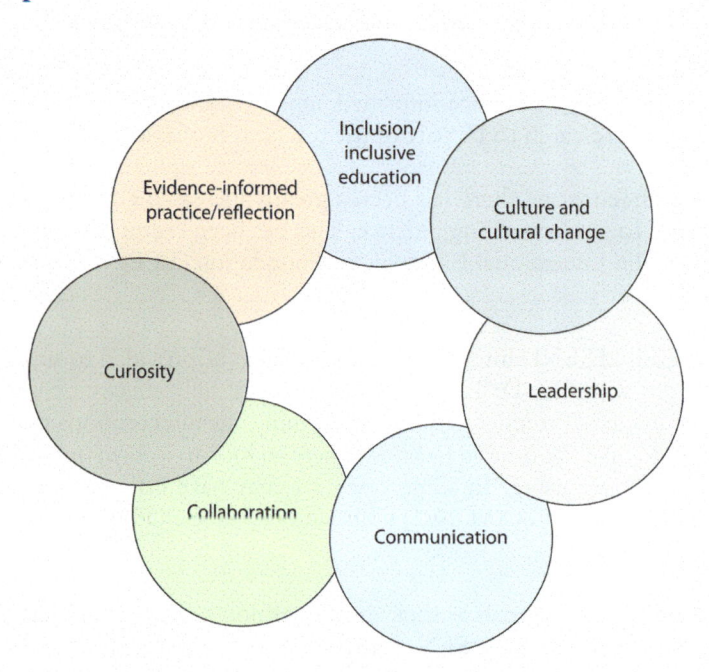

Figure 8.2 Key principles model

There are a number of principled areas for consideration in planning, monitoring and evaluating effective interventions and ***inclusion/inclusive education*** should be at the heart of what we plan for pupils. The Planning for Practice section will explore key principles such as: ***inclusion/inclusive education*** and ***culture and cultural change*** can ensure interventions are purposeful and have impact. The discussion will be linked to how recent research and ***evidence-informed approaches*** might inform practices and the interventions we select, as well as the ways in which we review and evaluate current provision.

Planning and delivering effective intervention 137

Once teachers have a basic understanding of the needs of children in their class, and ways that particular areas of SEND will impact on their learning, development and progress, teachers will then need support to carefully review and develop their understanding of effective whole class learning strategies to provide ***inclusive education***. ***Inclusive*** approaches will support all pupils to be able to access and make progress with their learning within the classroom context. Table 8.1 provides a framework to critically consider the planning of targeted interventions.

Table 8.1 EEF (2020: 29–30) Key critical questions to consider when planning targeted intervention

Key question	Issue	How does this relate to practice in your setting currently?
What are pupils missing by spending time away from the class?	Pupils are often withdrawn from their usual teaching for interventions, so it should be a prerequisite of any intervention programme that it at least compensates for time spent away from class. It is also important to consider whether the pupil might be missing subjects they enjoy and the social impact of not participating in the whole class.	
How does a pupil's experience in an intervention relate to whole-class teaching?	It should not be left to the pupil to make links between the content of the intervention and the curriculum covered back in the classroom. Given that supported pupils are often those who find accessing learning difficult in the first place, this would present a huge additional challenge. The integration of the intervention with the mainstream curriculum is, therefore, vital. Try ensuring that adequate time is set aside for regular liaison so that staff delivering interventions can meet and plan with main class teachers.	
Is the intervention the right one for the pupil?	Does the pupil really need the intervention? Targeted support has the potential to be detrimental if a pupil has been misallocated to an intervention they do not actually need and, as a result, miss out on whole-class activity. Do we have a good understanding of pupils' needs so that the support is well-targeted? Unless interventions are well-matched to address the barriers that pupils are experiencing in their learning, they are unlikely to be effective.	
Can we provide the support required for our staff to deliver the intervention well?	Do the staff have a good understanding of the teaching strategies required in the intervention? Would additional training be useful? Are we ensuring that pupils with the greatest needs have access to teaching from our most experienced staff?	
Are we able to dedicate the time and resources required to implement the intervention well?	Even the most promising intervention will fail with poor implementation. Once an approach has been identified, it is important to take the time to train the staff involved, monitor the delivery of the approach, and consider how to sustain it over time.	

Key principles underpinning effective provision

> **Reflective Activity**
>
> - How is provision planned and delivered in your school setting currently?
> - Whose responsibility is the planning of provision to meet the needs of all pupils, including those with SEND?
> - What works well?
> - Does the model that you currently have in practice meet the needs of pupils in your school setting?
> - How do you know?
> - Are there any areas to develop further?
> - How could this be achieved?

It is essential that teachers really understand the needs of pupils within the class, the next step will be to ensure that teachers understand the implications for effective teaching and learning approaches of the different SEND Areas of Need (Cognition and Learning, Communication and Interaction, Social, Emotional and Mental Health needs and sensory and/or physical needs) – see Chapter 2. Teachers will need to be supported, through robust Continuous Professional Development (CPD) opportunities to understand ways that each of the SEND Areas of Need can impact on learning, and the barriers to learning that they can create, as well as be taught and shown a range of strategies for overcoming those barriers to learning, as noted as a key finding of the DfE (2017a: 6) report:

> A key finding was the important role of training for all education professionals. Teaching assistants can provide good quality intervention if they are well trained, while even highly qualified professionals have less impact if they do not understand the principles and motivation behind the approach they are using.

Evaluating the effectiveness and impact of interventions

As discussed in Chapter 7, embedded into any effective approach to delivering intervention must be a rigorous approach to evaluating the effectiveness and impact of the intervention that is provided. To be able to do this, staff need to have a really clear understanding of the expected outcome of the provision, and ways that this reflects and meets the needs of the learners accessing the intervention. Staff also need to have a really clear understanding of ways to measure the progress made by pupils through the intervention and the impact that it may have.

In schools that might be data driven it is important to understand the individual at the centre (as noted in Chapter 10). As much as possible, it is important to follow the school systems and processes for monitoring and evaluating progress and attainment. However, for pupils with more complex needs SENCOs cannot always rely on the typical school data as providing a clear profile of the child. It may be that the steps of progress are so small they are not easily measured with the typical school system. It may be that they are making progress in areas outside of the academic curriculum, such as social interaction – this is possibly more difficult to measure. How we assess and record progress in interventions and the reliability of the data is fundamental to ensure that any target setting and supporting children to the next steps is specific, measurable, achievable, realistic and time-bound (SMART) as outlined in the Special Educational Needs and Disability Code of Practice (DfE/DoH, 2015). Essentially, we need to ensure that we draw on a range of information to inform judgements, not single narrow points of data.

Building on Chapter 2 where the four broad areas of need were outlined as a way to consider learners' needs and approaches, this section identifies some interventions that focus on specific skills development. This doesn't mean there cannot be flexibility in how the interventions are used and in some cases you may find that a child with Cognition and Learning as a primary need, may benefit from interventions supporting Communication and Interaction. This links to the underpinning principle of child-centred and ensuring that what we plan places the child first and foremost (Chapter 10).

In addition, this section will explore inclusive and assistive technology. Inclusive technology should be available to all in the class should they want to use this to support their learning and could include:

- Instructional apps – apps that provide instruction, modelling, or practice opportunities for a wide range of skills or
- Non-instructional apps – apps that provide tools to aid learning, such as note-taking apps
- Speech-generating apps to augment the communication skills of pupils with communication difficulties (EEF, 2020: 25).

Assistive technology is different because this is usually technology that is available to pupils who need something 'additional' or 'different' to what is included as part of the curriculum. This might include specialist technology such as eye-gaze software or ergonomic equipment, e.g. mice or keyboards.

Review the questions and complete Table 8.2 to consider how we use technology to support access to the curriculum and plan interventions using digital technologies.

Table 8.2 EEF (2021) Using Digital Technology to Improve Learning Guidance Report

Questions based on the EEF Using Digital Technology to Improve Learning guidance Report (EEF, 2021: 10)	Responses based on my school setting
• Is the right equipment available?	
• When should the programme be implemented, and what will the pupils miss?	
• What training is required for teachers and teaching assistants?	
• What initial support will be required to introduce pupils to the technology being used? Will some pupils need additional ongoing support to use it effectively?	
• Is there appropriate space within or outside the classroom for pupils to use the technology?	
• Should an adult be on hand to offer support, or will pupils be able to use the technology independently?	
• How will delivery of the approach be monitored to ensure that it is used as intended?	
• Is there an initial and ongoing financial cost? Is this affordable and justifiable?	

In addition to 'evaluating the effectiveness of the provision made for children and young people with SEN' (DfE/DoH, 2015: 107), the SEN Information report requires the school to provide annual, updated information on:

> arrangements for assessing and reviewing children and young people's progress towards outcomes.
>
> (DfE/DoH, 2015: 106)

> the expertise and training of staff to support children and young people with SEN, including how specialist expertise will be secured.
>
> (DfE/DoH, 2015: 107)

Table 8.3 is based on the four broad areas of need and the annual reporting to the DfE for the more specific needs – however this could be adapted depending upon your specific school profile. By completing Table 8.3, this will help you to identify:

- Gaps in the knowledge or skills of staff who might need to implement specific interventions
- Any gaps in resources to ensure we can accurately assess need to be able to then intervene if required.

Table 8.3 Audit for gaps in knowledge or skills of staff

Area of need	More detail	Training in my school	How we screen or assess
Broad area of need from the Code of Practice (DfE/DoH, 2015)	More specific needs aligned to annual reporting to the DfE	Include the date/s, staff involved and training completed, e.g. 'Neurodiversity awareness'	Include any specific resources or tools you have available to you in school, e.g. Grey Oral Reading Test 5th Edition; Speech and Language therapist 1 day a week
Cognition and Learning	Specific learning difficulty (SpLD), e.g. dyslexia		
	Moderate learning difficulty (MLD)		
	Severe learning difficulty (SLD)/Profound and multiple learning difficulty (PMLD)		
Communication and Interaction	Autism		
	Speech, Language and Communication Needs (SLCN)		
Social, Emotional and Mental Health			
Sensory and/or Physical	Hearing impairment (HI)		
	Visual impairment (VI)		
	Multi-sensory impairment (MSI)		
	Physical disability		
	Other difficulty or disability		

Developing a critical lens through evidence-informed approaches and research

Conducting research in school may seem time-consuming or daunting. However, embedded into the current statutory qualification for SENCOs is the need for SENCOs to evaluate and engage with evidence about teaching and learning in relation to pupils with SEND and also engage themselves in small-scale practitioner research within their own settings (DfE, 2014).

The current statutory qualification, the National Award for SEN Coordination, is undergoing change, but even if research is not an aspect that will feature in the new learning outcomes, it has value as an activity to support evaluation of practice. **Evidence-informed practice and reflection** may include critically looking at interventions: Why do we do what we do? Why is it important to continue with an approach? Why should we try something different? Are all questions which should be informed based on the research we engage in reading and the research we produce ourselves?

There are a range of accessible sources of information regarding evidence bases related to interventions. Table 8.4 is not an exhaustive list but provides a starting point.

Table 8.4 Table of evidence-informed resources

Education focused research – these organisations provide research on education more broadly, this can include research focused on SEND.
- Education Endowment Foundation (2023a) Guidance Reports Education Endowment Foundation | EEF
- Education Endowment Foundation (2023b) Teaching and Learning Toolkit Teaching and Learning Toolkit | EEF (educationendowmentfoundation.org.uk)
- Nuffield Foundation (2022) Education | Research | Nuffield Foundation
- Sutton Trust (2022) Our Research – Sutton Trust

SEND focused Websites – You can sign up to these websites for updates on the latest research and resources
- Whole School SEND (2023) Whole School SEND Home Page | Whole School SEND
- Nasen (2023) Home page | Nasen

SEND focused government reports
- DfE (2017a) SEN Support: A Rapid Evidence Assessment Research Report. Coventry: Coventry University
- DfE (2017b) SEN Support: a survey of schools and colleges. Coventry, DfE
- Department for Education (2017c) SEN support: research evidence on effective approaches and examples of current practice in good and outstanding schools and colleges. Available from: SEN_Support_Resource.pdf (excellencegateway.org.uk) (accessed 29.5.2023)

SEND Specific areas of need
- Communication and Interaction
  - Autism Education Trust (2023) Autism Competency Framework. Available from: Framework Documents | Autism Education Trust (accessed 29.5.2023)
- Social, Emotional and Mental Health
  - Emotionally healthy schools (2023) Home – Emotionally Healthy Schools
- Cognition and Learning
  - Lavan and Talcott (2020) Brook's What works for literacy difficulties (6th Edition). Available from: What Works for Literacy Difficulties – 6th edition – The School Psychology Service (accessed 29.5.2023)

Reflective Activity

Using evidence-bases to plan and evaluate the effectiveness of interventions

- Which of the above reports are you already aware of and using in your school setting to help to plan and evaluate the effectiveness of interventions?
- How were decisions made about the interventions that are prioritised and used in your school setting?
- Having reviewed the research reports above, do you still think that these are the most up to date and effective to meet the current needs of pupils in your school setting?
- Do any changes need to be made?
- What will be the implications of this for staff training and development needs?
- As you complete this review and audit, ensure that the planned focus of prioritised interventions is on input that cannot be provided through quality first teaching and effective differentiation within the classroom. The interventions that are planned should only be those which absolutely cannot be provided within the context of high-quality inclusive teaching.

It can be difficult to communicate the most effective strategies and approaches with teachers when using research reports – it can be useful to present the information in a different way. Based on the current research, providing a 'one page summary' for your colleagues in school, may be a way to enable you to keep colleagues updated in an accessible and practical way. Adopting an approach like this will mean that you also have a template to easily update information as new research becomes available. Figure 8.3 is an example for strategies to support memory, but you could create this for a range of different areas of need, e.g. literacy, social communication, fine motor, anxiety, emotional regulation, etc.

One page – Strategies to support Memory		
Repetition - provide opportunity to repeat new information	**Visuals** - Provide images to support written information	**Talk before writing** - Provide opportunities for pupils to talk about their work to help plan and create written response
Routine - Clear and consistent routines in class supports pupils to be less reliant on their memory	**Apps and Tech** - Recording information in other ways can be really helpful. Writing is a complex process and cognitively demanding. Use technology to help learners	**Making links** - Provide explicit links / associations for pupils
Cues - You can include different cues such as colour / a sound / an image to indicate or reinforce key instructions or information	**Small chunks** - Provide information in smaller 'chunks'. It can be difficult for pupils to hold information in their memory and then process what they need to do if there is a lot of information.	**Task planner** - This works like a checklist. It can link to each stage of the class activity and can include images

Figure 8.3 One page – Strategies to support memory

Reflective Activity – Memory Strategies

- What memory strategies are you already aware of, and how are these used to support learners in your school/ class setting?
- When and how do you use those strategies to support learners?
- How effective are those strategies?
- How do you know?

As well as reviewing and updating practice based on current research in the field, there are opportunities to undertake research in school to help us to understand and respond to priorities and needs in our own settings better. The following Case Study is from a student who completed action research (see Chapter 13) for the National Award in SEN Coordination. She has reflected on the impact this has had in practice:

144 *Planning and delivering effective intervention*

Case Study – SENCO Action Research

Laura Moss

Poster presented at the Well-being Scholarship Day on the 6th February 2020

Following the findings of this action research project (see Figure 8.4), the interventions within my school moved from more traditional programmes of study such as handwriting practice, nurture groups, pre-teaching of key vocabulary, to ones which then were focused around developing skills and effective learning characteristics. Interventions sat under four key umbrellas; the resilient learner, the optimistic learner, the creative learner and the learner as a key communicator. Children were grouped according to their current skill set and identified needs. By the end of the six-week intervention, learners would be assessed for their skill acquisition and transference of these skills across their academic profile.

Figure 8.4 SENCO Action Research – poster

Concluding comments and reflections

How we think about interventions and the ways in which we plan to take this forward in schools requires us to be critically reflecting on and reviewing our practice. Accurate and early assessment of need is essential as well as purposeful planning so that children are not missing classroom teaching:

> Small group and one-to-one interventions provide the opportunity to apply effective teaching strategies with a more intense focus on a smaller number of learning goals. They can be powerful tools but must be used carefully: they should not replace general efforts to improve the overall quality of teaching in the classroom.
>
> (EEF, 2020: 28)

Keeping in mind the key principles of child-centred practice, inclusive values, high-quality teaching and a Graduated Approach need to be central in our practice. Drawing on current evidence-informed interventions provides a robust foundation to enable us to meet the needs of pupils with SEND.

Individual Reflection

- What new information/ learning have you gained from this chapter?
- What are your key reflections?
- What are your next steps/ actions as a result?

References

Autism Education Trust (2023) *Autism Competency Framework*. Available from: https://www.autismeducationtrust.org.uk/framework-documents (accessed 29.5.2023).

Dale, E. (1969). *Audiovisual methods in teaching* (3rd Editon). New York, NY: Dryden Press.

DfE (2014) *National Award for Special Educational Needs Co-ordinator: Learning outcomes*. Available from: https://www.gov.uk/government/publications/mandatory-qualification-for-sencos (accessed 31.5.2023).

DfE (2017a) *SEN Support: A rapid evidence assessment research report*. Coventry: Coventry University.

DfE (2017b) *SEN Support: A survey of schools and colleges*. Coventry: DfE.

DfE (2017c) *SEN Support: Research evidence on effective approaches and examples of current practice in good and outstanding schools and colleges*. Available from: https://repository.excellencegateway.org.uk/SEN_Support_Resource.pdf (accessed 29.5.2023).

DfE (2022) *Promoting and supporting mental health and wellbeing in schools and colleges*. Available from: https://www.gov.uk/guidance/mental-health-and-wellbeing-support-in-schools-and-colleges (accessed 30.5.2023).

DfE/DoH (2015) *Special Educational Needs and Disability Code of Practice for 0 to 25 year olds*. Available from: https://www.gov.uk/government/publications/send-code-of-practice-0-to-25 (accessed 30.5.2023).

DfE/DoHSC (2023) *Special Educational Needs and Disabilities (SEND) and Alternative Provision Improvement Plan – Right support, right place, right time*. London: HMSO.

EEF (2020) *SEN in mainstream schools guidance report*. London: EEF.

EEF (2023a) *Guidance reports*. https://educationendowmentfoundation.org.uk/ (accessed 29.5.2023).

EEF (2023b) *Teaching and learning toolkit*. https://educationendowmentfoundation.org.uk/education-evidence/teaching-learning-toolkit (accessed 29.5.2023).

Ekins, A. and Grimes, P. (2009) *Inclusion: Developing an effective whole school approach*. Maidenhead: Open University Press.

Emotionally Healthy Schools (2023) *Home*. https://emotionallyhealthyschools.org/ (accessed 29.5.2023).

Lavan, G. and Talcott, J. (2020) *Brook's what works for literacy difficulties: The effectiveness of interventions schemes* (6th Edition). The School Psychology Service. Available from: https://www.theschoolpsychologyservice.com/what-works-for-literacy-difficulties-6th-edition/ (accessed 29.5.2023).

Nasen (2023) *Home page*. https://nasen.org.uk/ (accessed 29.5.2023).

Norbury, C.F., Gooch, D., Wray, C., Baird, G., Charman, T., Simonoff, E., Vamvakas, G. and Pickles, A. (2016) 'The impact of nonverbal ability on prevalence and clinical presentation of language disorder: Evidence from a population study'. *Journal of Child Psychology and Psychiatry, and Allied Disciplines* 57(11), 1247–1257.

Nuffield Foundation (2022) *Education | Research*. https://www.nuffieldfoundation.org/research/education (accessed 29.5.2023).

Office for Health and Improvement Disparities (2022) *4. Children and Young People*. Available from: https://www.gov.uk/government/publications/covid-19-mental-health-and-wellbeing-surveillance-report/7-children-and-young-people (accessed 30.5.2023).

OFSTED (2010) *The special educational needs and disability review: A statement is not enough*. Manchester: Crown Copyright.

OFSTED (2019) *Education Inspection Framework*. Available from: https://www.gov.uk/government/publications/education-inspection-framework (accessed 30.5.2023).

OFSTED (2022) *Education recovery in the early years providers – Spring 2022*. Available from: https://www.gov.uk/government/publications/education-recovery-in-early-years-providers-spring-2022/education-recovery-in-early-years-providers-spring-2022 (accessed 30.5.2023).

Speech and Language UK (2023) *Speech and Language UK: Changing young lives*. Available from: https://speechandlanguage.org.uk/ (accessed 30.5.2023).

Sutton Trust (2022) *Our Research – Sutton Trust*. https://www.suttontrust.com/our-research/ (accessed 29.5.2023).

The Speech, Language and Communication Framework (2023) *Home*. Available from: https://www.slcframework.org.uk/ (accessed 30.5.2023).

Whole School SEND (2023) *Home page*. https://www.wholeschoolsend.org.uk/ (accessed 29.5.2023).

9 Developing effective working relationships with teaching assistants

> In this chapter, we critically examine and explore the following key aspects:
>
> - Changes in the teaching assistant workforce in schools
> - Research relating to the effectiveness of teaching assistants
> - Continuing Professional Development (CPD) and training approaches for teaching assistants
> - Communication between teachers and teaching assistants
> - Models for effective deployment of teaching assistants

Key issues

Teaching assistants (TAs) make up over a quarter of the school workforce (approximately 35% primary and 14% secondary) and 'over the last decade or so, the number of full-time equivalent TAs has more than trebled since 2000: from 79,000 to 243,700' (EEF, 2018: 5). However, there has been an ongoing discussion in recent years regarding the impact TAs have in the classroom and the value for money as a resource to support pupil outcomes. Recent research serves to validate the TA as a key resource available to schools (e.g. EEF (2018) Making the best use of teaching assistants guidance report) and the EEF report Special Educational Needs in Mainstream Schools (EEF, 2020: 1) identifies a separate strand on how to 'work effectively with Teaching Assistants'. It is, therefore, essential that the effective deployment and development of this key staffing resource is carefully planned and central to whole-school strategic planning to meet the needs of all pupils in the school setting.

The SENCO Learning Outcomes (DfE, 2014: 7) note the following requirements within the training:

- Lead the professional development of staff so that all staff improve their practice and take responsibility for removing barriers to participation and learning.
- Deploy and manage staff effectively to ensure the most efficient use of resources to improve progress of children and young people with SEN and/or disabilities.

In this chapter, we will focus on the ways in which Special Educational Needs Coordinators (SENCOs) can enact these requirements in practice through equipping teachers and TAs to hold relevant knowledge and skills. Ensuring there is effective CPD, so teachers are confident and are able to work effectively with TAs in their classrooms is a pressing

DOI: 10.4324/9781003033554-9

issue we face in schools. Exploring models for the deployment of TAs based on the current research will provide a platform for reviewing practice. Therefore the following key issues will be explored further in this chapter:

1. Continuing Professional Development (CPD) and training approaches for teaching assistants
2. Supporting teachers and TAs in more effective ways of working together
3. Models for effective deployment of TAs in schools

The EEF (2020: 24) guidance clearly foregrounds that the main underlying principle is that TAs must be viewed as a supplement to teachers and not a replacement. All 'remaining recommendations in [the] guidance are either exemplifications of that principle (e.g. the careful use of TA-led interventions) or ways of achieving it (e.g. ensuring TAs and teachers understand their complementary roles)'.

Current policy/research context

CPD and training approaches for teaching assistants

There are a range of support staff roles within school who aid the day to day smooth operation and this can include laboratory technicians, lunchtime supervisors, administration roles, librarian, etc. Some of these roles have been in existence for some time, but TAs predominantly joined the workforce in schools in response to the changes in legislation to introduce Statements of Special Educational Needs (Education Act, 1981) where children with complex needs were educated in mainstream schools and needed additional support to access the school facilities and curriculum. The TA role has changed quite considerably over time, from historic perceptions of TAs as a 'Mum's Army' (Kerry, 2001) leading to assumptions that could be viewed as derogatory regarding the level of skill and knowledge for the role. Increasingly there has been a focus on training, professionalisation and accountability, with political drivers related to an increased focus on outcomes for pupils and the need to ensure value for money. The EEF (2018: 5) refer to the 'rise and rise of TAs' noting:

> While the proportion of teachers in mainstream schools in England has remained relatively steady over the last decade or so, the proportion of full time equivalent TAs has more than trebled since 2000: from 79,000 to 243,700.

This increase in numbers of TAs within the workforce has been in response to a number of changes. One is the government commitment to reducing teachers' workload in 2003 with The National Agreement and School Workforce Remodelling (DfES, 2003). The increasing focus on inclusion of pupils with Special Educational Needs and Disability (SEND) in mainstream is another factor, as well as support for those who are more vulnerable and entitled to Pupil Premium (NFER, 2012).

Therefore, due to the increase in the TA workforce and the changes and increased focus on outcomes/value for money, it is important to consider the training and opportunities in place for TAs to fully equip them to meet the demands now in place. It is important to carefully consider the approach regarding the 'need for continuing professional development for SEND and greater access to staff or practitioners with specialist SEND expertise'

(DfE, 2021, n.p). From a recent review on the deployment of TAs, the training taking place in schools were identified:

Across interviewees, TAs were described as being trained on:

- Teaching support – including being involved in whole school training on areas such as metacognition and providing effective feedback
- SEND – including on understanding types of SEND, possible manifestations, and support strategies
- Particular interventions and programmes

(DfE, 2019: 31)

The Government (DfE/DoHSC, 2023: 56) identify the importance of good quality training for TAs in their recent proposals, planning to: 'develop a longer-term approach for TAs to ensure their impact is consistent across the system and the different responsibilities they take on. We want TAs to be well-trained and to be able to develop specific expertise, for example in speech and language interventions'. The systems and processes in school are key and link to the notion of an inclusive, learning environment as being conducive to support quality training of the staff (as outlined in Chapters 2 and 13). SENCOs need to ensure the offer of training responds to the school profile of need, the staffing requirements and the school's models for deployment of TAs (which will be discussed later in this chapter). School leaders identify the SENCO as central to the training needs of TAs:

Headteachers, Deputy and Assistant Headteachers, and SENCOs reported that the main support that teaching assistants received was through training. This could be delivered either through external courses or, more commonly, within setting. In primary and secondary schools it was reported that SENCOs played an 'important role in supporting teaching assistants either through regular meetings to discuss their work and by sharing information or through modeling strategies'.

(DfE, 2017: 9)

The proposals (DfE/DoHSC, 2023: 56) also note the commitment from the government to set out clear guidance for the effective use and deployment of TAs, and training to enable them to support pupils: 'We will do this through the new SEND and alternative provision practice guides, enabling TAs and learning support assistants to make best use of the available provision set out in the National Standards and setting expectations for good practice in meeting the needs of individual children and young people'.

In addition to quality training, the progression available to TAs, is an area to consider when we ask them to take on more responsibility in their roles. Higher level teaching assistant (HLTA) is an option which may provide recognition and professionalises the role through a progression route. In schools, HLTAs could take more of a lead on areas of expertise, e.g. specialist in Cognition and Learning, Communication and Interaction, etc. Working with outside agencies, TAs could build capacity within the school, for example HLTAs assigned to programmes with external professionals which they can then replicate in-house. HLTAs could also take on more responsibility for supporting teachers and managing TAs within their areas of expertise. Attending multi-agency meetings and delivering training for parents/carers, etc. could be included as additional responsibilities to differentiate the role from a TA. In the long-term expertise of the HLTAs could be shared with other settings/schools to provide a source of income.

Supporting teachers and teaching assistants in more effective ways of working together

The SENCO might manage the day to day deployment of the TAs and may also line manage the TAs, yet teachers are responsible for directing support staff in their classes. It is therefore essential that teachers have a good understanding of how best to deploy their TA in the classroom.

We need to consider how we work with TAs in school to have the best possible impact. Communication between the TA and teacher is key and can pose quite a challenge in a large secondary model where children and staff are moving to different classes. Facilitating time to liaise together to enable staff to develop effective collaborative practices is important:

> Interventions are often quite separate from classroom activities and the lack of time for teachers and TAs to liaise means there is relatively little connection between what pupils experience in and away from the classroom. This means it can be left to the pupil to make links between the coverage of the intervention and the wider curriculum coverage back in the classroom. Given that supported pupils are usually those who find accessing learning difficult in the first place, this presents a huge additional challenge.
>
> (EEF, 2020: 23)

This illustrates that the hard work taking place to support pupils with evidence-informed interventions can so easily be undone if there is a lack of time to be able to effectively communicate between the teacher and TA to help the pupil with making connections and applying their understanding in when they return to class. In fact Recommendation 7 of the Making Best Use of Teaching Assistants Guidance Report states schools should 'ensure explicit connections are made between learning from everyday classroom teaching and structured interventions' (EEF, 2018: 3).

It is not only time that can be a barrier to the effective deployment of TAs by teachers, it can include other factors as outlined here:

> Class teachers reported some barriers they experienced when deploying teaching assistants effectively in lessons. These barriers included lack of time to plan together and teaching assistants not being available for entire lessons or consistently due to other commitments in school making continuity of support difficult.
>
> (DfE, 2017: 10)

This is further reinforced with the findings of the EEF Guidance report (2018: 9) which identifies that the most teachers, and particularly so in secondary, have no time to plan or for feedback with the TA. They also noted there was 'no training in relation to managing, organising or working with TAs'. The EEF Recommendation 4 which referred to TAs being fully prepared for their role notes that: 'Schools should provide sufficient time for TA training and for teachers and TAs to meet out of class to enable the necessary lesson preparation and feedback' (EEF, 2018: 10). Therefore looking at ways to strategically provide more consistency, opportunities to communicate and time for planning are important.

The SENCO, therefore, not only needs to consider the training needs of the TAs, but also how well the teachers and TAs are able to communicate about the work they are undertaking. Ensuring the teachers are able to work with and effectively deploy the TAs.

Models for effective deployment of teaching assistants in schools

TAs and support staff play a vital role in supporting us to be able to meet the needs of pupils with a range of SEN in our school settings. Yet, increasingly school budgets have been tightened and additional staffing has to have a very clear purpose and role. It is, therefore, essential that the effective deployment and development of this key staffing resource is carefully planned and central to whole-school strategic planning to meet the needs of all pupils in the school setting. As the EEF (2020: 34) have identified, 'when well trained and supported TA's can have a positive impact. Unfortunately, where the deployment of TAs is not carefully considered by school leadership, it can have a negative impact on pupils' learning and wellbeing'.

TAs are quite an expensive resource (EEF Toolkit, 2023) which consequently led to much research into the effectiveness of support staff over recent years. This has included the following papers and reports:

- Blatchford et al., (2009) Deployment and Impact of Support Staff (DISS) project
- Blatchford et al., (2012) Challenging the role and deployment of teaching assistants in mainstream schools: The impact on schools. Final report on the Effective Deployment of Teaching Assistants (EDTA) project
- Webster & Blatchford (2013) The Making a Statement (MAST) Study Final Report. A study of the teaching and support experienced by pupils with a statement of Special Educational Needs in mainstream primary schools
- Webster et al. (2015) Maximising the Impact of Teaching Assistants (MITA): Guidance for School Leaders and Teachers
- Webster & Blatchford (2017) The Special Educational Needs in Secondary Education (SENSE) study Final Report
- EEF (2018) Making the Best use of Teaching Assistants
- EEF (2020) Special Educational Needs in Mainstream Schools.

Often, the focus of the role of the TAs and support staff is solely on providing direct support to pupils with SEND (Blatchford et al., 2009) yet, 'the typical deployment and use of TAs, under everyday conditions, is not leading to improvements in academic outcomes' (EEF, 2020: 6). Resources are precious and this is now increasingly the case where school budgets have been tightened and additional staffing has to have a very clear purpose and role. As a result, schools are adopting a range of models for using TAs support. In some cases there has been a reduction of TAs, or even removal of TAs as support in classes. As noted in the EEF report (2018: 36) 'Making the best use of teaching assistants is a leadership issue; a lack of proper support and training is not the fault of TAs themselves'. Therefore, it is important to explore different models for effective deployment of teaching assistants in schools. The DfE (2019) publication Deployment of Teaching Assistants in schools includes the following models:

1 **Whole-class support**

   Deployment of TAs as a general support to the whole class was the common mode of deployment stated by primary schools. No secondary schools reported allocation of TAs in this way (DfE, 2019: 6).

2 **Targeted in-class learning support**

   Allocating TAs for targeted in-class support was the most commonly reported mode of deployment by secondary schools and the second most common method of TA deployment by primary schools (DfE, 2019: 6).

3 **Targeted intervention delivery**

Primary and secondary schools also reported deploying TAs to withdraw pupils for intervention delivery. Interventions took place either in addition to class taught lessons (such as lunchtime or tutor time) or instead of class taught lessons (such as withdrawing pupils from Modern Foreign Language lessons or alternating withdrawal from different subjects or lessons) (DfE, 2019: 6).

These three models are not necessarily exclusive, you may find that schools adopt more than one model concurrently in order to be able to meet the needs of learners.

Despite research outlining the low-impact or sometimes negative effect TAs can have on outcomes (Blatchford et al., 2009; Webster & Blatchford, 2013), it is important to consider the impact reactionary changes can have if they are not implemented with sufficient foresight, 'it is difficult to see how mainstream schools would accommodate the inclusion and teaching of pupils with high-level SEND in the long term, if TAs were to disappear from classrooms tomorrow' (Webster & Blatchford, 2017: 6). This reinforces the need to carefully consider all models. In models 1 and 2 (above) additional adult support in class may have an impact which is not easy to measure in a tangible way, but could be critical to teacher well-being, pupil confidence, managing low-level disruption, etc.

Some schools have reported allocating very little TA support to the classroom, with their focus being on teachers offering high-quality, inclusive teaching for pupils:

> Allocated little targeted TA in-class support – preferring to train, advise and support teachers to better differentiate and make reasonable adjustments in lessons. TAs then delivered interventions in non-taught times to help pupils catch or keep up, or to address specific additional needs.
>
> (DfE, 2019: 22–23)

Both high-quality teaching and inadequate teaching can impact upon the effectiveness of TA support in the class. Where teaching is high quality and inclusive this could lead to the TA support as becoming redundant because the lesson is accessed well by the pupils without the need for additional support. Where teaching is inadequate the TA support might be ineffective because there might be little challenge in relation to the tasks set, so the TA is therefore not able to aid effectively in supporting the learning activities. It is important that there are processes in place to monitor the effectiveness of teaching with a lens as to how this might relate to the deployment of TA support. In all cases, removing TAs from class, requires teachers to be confident in removing barriers to learning for those children in their class who have more significant needs. Some schools reported not using TAs for targeted interventions where pupils are removed from the class. This is illustrated in the example below:

> Delivered no interventions, instead delivering all support using the targeted in class approach. This approach was often used because these schools had found that, although the target skill was developed by an intervention, this did not necessarily translate to the wider curriculum or learning.
>
> (DfE, 2019: 22)

Equally, model 3 (above) has its merits. Where TAs have high-quality support and training from structured settings, research has shown: 'delivering targeted interventions in one-to-one or small group settings shows a consistent impact on attainment of approximately three to four additional months' progress' (EEF, 2018: 19). Using model 3 (above) to develop TAs with expertise in specific areas of need and appropriate evidence-informed interventions with clear baseline and exit data, means the impact can be more easily measured in school. Having expert TAs in school can build capacity by working with teachers to improve quality first teaching strategies in the class.

The SENCOs role is therefore quite substantial in leading on the training of TAs, but also in training and supporting the teachers in how to best deploy TAs in their class. In addition the strategic oversight of the different model/s for deployment of the TAs in school to most effectively meet needs and use the TAs skills and expertise to have the greatest impact on pupil outcomes.

Planning for practice

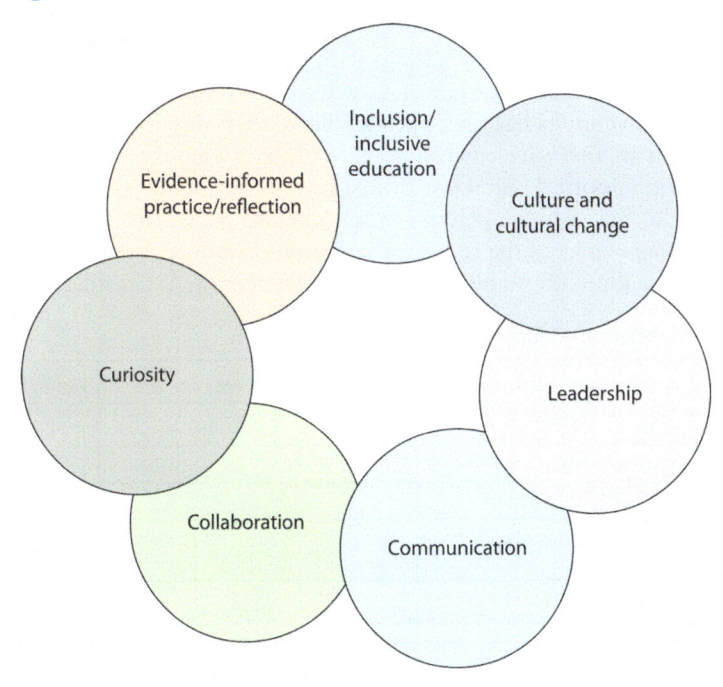

Figure 9.1 Key principles model

To be able to really ensure that staff feel confident and able to undertake CPD that will have an impact on their practice there needs to be ***leadership*** in place which values CPD and has strategic oversight of the profile of the school, the training needs of staff as well as an understanding of the effective research-based models for the deployment of TAs. The SENCO is often leading training for staff, so ensuring there is appropriate time and allocation of resources is important to foster an ***inclusive environment*** where TAs and teachers can engage in training and working together. Ultimately, what happens in the class is key and so the effective ***communication*** between TAs and teachers is essential to ensure the working relationships serve to meet the needs of the pupils. In some cases ***curiosity*** has led to new models of working and ways to really utilise knowledge and skills and build capacity in schools.

CPD and training approaches for teaching assistants

> **Reflective Activity**
>
> - What models of TA support and deployment to you currently have in place in your school setting?
> - Are these models effective to meet the current and changing needs of pupils within your school?
> - How do you know?
> - Is there a carefully structured CPD model to support all TA's to develop the skills needed to be able to work effectively with some of our most complex learners?
> - Are there any gaps that need to be addressed?

Fostering an environment where staff are able to engage in training impacts on outcomes, it was identified that only 'structured settings with high quality support and training' (EEF, 2018: 11) led to positive outcomes where TAs delivered interventions. Poor understanding or poor delivery of interventions has the opposite effect. Therefore looking at ways to provide effective training in an *inclusive* environment where everyone is valued is important. The Index for Inclusion (Booth & Ainscow, 2002) provides a model with useful templates to review and consider the inclusive practice in schools and gaps that might need addressing. Table 9.1 includes an extract of the Index for Inclusion (Booth & Ainscow, 2002) noting the indicators for A.1 Building community which is from Dimension A: Creating inclusive cultures.

Table 9.1 Index for Inclusion – indicators for building community

Indicators	RAG rating of current practice*	Example and comments
A.1.1 Everyone is made to feel welcome		
A.1.2 Students help each other		
A.1.3 Staff collaborate with each other		
A.1.4 Staff and students treat one another with respect		
A.1.5 There is a partnership between staff and parents/carers		
A.1.6 Staff and governors work well together		
A.1.7 All local communities are involved in the school		

* Red = Not evident in practice; Amber = some aspects evident in practice; Green = Fully evident in practice.

The SENCO, but also the wider leadership team are key to the effective deployment of TAs because it can be a 'complex process, requiring changes across the school (senior leadership, middle leadership, teachers, TAs), addressing existing ways of working, training at all levels, and sometimes structural changes in terms of timetabling and working arrangements' (EEF, 2018: 24).

The Professional Standards for teaching assistants (MITA, 2016) can be used by SENCOs to evaluate induction and the provision of CPD for TAs. It gives guidance focused on four themes:

1 Personal and professional conduct
2 Knowledge and understanding

3 Teaching and learning
4 Working with others

The standards within these themes can help to inform processes for identifying training and development needs. In addition, effective audits of existing SEND knowledge and understanding are useful to be able to track and respond to the training needs across the school.

The MITA (2023) project website includes a range of free resources, which includes a self-review form for schools (Nasen/WSS, 2020) regarding current levels of training and ways TAs are deployed in the setting. Use the statements in Table 9.2, specific to 'Preparation and Training' to consider these aspects in your practice.

Observations of practice are also important to ensure training that has taken place is being applied in practice. The EEF (2018: 26) TA observation schedule is a useful resources to review practice in class.

Additionally key questions to ask when conducting observations of interventions is useful in reviewing the provision for pupils and the impact on their learning: The Intervention Health Check (EEF, 2018: 26) is another helpful resource: https://d2tic4wvo1iusb.cloudfront.net/production/eef-guidance-reports/teaching-assistants/TA_Health_Check.pdf?v=1701955474 (accessed 31.5.23).

Too often TAs will attend external training or a course, but then when they return to school it can be difficult to schedule the time to evaluate the impact of this new knowledge in relation to practice. A useful tool to reflect on the impact of training and TAs ability to support pupils in class more effectively is utilising a reflection tool linked to the 'Five-a-day' (see Figure 9.2). The 'Five-a-day' is intended to support pupils with SEND to make increased academic progress (see Chapter 5).

However, this can be used alongside a reflection tool which contains questions and prompts for TAs to respond to related to each focus (see EEF, 2020).

Table 9.2 Preparation and Training school self-review

Nasen/WSS (2020) 'Preparation and Training' *statements from the school self-review*	What this looks like in my setting
Teachers have received extensive and on-going training on how to manage, organise and work with TAs.	
Teachers plan tasks matched to individual's needs, broken down into smaller achievable actions (where needed).	
For new TA appointments, there are minimum requirements in terms of qualifications/experience and subject knowledge.	
Ahead of lessons, TAs have a clear understanding of concepts and information to be taught, skills to be learned and applied, intended learning outcomes and specific learning needs of pupils they will work with.	
There are mechanisms in place to capture meaningful feedback for teachers, which is used to inform the next stages of learning within and/or after lessons.	
There is allocated time outside of lessons for teachers and TAs to plan and review lessons together. SLT set clear expectations on how this time is used, and monitor regularly.	

Source: Available from: https://irp.cdn-website.com/acefe6d4/files/uploaded/tadeploymentreviewguideweb.pdf (accessed 31.5.23).

156 *Effective working relationships with teaching assistants*

High quality teaching benefits pupils with SEND
The 'Five-a-day' principle

The research underpinning the EEF's guidance report 'Special Educational Needs in Mainstream Schools' indicates that supporting high quality teaching improves outcomes for pupils with SEND. Five specific approaches—the 'Five-a-day' indicated below—are particularly well-evidenced as having a positive impact. Teachers should develop a repertoire of these strategies, which they can use daily and flexibly in response to individual needs, using them as the starting point for classroom teaching for all pupils, including those with SEND.

1 Explicit instruction
Teacher-led approaches with a focus on clear explanations, modelling and frequent checks for understanding. This is then followed by guided practice, before independent practice.

2 Cognitive and metacognitive strategies
Managing cognitive load is crucial if new content is to be transferred into students' long-term memory. Provide opportunities for students to plan, monitor and evaluate their own learning.

3 Scaffolding
When students are working on a written task, provide a supportive tool or resource such as a writing frame or a partially completed example. Aim to provide less support of this nature throughout the course of the lesson, week or term.

4 Flexible grouping
Allocate groups temporarily, based on current level of mastery. This could, for example, be a group that comes together to get some additional spelling instruction based on current need, before re-joining the main class.

5 Using technology
Technology can be used by a teacher to model worked examples; it can be used by a student to help them to learn, to practice and to record their learning. For instance, you might use a class visualiser to share students' work or to jointly rework an incorrect model.

More information about finding better ways to support pupils with SEND, including these five principles and more specialist interventions, can be found in the EEF's guidance report '*Special Educational Needs in Mainstream Schools*'.

Education Endowment Foundation

Figure 9.2 EEF (2020) Five-a-day principle

Source: https://d2tic4wvo1iusb.cloudfront.net/eef-guidance-reports/send/Five-a-day-poster_1.1.pdf?v=1643188181 (accessed 31.5.23).

Effective working relationships with teaching assistants 157

The reflection tool can be used as a starting point for TAs to consider their practice, but could then be returned to, in order to consider how the new knowledge and skills from training will have helped to develop their practice. 'It can help TAs to consider how their own practice can align with the evidence around what supports pupils with SEND to make good academic progress' (Aubin, 2022: n.p).

Supporting teachers and teaching assistants in more effective ways of working together

TAs should supplement, not replace, teaching from the classroom teacher. The EEF's guidance report Making Best Use of Teaching Assistants (EEF, 2018) provides detailed recommendations. The recommendations include the following areas of focus:

- the effective use of TAs under everyday classroom conditions,
- the effective use of TAs in delivering structured interventions out of class,
- integrating learning from everyday classroom contexts and structured interventions.

Effective deployment of TAs is critical. School leaders should pay careful attention to the roles of TAs and ensure they have a positive impact on pupils with SEND.

A key finding and a recurring issue related to the time and opportunity to ***communicate*** between the teachers and TAs. The TA preparedness (EEF, 2018: 16) noted in Figure 9.3 identifies some suggestions as to how to address this issue:

Teacher-TA liaison	Ensure TAs have the lesson plan 'need to knows' in advance
• Adjust TA's working hours: start early, finish early	• Concepts, facts, information being taught
• Timetabling: use assembly time	• Skills to be learned, applied, practised or extended
• TAs join teachers for (part of) PPA time	• Intended learning outcomes
• SLT set expectations for how liaison time is used	• Expected/required feedback

Figure 9.3 EEF (2018) making the best use of teaching assistants

Source: https://educationendowmentfoundation.org.uk/education-evidence/guidance-reports/teaching-assistants (accessed 29.5.23).

Another strategy that could be adopted is a TA/Teacher agreement. Table 9.3 is based on the EEF (2018: 26) Teacher-TA agreement template. It can be used as an agreement between the teacher and TA on the agreed examples of how TAs can support a class. It can be a way to foster ***communication*** on the roles and responsibilities of TAs and teachers in class.

Table 9.3 EEF (2018) Teacher-TA agreement template

When?	What?
During the lesson introduction	- Check learning objectives are written in books - Refocus pupils - Ensure relevant learning materials and equipment are out/available
During whole-class work	- Use the 'Scaffolding framework' to ensure pupils are offered the 'least amount of help first' - Encourage responses from [names of target pupils] - Emphasise key vocabulary; record key words - Model or role-play activities with teacher - Ensure pupils refer to success criteria - Observe and note learning difficulties and achievements and feed back to the teacher
In group work	- If necessary, check pupils understand what they need to do, what they will learn and what outcome is expected by the end of the session - Provide prompts on group objectives and roles required. Give time checks - Note issues, mistakes, misconceptions and difficulties for follow-up by teacher - Encourage interaction with others
In plenary sessions	- Encourage pupils to reflect on their learning. Prompt recall and use of relevant strategies if necessary - Monitor and record responses of [names of target pupils] (note difficulties and achievements)
At the end of the lesson	- Clarify next steps in pupils' learning - Ensure pupils understand homework and are clear about any follow-up required. Ensure homework is written in planners
After the lesson	- Provide feedback on any misconceptions, difficulties, etc.; issues with behaviour for learning

> **Reflective Activity**
>
> The Teacher-TA agreement template (EEF, 2018) is useful to determine clear roles and expectations for in-class support. However, it could also be used in the following ways:
>
> - shared with the TAs in a meeting to discuss and create a school version on what constitutes good practice in the class
> - used by TAs to conduct peer observations and supportive feedback on how to improve on practice
> - used as a training tool, supporting TAs and teachers to reflect on practice and ways in which they work together
>
> Reflect on some of these different ways to use the resource and identify any actions you could take forward in practice to improve on the communication between teachers and TAs.

Effective working relationships with teaching assistants 159

The Nasen/WSS (2020) TA Deployment Review Guide includes template questionnaires for both teachers and TAs to explore the ways in which they work together. The questionnaire for teachers (see Figure 9.4) includes questions which help them to critically reflect on how they deploy TAs, the first page is below:

ANNEX 2
Staff survey
QUESTIONS FOR TEACHERS
For the first few questions, you will need to think about the LAST lesson in which you received support from a TA.

1 Thinking about what you did in that lesson, put the list of five activities into rank order from 1 to 5. Use 1 to indicate the activity you spent the MOST time doing in that lesson, and 5 to indicate the activity you spent the LEAST time doing.

	RANK
Working one-to-one with a pupil	
Working with a pair or group	
Walking around the classroom (monitoring pupils)	
Leading or teaching the class	
Other (e.g. marking)	

2 To what extent are the answers you provided in Q1 typical of what you do in other lessons?

Very typical	
Fairly typical	
Not very typical	
Not at all typical	

3 Once again, thinking about what you did in that lesson, which two groups of pupils did you spend the MOST time supporting?

	HIGHER ATTAINING PUPILS	AVERAGE ATTAINING PUPILS	LOWER ATTAINING PUPILS	PUPILS WITH SEND	MIXED ATTAINING PUPILS
Most time with…					
Second most time with…					

4 To what extent are the answers you provided in Q3 typical of what you do in other lessons?

Very typical	
Fairly typical	
Not very typical	
Not at all typical	

Figure 9.4 Teachers' questionnaire

The questionnaire for TAs (see Figure 9.5) mirrors the questions for teachers, so it provides a really good opportunity to identify any similarities and differences in the perceptions over the support in place.

Nasen/WSS (2020) explain this is part of a process of auditing the TA provision through self-evaluation before then taking steps towards commissioning a TA deployment review.

Reflective Activity

- How might you use the Nasen/WSS (2020) questionnaires to audit the current provision?
- Once you have completed the questionnaires with staff how would you feed this back?
- How might you use this to determine the future ways in which teachers and TAs work together?

160 *Effective working relationships with teaching assistants*

ANNEX 2
Staff survey
QUESTIONS FOR TEACHING ASSISTANTS

1 Thinking about what you did in that lesson, put the list of five activities into rank order from 1 to 5. Use 1 to indicate the activity you spent the MOST time doing in that lesson, and 5 to indicate the activity you spent the LEAST time doing.

	RANK
Working one-to-one with a pupil	
Working with a pair or group	
Walking around the classroom (monitoring pupils)	
Leading or teaching the class	
Listening to the teacher teach	
Other (e.g. marking)	

2 To what extent are the answers you provided in Q1 typical of what you do in other lessons?

Very typical	
Fairly typical	
Not very typical	
Not at all typical	

3 Once again, thinking about what you did in that lesson, which two groups of pupils did you spend the MOST time supporting?

	HIGHER ATTAINING PUPILS	AVERAGE ATTAINING PUPILS	LOWER ATTAINING PUPILS	PUPILS WITH SEND	MIXED ATTAINING PUPILS
Most time with...					
Second most time with...					

4 To what extent are the answers you provided in Q3 typical of what you do in other lessons?

Very typical	
Fairly typical	
Not very typical	
Not at all typical	

Figure 9.5 Teaching Assistants' questionnaire

Models for effective deployment of teaching assistants in schools

After considering the different models of deploying TAs, stop to reflect on practice in school and what model/s are already in place or what you might want to introduce. It can be difficult to change embedded structures or approaches, especially when this affects people's roles, duties and expectations. Therefore, 'Breaking away from a model of deployment where TAs are assigned to specific pupils for long periods requires more strategic approaches to classroom organisation' (EEF, 2018: 10).

Reflective Activity

- What might ineffective TA/support staff deployment look like?
- How would you know if it is ineffective or not?
- What would you need to prioritise to change or develop?

Now consider your reflections against Table 9.4 based on the EEF (2020) overview of what ineffective teaching assistant deployment looks like and identify ways that you would address each of those points with more positive examples of practice and deployment, and ways that you will develop those in your own school setting.

Table 9.4 EEF (2020) ineffective and effective deployment of TAs

Considering the ineffective, and effective, deployment of TA's – adapted from EEF (2020: 34)

What does ineffective deployment of TA's look like (taken from EEF, 2020: 34)	RAG rating of current practice*	What actions would you take to change this into practices which would mean that the deployment of the TA is effective in your own setting?
TAs take responsibility for planning, and delivering, the teaching for pupils with SEND. TAs take on a primary teaching role but have not been trained or supported to provide effective teaching.		
Pupils with SEND are often segregated from the rest of the class at an individual table with a TA. TAs conduct 'stereo-teaching' where their interactions with the pupil cut across the teacher's whole class delivery.		
Pupils with SEND receive a very different classroom experience when working with a TA. Tasks can be inappropriately targeted, repetitive, or undemanding. TAs might decide what to do based on what they think the pupil can do or understand, This is well-intentioned but may not provide appropriate challenge.		
The classroom teacher is not confident in addressing the sometimes complex and challenging needs of the pupils in their class. They might not have received training on teaching pupils with SEND. Their lesson planning is not sufficiently addressing the needs of pupils with SEND and this has become the responsibility of the TA.		

* Red = This ineffective practice is firmly embedded; Amber = some aspects of this ineffective practice are still in practice; Green = This ineffective practice is not evidenced in practice.

Leading on the whole school approaches to deploy TAs aligns to the research and is fundamental. However, to avoid resistance to changes it is crucial to collaborate with TAs and wider staff in introducing any changes. One way to ensure TAs do not feel disaffected and excluded from 'top-down' decisions is to involve them fully in the process, the discussions and the planned developments. By collaborating on the planned changes, it will hopefully serve to increase the genuine 'buy-in' from the TAs. If they have a voice in what the support will look like it is more likely they will be invested in making it work. The EEF (2018: 26) provides a tool for a 'visioning exercise' when considering the schools direction and planning for their TA workforce (see Figure 9.6). This leadership is key to informing the next steps based on the school priorities and the longer term action plan. The exercise may help with discussions on what stakeholders require and recording what they want to see as a result of implementing a change to improve on ways in which TA support is deployed in school:

MAKING BEST USE OF TEACHING ASSISTANTS
Visioning exercise

Schools need to develop a clear vision for their TA workforce to informing the steps of their action plan. One way of starting this process is to think about where you want to be in the future. Use this sheet to support discussions throughout your school about what differences you and your staff want to see as a result of improving your use of TAs. Keep discussions open and positive.

Think about what you will see and hear that are different two years from now, which will indicate whether your changes have been successful. What kinds of things will pupils be saying more or less of? What kinds of things will teachers and TAs be doing more or less frequently? What comments do you hope to hear from parents?

Teachers | TAs

What will you see more and less of in two years' time?

Pupils | Others (e.g. parents)

Education Endowment Foundation

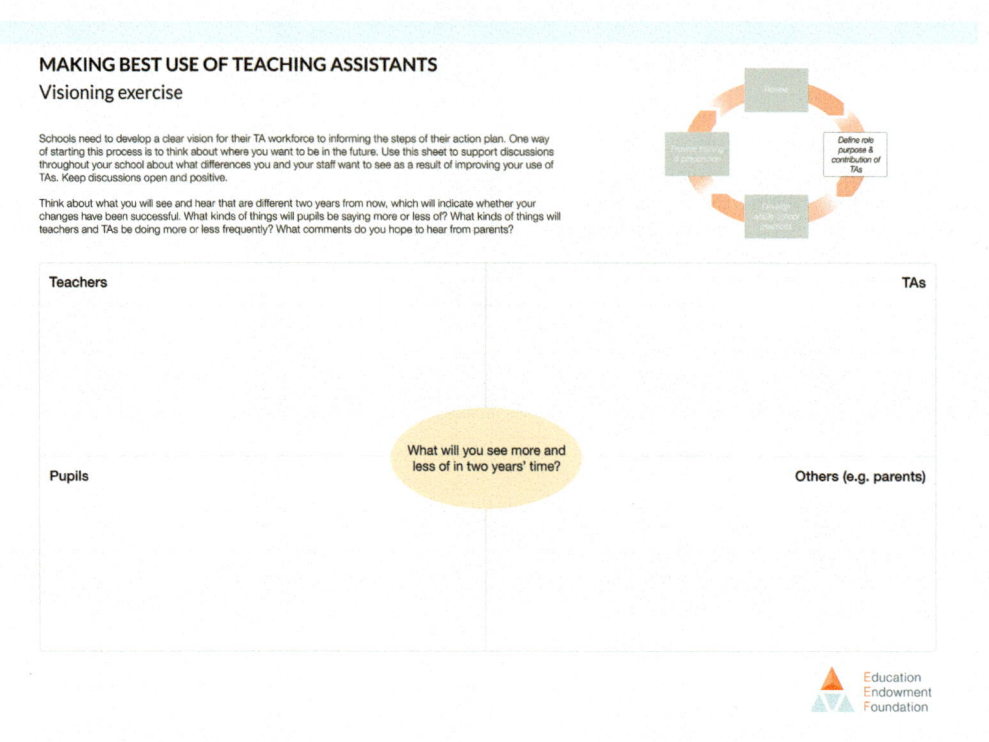

Figure 9.6 EEF (2018) Visioning exercise tool

Schools are having to think more creatively about how to use resources to meet the needs of pupils because funding continues to reduce:

> Schools reports that a reduction in available funds was happening at the same time as levels and types of needs in pupils were seen as increasing. Schools detailed that this increase was due to more pupils with SEND being in the mainstream system and more pupils facing issues, which can result in barriers to learning.
>
> (DfE, 2019: 36)

In some cases, when TAs have high levels of expertise, this can be utilised in different ways and can provide a more cost effective way to use resources in school. Having the *curiosity* to explore this can lead to positive outcomes as noted in the Case Study below:

Case Study – TAs Teaching the Teachers

In a secondary school in the South East of England, the TAs were all trained in specific areas of expertise. This included subject areas and also areas of need, e.g. literacy, speech and language, emotional regulation, etc. The SENCO identified the areas

TAs felt most confident in through the Performance Management cycle. Through discussion at these points in the year, the SENCO could identify curriculum areas the TAs were more confident in as well as their personal interests. This meant that TAs were more engaged because their personal and professional needs were acknowledged. TAs were predominantly deployed to curriculum areas, but with the understanding that they may need to cover other curriculum areas too.

The development of expertise in specific areas of need led to outcomes that were not originally anticipated. Two examples are outlined below:

1 A TA trained in 'The Incredible Five Point Scale' (Buron & Curtis, 2003) supported training of the pastoral team in the school so that children using this in class could also use it as part of their communication with year heads should something have happened. This then led to the SENCO delivering a session with parents/carers so they had a better understanding of the intervention – this meant it was a more holistic form of communication for the child, which enabled them to better regulate and manage in class, outside of class and at home
2 One TA developed specialism in supporting pupils who had English as an Additional Language (EAL). There was an increasing need to support children arriving in school with very little English, but having to attend General Certificate of Secondary Education (GCSE) focused lessons. It was necessary to support teachers in how best to ensure the pupils were included and able to access the curriculum. A session was organised which the TA led for the teachers. This had really positive impact compared to arranging for an external visitor to deliver training because the TA was able to talk about specific children in school, the strategies that worked for them and was also able to take away any actions that might be necessary based on some of the teachers' comments.

These models where TAs are leading training for staff in the school really served to value their expertise in a wider sense across the school rather than just seeing them in a 'support' role – illustrating in practice how 'school leaders recognise the value and importance of teaching assistants and should ensure teaching assistants have parity of esteem with fellow education professionals' (MITA, 2016: 5). It also had the effect of building capacity from within. So not always being dependent on outsider specialists for delivering training to teachers which reduces costs and makes use of the excellent resources available within the school.

Reflective Activity

- Reflect on ways you can move away from the sole SENCO-expert model. Based on your reading in this chapter, list as many examples as you can on ways you could draw on expertise from the school to support future training
- Now reflect on how you will plan to share this knowledge and expertise you have identified.

Concluding comments and reflections

TA deployment involves complexities (EEF, 2018) and so adopting approaches that are strategic and clearly align to the evidence-bases (EEF, 2018, 2020) will help us to make best use of resources and support teachers in delivering high-quality teaching. The opportunity for teachers and TAs to communicate to have very clear awareness of their roles and responsibilities will help to improve on competence in managing deployment in class. It is essential that we ensure the most vulnerable pupils in our schools are appropriately taught and supported. An essential aspect to remember is that 'The evidence on effective TA deployment, training and use can be summarised in one clear principle – "Use TAs to supplement what teachers do, not replace them"' (EEF, 2018: 24).

> **Individual Reflection**
>
> - What new information/ learning have you gained from this chapter?
> - What are your key reflections?
> - What are your next steps/ actions as a result?

References

Aubin (2022) *EEF's Gary Aubin, Content Specialist for SEND introduces this new blog and tool.* Available from: https://educationendowmentfoundation.org.uk/news/eef-blog-five-a-day-for-send-how-does-it-transform-the-ta-role (accessed 31.5.23).

Blatchford, P., Bassett, P., Brown, P., Koutsoubou, M., Martin, C., Russell, A., Webster, R. and Rubie-Davies, C. (2009) *The impact of support staff in schools. Results from the Deployment and Impact of Support Staff (DISS) project.* London: Department for Children, Schools and Families.

Blatchford, P., Webster, R. and Russell, A. (2012) *Challenging the role and deployment of teaching assistants in mainstream schools: The impact on schools. final report on the Effective Deployment of Teaching Assistants (EDTA) project.* London: Institute of Education. http://www.schoolsupport-staff.net/edtareport.pdf (accessed 31.5.23).

Booth, T. and Ainscow, M. (2002) *Index for Inclusion.* Bristol: CSIE.

Buron, K.D. and Curtis, M. (2003) *The incredible 5-point scale.* Shawnee Mission, KS, Autism Asperger Publishing Co.

DfE (2014) *National Award for Special Educational Needs Co-ordinator: Learning outcomes.* Available from: https://www.gov.uk/government/publications/mandatory-qualification-for-sencos (accessed 31.5.2023).

DfE (2017) *SEN Support: A survey of schools and colleges.* Coventry: DfE.

DfE (2019) *Deployment of Teaching Assistants in Schools.* Available from: https://assets.publishing.service.gov.uk/government/uploads/system/uploads/attachment_data/file/812507/Deployment_of_teaching_assistants_report.pdf (accessed 29.5.23).

DfE (2021) *Supporting SEND: A summary for children and young people.* Available from: https://www.gov.uk/government/publications/supporting-send/supporting-send-a-summary-for-children-and-young-people (accessed 20.12.22).

DfE/DoHSC (2023) *Special Educational Needs and Disabilities (SEND) and Alternative Provision Improvement Plan – Right support, right place, right time.* London: HMSO.

DfES (2003) *The National Agreement and School Workforce Remodelling.* Available from: https://publications.parliament.uk/pa/cm200304/cmselect/cmeduski/1057/3070902.htm (accessed 29.5.23).

Education Act (1981) *Education Act 1981*. Available from: https://www.legislation.gov.uk/ukpga/1981/60/enacted (accessed 29.5.23).

EEF (2018) *Making the best use of teaching assistants guidance report*. London: EEF.

EEF (2020) *SEN in mainstream schools guidance report*. London: EEF.

EEF (2023) *Teaching and learning toolkit*. Available from: https://educationendowmentfoundation.org.uk/education-evidence/teaching-learning-toolkit (accessed 29.5.23).

Kerry, T. (2001) *Working with support staff: Their roles and effective management in schools*. Harlow: Pearson Education Limited.

MITA (2016) *Professional Standards for Teaching Assistants*. Available from: https://www.maximisingtas.co.uk/resources/professional-standards-for-teaching-assistants (accessed 29.5.23).

MITA (2023) *Maximising the Impact of Teaching Assistants*. Available from: https://www.maximisingtas.co.uk/ (accessed 29.5.23).

Nasen/WSS (2020) *TA Deployment Review Guide*. Available from: https://asset.nasen.org.uk/ta_deployment_review_guide_web.pdf (accessed 29.5.23).

NFER (2012) *Teacher Voice Omnibus Survey: The use of the Pupil Premium*. London: The Sutton Trust.

Webster, R. and Blatchford, P. (2013) *The Making a Statement Study (MAST) Final Report. A study of the teaching and support experienced by pupils with a statement of special educational needs in mainstream primary schools*. Available from: https://discovery.ucl.ac.uk/id/eprint/10096862/ (accessed 16.07.17).

Webster, R. and Blatchford, P. (2017) *The Special Educational Needs in Secondary Education (SENSE) study final report*. London: UCL Institute of Education.

Webster, R., Russell, A. and Blatchford, P. (2015) *Maximising the impact of teaching assistants: Guidance for school leaders and teachers* (2nd Edition). Abingdon: Routledge.

10 Working with pupils: developing effective person-centred planning

In this chapter, we critically examine and explore the following key aspects:

- Understanding person-centred planning
- Involving and valuing everyone's individual voice
- Exploring pupil participation and engagement
- Investment and resources for person-centred planning
- Embedding person-centred planning across the school
- Frameworks to support person-centred planning

Key issues

Person-centred planning places pupils and families as central to what we do as Special Educational Needs Coordinators (SENCOs). The underpinning principles of the SEN and Disability Code of Practice (DfE/DoH, 2015) illustrate this commitment with the following reference to the requirements for regard to:

- the views, wishes and feelings of the child or young person, and the child's parents/carers
- the importance of the child or young person, and the child's parents/carers, participating as fully as possible in decisions, and being provided with the information and support necessary to enable participation in those decisions
- the need to support the child or young person, and the child's parents/carers, in order to facilitate the development of the child or young person and to help them achieve the best possible educational and other outcomes, preparing them effectively for adulthood.

(DfE/DoH, 2015: 19)

Person-centred planning therefore places those directly involved – the pupils themselves – at the centre of the Special Educational Needs and Disability (SEND) processes and the decisions being made. This will hopefully avoid historic practices whereby pupils and families have sometimes been 'done to' rather than being involved and able to voice their views and opinions regarding the decisions that might affect them. This chapter focuses mainly on the voice of the pupil because the next chapter outlines more specifically ways to work with families and to foreground their voice.

DOI: 10.4324/9781003033554-10

The issues related to understanding and implementing person-centred planning will be focused on three fundamental areas:

1 Understanding person-centred planning
2 Involving and valuing everyone's individual voice
3 Embedding person-centred planning across the school.

Person-centred planning is a term that can include placing children and families at the centre of planning, where the focus in this chapter is more specifically on pupils the term child-centred will be used.

Current policy/research context

Understanding person-centred planning

Placing people at the centre of our planning is a principle that is generally agreed upon. The House of Commons Education Committee (2019: 3) identified that the underpinning ethos of the SEND reforms were considered as 'the right ones', yet the practicalities of implementing this approach in busy schools leads to persistent issues. There needs to be a values-based approach to working with people, but in order to provide this approach, professionals need to be provided with the time and resources to undertake activities which will enable pupils and families to be placed at the heart of what we do.

Children's expression in matters affecting them has been a fundamental right in force in England based on the United Nations Conventions on the Rights of the Child (UNCRC) ratified in 1991. Article 12 is outlined below:

> States Parties shall assure to the child who is capable of forming his or her own views the right to express those views freely in all matters affecting the child, the views of the child being given due weight in accordance with the age and maturity of the child.
>
> (United Nations, 1989: 5)

Furthermore, the Council for Disabled Children (2023: n.p) identifies why this right to expression is so important in practice, by noting that when 'children are meaningfully involved, this can change their attitude, behaviour and learning and make them active partners who work with adults to bring about change'.

In relation to Education, Health and Care Plans (EHCPs) the SEN and Disability Code of Practice (DfE/DoH, 2015) outlines the following guidance for involving pupils in the assessment and planning process:

- focus on the child or young person as an individual
- enable children and young people and their parents/carers to express their views, wishes and feelings
- enable children and young people and their parents/carers to be part of the decision-making process
- be easy for children, young people and their parents/carers to understand, and use clear ordinary language and images rather than professional jargon
- highlight the child or young person's strengths and capabilities

- enable the child or young person, and those that know them best to say what they have done, what they are interested in and what outcomes they are seeking in the future
- tailor support to the needs of the individual
- organise assessments to minimise demands on families
- bring together relevant professionals to discuss and agree together the overall approach, and
- deliver an outcomes-focused and coordinated plan for the child or young person and their parents.

(DfE/DoH, 2015: 147–148)

Engaging pupils effectively in discussions about their own learning and support needs is essential. Pupils should be at the centre of planning for and about their needs – they have a unique understanding and perspective on their own needs and a right to have their voice and opinion heard and respected.

Involving and valuing everyone's individual voice

Working with pupils who have more complex SEND can mean that we need to invest more time and creative thought as to how we ensure their voices are heard and listened to. In some cases, communication can present challenges and it is important to realise we might communicate in different ways and these different forms of communication need to be valued. Poor experiences of school or school systems and processes can also make communication more difficult. It is important to consider the ways we work to ensure that we can elicit effective communication with children and young people and their families so we can impact and improve on outcomes.

Child-centred practice was foregrounded with Hart's (1992) paper for the United Nations identifying the benefits of children as being active participatory members of society. Hart's (1992) Ladder of Participation (see Figure 10.1) is a useful model to consider the levels of participation and how we can foster more participatory practices in our school settings.

There has been a societal move towards recognising that children do have a voice and can contribute to their lives and education in a constructive way. It builds self-worth and confidence to engage in community and society more widely. Hart (1992: 37) argues that '[s]chools, as an integral part of the community, should be an obvious venue for fostering young people's understanding and experience of democratic participation'. It is important to recognise that if we want children to become effective members of society it is important to facilitate opportunity otherwise, when they become adults, this may be more challenging for them. Can we say we are truly living in a democratic society if we do not take account of the individuals within society by excluding children's voices?

There were changes in the SEND reforms to support the move towards improvements in foregrounding the voice of the child, for example the inclusion of Section A (DfE/DoH, 2015: 161). Section A is placed first in the EHCP which could indicate the voice of the pupil and their family as having priority. Another change included the requirement to foreground the young person's wishes over the parental wishes once they reach 16 years of age. If the young person has the capacity to make their own decisions, then they must be listened to and their views are taken forward. Additionally, the changes to the terminology in EHCPs to include the word 'outcomes' as opposed to 'objectives' (which were used prior to 2014 on Statements of Special Educational Needs) is a measure taken to try and address the historic challenges of low expectations for learners with SEND by building in a measurable 'outcome'.

The Ladder of Participation

8. Child-initiated, shared decisions with adults
7. Child-initiated and directed
6. Adult-Initiated, shared decisions with children
5. Consulted and informed
4. Assigned but informed

Degrees of Participation

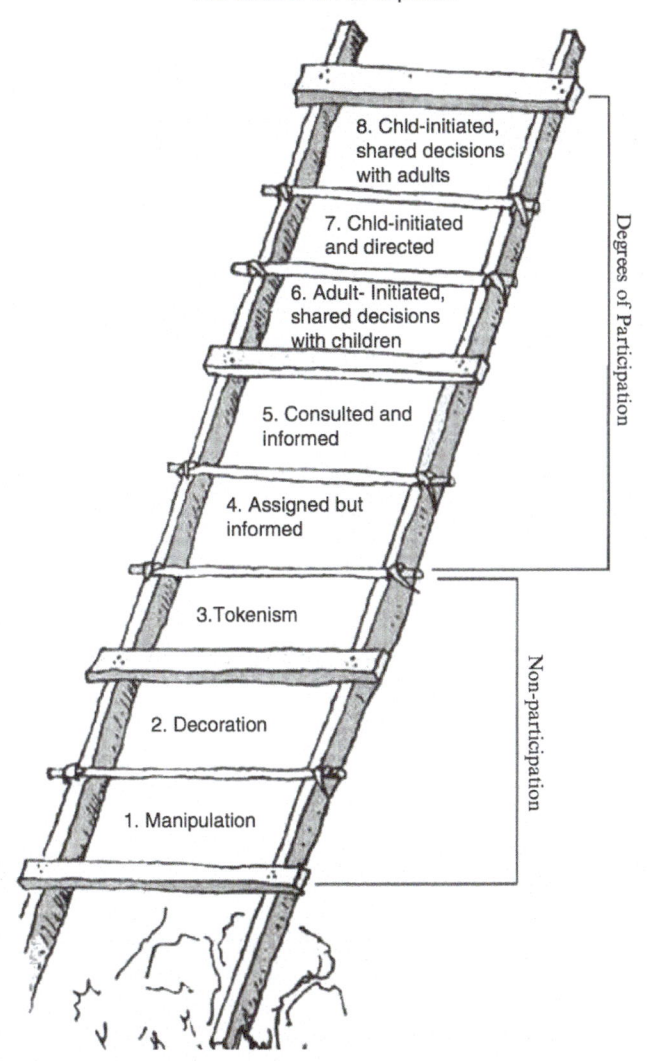

3. Tokenism
2. Decoration
1. Manipulation

Non-participation

Figure 10.1 Hart (1992) Ladder of Participation

As SENCOs, considering adulthood and employment for the pupils we work with might be difficult because we focus on their current need, but it must be part of the longer-term consideration and planning because we have a duty to ensure that children are fully prepared for future stages of their life. Historically there have been challenges leading to poor outcomes. This was identified in the DfE Careers Strategy (2017a) which aims to improve social mobility:

Careers advice for young people with special educational needs and disabilities (SEND) can often be poor and lacking in aspiration. We want careers advice for these young people to be aspirational, personalised and well informed.

(DfE, 2017a: 29)

Chapter 3 of the SEND and Alternative Provision Improvement plan (DfE/DoHSC, 2023) is entitled 'Successful transitions and preparation for adulthood' demonstrating the commitment to make improvements to the lives of young people to 'develop independence, contribute to their community, develop positive friendships, be as healthy as possible, and, for the majority of young people, prepare them for higher education and/or employment' (DfE/DoHSC, 2023: 44). This clearly places a duty on us all to have progression to independence and success in adulthood in mind even if we are working with children in the very early stages of their lives.

However, it is important to recognise that the principles of child-centred practice need to be in place for all children with SEND and not just those with EHCPs. How we foreground voice might take on a range of creative approaches. Article 13 states:

> The child shall have the right to freedom of expression; this right shall include freedom to seek, receive and impart information and ideas of all kinds, regardless of frontiers, either orally, in writing or in print, in the form of art, or through any other media of the child's choice.
>
> (UNCRC, 1989: 5)

We need to be particularly sensitive to this notion because a child's need may impact on their ability to communicate.

Embedding person-centred planning across the school

In a broader sense children's participation in education is fundamental to aid learning and development. If children are passive and disengaged, learning opportunities may be limited. The implementation of strategies to foster active learning, assessment for learning, development of metacognition and independence as well as self-regulation are all aspects of learning where the child should have some engagement and autonomy or voice in the direction of their learning. It is dialogic rather than didactic. It is important that children with SEND have these same opportunities and this is why it is crucial that all staff foster a child-centred approach. These activities take place in the classroom, so teachers need to be able to understand how pupils can contribute if they find communication in the conventional sense more difficult. Often times this is about an ongoing conversation and conversations taking place in a broader sense. So this could include a teacher understanding body language, mannerisms and typical behaviours to inform their understanding of the pupil

School ethos is central to embedding child-centred practices. Culture and power differentials can impact on how successful this is in practice (Rudduck & Fielding, 2006). Unless we create an environment where the child is truly valued then child-centred practice is not likely to be successful. As discussed in Chapters 4 and 7, leadership and a whole school approach is required to embed child-centred practice. Without a child-centred ethos in all areas of SEND, including at State level, anything in policy will be limited in its implementation. The SEND green paper called for 'co-production embedded at every level of the SEND system' (DfE/DoHSC, 2022: 66).

Child-centred practice is an approach which requires time and investment (Rudduck & Fielding, 2006). The challenge faced by SENCOs is the increasing demands related to their workload which then places limits upon their time. In the Workload survey report The time is now Curran et al. (2020: 10) note that 'nearly three-quarters of SENCOs (74% *n* = 1,058) cited administration tasks as taking up the majority of their allocated SENCO time (previous survey 71%). This is a significant issue if SENCOs are appointed to be the strategic leaders for inclusion in schools. One SENCO who participated in this survey stated:

> I cannot bear the fact that I now spend my time doing paperwork and not using my skills, experience and understanding of learners with additional needs to work with learners, work with colleagues, to support learners with additional needs or be co-productive with parents of learners with additional needs.
>
> (Curran et al., 2020: 10)

The SEN and Disability Code of Practice (DfE/DoH, 2015) clearly outlines the requirement for child-centred practice and yet if SENCOs are not provided with time to undertake their role fully, it will impact on the support and provision that can be put into place. Without the resources, including the allocation of time, person-centred practices cannot be integrated into practice.

Planning for practice

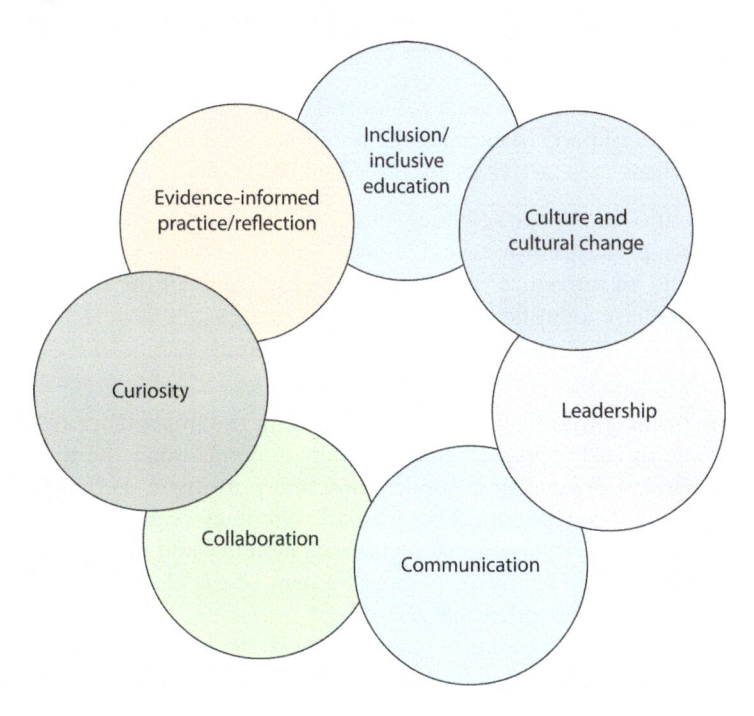

Figure 10.2 Key principles model

To be able to really ensure that pupils are meaningfully involved in decisions and planning for their provision, support and educational outcomes requires a commitment to ***inclusive values***, which underpin and ensure that barriers to participation and access are removed and there is an ***inclusive*** strengths-based focus rather than a deficit difficulties-led approach. Developing and adapting ***communication and collaborative practices*** so that they are accessible and meet the needs of the child and an approach based on ***professional curiosity*** where we actively seek deeper understanding by asking questions and showing a sincere and genuine interest in the child as an individual are essential.

Understanding person-centred planning

Developing an *inclusive culture* that recognises the value of placing children at the centre throughout their educational journey is essential. Fostering these practices in educational settings will enable children to be part of society and understand their voices are important and should be heard in the community in adulthood too.

Reflective Activity

- What do staff in your setting currently understand by the term 'person-centred planning'?
- Is this a term that is used and understood by all – pupils, staff and parents/carers?
- How do you know?
- What is currently in place and working effectively?
- What could be done to develop understanding further?
- Make a list of activities in your school which you would consider are child-centred, e.g. school council, target setting, peer-mentoring, interventions, annual reviews for EHCPs, etc.
- Now use the diagram of the ladder (Figure 10.1) to place each of these activities against the level of participation for the pupils involved in that activity.
- Reflect on where these activities are placed on the ladder.
  - Is the positioning of the activities suitable?
  - Would you prefer to move them higher?
  - What could be introduced to reach the higher rungs of the ladder for the activities you have identified?

A key part of person-centred planning is understanding the importance of individualised outcomes relevant to each pupil. In this, broader outcomes than the narrow academic and attainment outcomes need to be understood and prioritised, as these will be key to the individual child's development. These broad outcomes (e.g. social communication and interaction development; emotional regulation; memory and organisational skills) are arguably more important in terms of the development of the child as a whole, preparing them holistically for an independent life ahead.

The House of Commons Education Committee (2019: 21) identified that pupils with SEND are not effectively supported into adulthood:

> The 2014 reforms were not just about education. We are particularly concerned to hear that there is a lack of support and development for wider outcomes than just education and employment opportunities. We heard a significant amount of evidence, particularly from children and young people, about the importance of their support addressing their life goals and future plans. We were disappointed to hear that these important aspects of children and young people's lives were not suitably addressed in the support and plans for children and young people with SEND.

In the development of those broader outcomes, there is a need to ensure that the focus for the outcomes and associated provision is truly child-centred – based on what is important and relevant to the individual pupil, rather than based on deficit models of thinking relating to what 'we' believe, decide, or presume, the 'other' needs to do, or learn. Such an approach challenges traditional ways of determining what is 'normal' and therefore to be valued. Fortunately, such historic practices are now increasingly being challenged, particularly through, for example greater understanding and research around neurodiversity, with greater acceptance of the different ways that neurodiverse individuals will interact and relate to their environment and that those different ways need to be accepted and valued, rather than undermined and seen as something to be changed.

Instead of adopting approaches which de-value individual strengths and force conformity to a traditional sense of 'normal' – for example setting a target requiring eye contact and then placing emphasis on ensuring that pupils with autism must continually focus on improving eye contact, effective practices now focus on collaboratively target setting on an aspect they have a desire to improve on through a child-centred approach. Outcomes and provision targets can focus on what is more appropriate and meaningful for the individual if they are part of the conversation and personally invested.

Thus, as the DfE (2017b: 13) note:

> A key issue to consider is the goal of any support or intervention. In recent years there have been a number of debates raised about different interventions which have been put in place to support children and young people, particularly with regard to individuals with autism spectrum conditions …. It is important to remember that therapy or support should be based around the needs of the individual learner and their family's views rather than a desire to make a child "fit in" to a classroom situation.

Pupils will have a unique experience and understanding of their own needs and approaches that are supportive for them. We therefore need to focus on how to value and capture their unique insights and use that as a way to inform and guide the development of provision and practice moving forward.

Reflective Activity

- What systems and processes are currently in place to really listen to, understand and respond to pupil's unique insights into their own experience, needs and approaches that support them?
- What works well?
- Is this consistent across the whole school?
- Are there other approaches that could be developed further?
- How are broader outcomes understood in your school setting?
- What is in place to develop and prioritise the holistic development of all pupils, particularly those with SEND?
- How is the child engaged and involved in meaningful collaboration and partnership to identify the focus for those broader outcomes?
- Do the broad outcomes that are identified respect the individual's needs, rather than focus on outdated expectations of what is 'normal/expected'?
- Do all staff understand the importance of a focus on broader outcomes, or is this still narrowed in the classroom to a focus on academic outcomes?
- How could this be positively addressed?

Developing and integrating child-centred practices will take time and investment. It involves **culture-change** and so this is not something that can be quickly achieved with a change to process. However, that said, there are useful templates to support effective methods, which are steps towards supporting, developing and evaluating child-centred practices in schools – e.g. Helen Sanderson Associates (2023) Person-centred Thinking tools (http://helensandersonassociates.co.uk/person-centred-practice/person-centred-thinking-tools/). Some of the practical tools include:

- **The perfect week** – requires the pupil to outline their perfect week, but can then be used to personalise aspects of their support
- **The doughnut** – clarifies roles and responsibilities. This is helpful when looking at multi-agency working, setting the expectations and how to work creatively together
- **Presence to contribution** – this is a visual representation which illustrates different levels of engagement and helps to consider possibilities for taking actions to make positive change.

Involving and valuing everyone's individual voice

Once an understanding of what person-centred planning is has been established in school, there will be a need to develop this further by considering the practical ways that children are positively enabled to participate and have their voice heard.

Some children and adults may not be in a position to contribute in conventional ways and this may require us to view *communication* in innovative ways. Children with SEND may not have the language and communication skills to be able to fully understand and explain barriers to learning that they experience or the support that they might need. Careful consideration needs to be given to ways that all pupils with SEND can be effectively supported to provide meaningful feedback. We need to be *curious* to help explore communication in a broader sense.

Case Study – Supporting pupils who are pre-verbal to share their thoughts and views

Mark Roberts

The information below is summarised from my doctoral thesis which focused on questioning and reflecting on the challenges that pupils who are pre-verbal or who have very limited communication systems are able to meaningfully share their thoughts and views.

In my research I explored the ways in which a Special School listened to pupils with complex communication needs, how the school enabled the pupils to express themselves and how the staff responded to these expressions.

I conducted this research through the creation and analysis of four detailed case studies, constructed from a range of evidence. From this research I have identified the following recommendations relevant to SENCOs.

Recommendations

Education Health and Care Plan (EHCP)

Ensure that the Section A is a document which grows each year and into which pupils and parents/carers are invited to engage with their previous comments, alongside adding their latest views and experiences. This builds a much richer picture of pupil and parents/carers views of school and enables a dialogue to emerge.

Regularly (three or four times a year) review the Section A to avoid it becoming a yearly 'tick box' and engage parents/carers in the evolving narrative of their child's views about school and learning.

Use local authority formats as guides rather than as a series of 'questions to answer' and give time and space for pupils to comment.

Avoid seeking or encouraging pupils to give 'correct' answers to prompts and instead be open to the answers that pupils give and be willing to explore them further.

Ensure that these views (from the Section A) are shared widely with staff.

Classroom practice

Ensure teachers are confident and comfortable with any specific communication approaches – not just the TA and 1:1. The teacher is planning the lessons and learning experiences and needs a deep knowledge of the ways in which pupils will be able to respond in order to ensure that activities are inclusive.

Take a 'total communication' approach and value all the ways in which pupils choose to communicate to create an inclusive classroom approach to communication. Do not limit pupil's routes to expression or value one communication method over another.

Be aware of the tendency to over-interpret pupil's responses and invent narratives which explain their behaviours and answers. Ensure that you 'listen' to what the pupil is communicating and do not adjust their answers to fit your context or expectations.

Be consistent in the use of symbols and their meanings, and ensure these are taught and understood.

Establish systems to accurately record what was communicated which include the manner of the communication, the context, and the support and prompts that elicited and facilitated the communication.

When possible, avoid 'time pressured' communication and encourage approaches which provide children with additional time – or time to give pre-prepared answers which pupils have been asked and answered in advance.

Focus upon core vocabulary, rather than providing key word sheets which can provide pupils with an answer sheet. Flip questions to ensure that core vocabulary is needed to answer rather than subject specific vocabulary (What happens when a rock is eroded?)

Treat pupils communication seriously and avoid identifying the communication system as the issue, rather than their engagement, understanding or attitude to learning.

176 *Developing effective person-centred planning*

As SENCOs we need to ensure our schools can adopt creative ways to value communication in its different forms. A 'Total Communication' (SENSE, 2023) approach supports individuals to connect using the methods which are suitable to them personally. Communication can take on a range of forms which might include speech, sign, touch, movement, gesture, sound, art or dance

Below are some examples from the SENSE (2023) website (https://www.sense.org.uk/information-and-advice/communication/total-communication/) of different formal and non-formal types of communication that can be used:

- **Non-verbal**: including body movements, breathing patterns and eye pointing. Textures, smells, temperature, intensive interaction and routine can also support communication by allowing an individual to anticipate what is going to happen next
- **Language-based communication**: including speech, lip reading, Tadoma, deafblind manual alphabet, giving and receiving information in large print, braille and block alphabet, and sign systems, including British Sign Language (BSL) and Makaton. Sign systems may be independent sign, on body sign or hand under hand sign
- **Symbol systems**: including using objects of reference (real objects and object symbols), Bliss, Widgit, Mayer-Johnson, Picture Exchange Communication System (PECS), line drawings, pictures and photographs.

(Sense, 2023)

Embedding person-centred planning across the school

Person-centred planning should be embedded into the ethos of school in order for it to be truly effective. A SENCO alone may be able to implement certain practices when meeting with parents/carers or reviewing provisions, but unless the school as a whole is placing the child as central to planning then practice will not improve. There are ways in which to influence the school systems and processes which could in turn provide more inclusive learning opportunities.

> **Reflective Activity**
>
> - What systems and processes do you already have in place to gather pupil feedback in effective and meaningful ways?
> - How do you know what pupils think about the support that they have in place and any additional support needs?
> - What do you do with the feedback that you receive?
> - How do pupils know how you use and value the feedback that is given by them?

As we have explored previously (Chapters 5 and 6), the EEF's (2020: 10) first recommendation in the Special Educational Needs in Mainstream Schools Guidance Report is to 'Create a positive and supportive environment for all pupils, without exception'. Child-centred practice is clearly highlighted in the practical activities that can be adopted in the classroom to include all pupils to be active participants. This just requires careful thought and planning on including pupils who may find it difficult to share their views in a class situation:

> Asking children to 'share what their partner said' allows quieter children to have their answers shared without needing to feel exposed by having to share it themselves. Similarly, allowing a child the chance to write their answer instead of voicing it, or giving them warning time before sharing an answer, supports maximum participation.
>
> Other approaches schools could consider include:
> - cards with questions stems as scaffolds;
> - non-verbal answers to questions—pupils can stand and sit, or give a thumbs up or thumbs down, to agree or disagree with an answer; and
> - using post-it notes to encourage pupils to add their views to topics.
>
> (EEF, 2020: 12)

Importantly, the report also identifies that:

> this does not require a comprehensive understanding of every type of SEND found in classrooms. Effective teachers of pupils with SEND are focused on learning more about the individual profiles of the pupils they teach and maximising the effectiveness of their teaching.
>
> (EEF, 2020: 12)

Reflective Activity

- Based on the suggestions in the report, what practical strategies could you encourage teachers to adopt in the class?
- How could you encourage teachers to adopt these strategies, for example supporting them to see the benefits, drawing on their motivation to improve outcomes for pupils?
- How can we be more critical of our own potential bias when communication is more challenging? For example recognising communication is more broad than just speech.

Rudduck and Fielding (2006: 219) refer to the perils of popularity in relation to child-centred practices, which could lead to 'surface compliance' which they explain is a 'a quick response that focuses on "how to do it" rather than a reflective review of "why we might want to do it"'. Child-centred practice is not a 'tick-box' exercise. The key principles of *leadership* in *inclusive values* will be at the heart of a school with a child-centred ethos. Settings where the child's voice is embedded and considered at all levels are likely to be successful. For example there are a range of processes and aspects of school which do not necessarily foreground child-centred practices, yet if these were viewed with a child-centred lens, it can become clearer as to how we can become more successful. Complete Table 10.1 to reflect on the child-centred nature of activities in your school setting:

178 Developing effective person-centred planning

Table 10.1 Table to review child-centred practices

Process	Not child-centred	Child-centred	My school
Writing pupil profiles	The staff member writes the profiles based on their knowledge of the child	The pupils collaboratively contribute to, or write their profile to share with staff.	
School council meetings	School council meetings are led by staff who control the conversation and the recorded outcomes.	Child-led e.g. pupils chairing the meetings etc. There is good representation from the different groups of children in the school.	
Interviews for new staff	Pupils are not part of the process of interviewing staff. They have no say in who will be appointed.	Pupils take an active role in interviewing new staff. Their views are taken into consideration.	

Wall et al. (2019) include eight factors for supporting participation from children from the earliest age, which include the following:

Definition
Power
Inclusivity
Listening
Time and Space
Approaches
Processes
Purposes.

They note that 'each factor may be considered individually, it is also important that they are treated as interconnected and interdependent' (Wall et al., 2019: 275). The first factor from the list 'Definition' has been chosen as a focus. The supporting prompts (or questions) have been used to create an activity related to 'voice' and how we ensure we include all voices in our schools. Use the following grid as a reflective exercise (Table 10.2), which includes others in the school to help to conceptualise what child-centred is for your setting. By triangulating the responses, this could enhance your understanding of your school, feed into the development of your policies and may also support the direction of training in this area.

Table 10.2 Key factor of 'Definition' based on Wall et al. (2019)

Key factor of 'Definition' based on Wall et al. (2019)	My responses to the questions	Others' responses to the questions (could be children, teachers, leaders, etc.)
What does voice look like/sound like in my setting?		
How do I identify voice in practice?		
How do I tune into different types of voice (s)?		
How do I listen to silence?		
If voice is important, what is it more important than?		
How does voice change over time?		

Developing effective person-centred planning 179

Wall et al. (2019: 268) note the eight factors 'are not presented as an answer or recipe, but rather as the starting point to dialogue. We assert that for children's talk to be encouraged, adults have to be engaged in talk too'. Therefore their principled approach is to underpin every aspect of person-centred practice with dialogue. The premise that 'dialogue' is more than one voice or position, support an inclusive and valued understanding of all individuals' perspectives. By completing Table 10.2, it will help you to facilitate this approach in practice by capturing your own and a range of perspectives from others. After completing this activity return to your own responses to reflect and consider if you have adjusted your position.

Arnott and Wall (2022) Talking Point Posters were created from a graphic facilitator process. The 'Enable' Talking Point Poster (see Figure 10.3) is one of eight posters developed by the Look Who's Talking Project run by members of the School of Education at the University of Strathclyde. All posters are freely downloadable from the project website: https://www.voicebirthtoseven.co.uk. The posters can be a way to open up dialogue with colleagues, for example the 'Enable' poster might be useful to discuss in a staff meeting to help conceptualise child-centred practice in school. Wall et al. (2019) argue, that dialogue is required to be able to value the position of others, it is not just a simple tick list. It is part of what we do every day and how we interact with others. Talking with staff is a key part of the process.

Figure 10.3 Arnott and Wall (2022) Talking Point Poster – 'Enable'

Another important aspect we need to adopt are more holistic approaches. Bronfenbrenner's (1979) ecological systems theory places the individual at the centre and considers the importance of the wider connections and influences in school, outside of school, the wider community and even macro influences such as the political context. The following Case Study outlines how this might relate to working with a child in school.

Case Study – Working with Pupils to Develop Effective Person-Centred Planning

Ali Keysell

This case study focuses on developing effective person-centred planning for a pupil with Social, Emotional and Mental Health (SEMH) specifically, Attention Deficit Hyperactivity Disorder (ADHD) needs using the holistic approach recommended by the EEF (2020) Special Educational Needs in Mainstream School Guidance Report. It draws on Psychologist Urie Bronfenbrenner's (1979) Ecological Systems Theory of Child Development. Some reflections are also taken from Paul Dix (2017) When the Adults Change Everything Changes.

Pupil A attends a large mainstream secondary school. Pupil A has a diagnosis of ADHD and is medicated. There are a range of home-based factors currently impacting on his emotional regulation and sense of belonging.

The intensity, frequency and duration of Pupil A's behaviour indicated that his needs were not being fully met from when he started in year 7. Pupil A quickly became a pupil who was receiving multiple, daily 'on-calls' from lessons which meant that he was spending a large amount of time in 'reflection' and 'detention'.

The first step was to look at the four areas set out below (Figure 10.4) in the planning quadrant to 'Build a holistic picture of the pupil's learning needs from several sources, such as the pupil, parents/carers, colleagues and external professionals' (EEF, 2020: 15).

What are the barriers to learning that the pupil is experiencing and in which subjects? • RAG rating of pupil's timetable • Round Robin to teachers • Classroom observations / Learning walks • Reviews of current strategies in place • Face to face meeting with parents/carers • Parental review with the ADHD medication nurse	What are their strengths, interests, and aspirations? • CAT scores and Reading Age both above average • Good relationships with SENCO, Head of Year 7 and Student Support Manager • Likes animals, especially dogs
What support do they need to access the curriculum? • Personalised timetable (time-limited) • 1:1 Mentor support • 1:1 Emotion Coaching (the Incredible 5 point scale) • An adult 'Champion' (Rita Pierson, Educator) • Time with the therapy dog • Restorative justice time when things go wrong	How can the school's provision be improved to support this pupil to learn? • Communication with staff • Communication with parents/carers • Staff training ('Tea and Toast Tuesdays', 'Wednesday Workshops', CPD shorts) • Emotionally literate staff body • Emotionally literate team of support around the pupil

Figure 10.4 EEF (2020: 15) planning quadrant – Special Educational Needs in Mainstream Schools Guidance Report

The implementation of the plan involved several key staff members. Responsibility for overseeing of the plan and communicating regularly with all involved was taken on by the SENCO. A programme of restorative justice was implemented by the Head of Year as an alternative to the pupil sitting in 'Reflection' without any of the issues arising from the lesson being addressed. The pupil received time with the therapy dog, 1:1 emotion coaching and 1:1 mentor support in the times that he was not in lessons that were currently proving too stressful for him (identified by pupil, staff and parents/carers). Regular meetings with parents/carers also played a key role in the cycle.

It was apparent that a holistic approach to this pupil's needs was necessary, as home life was sometimes stressful for Pupil A, his parents/carers and siblings (reported by parents/carers at the Assess stage of the Graduated Approach).

'Bronfenbrenner's ecological systems theory views child development as a complex system of relationships affected by multiple levels of the surrounding environment, from immediate settings of family and school to broad cultural values, laws and customs (Figure 10.5). To study a child's development then, we must not only look at the child and their immediate environment, but also the interaction of the larger environment as well' (Simply Psychology, 2023: n.p).

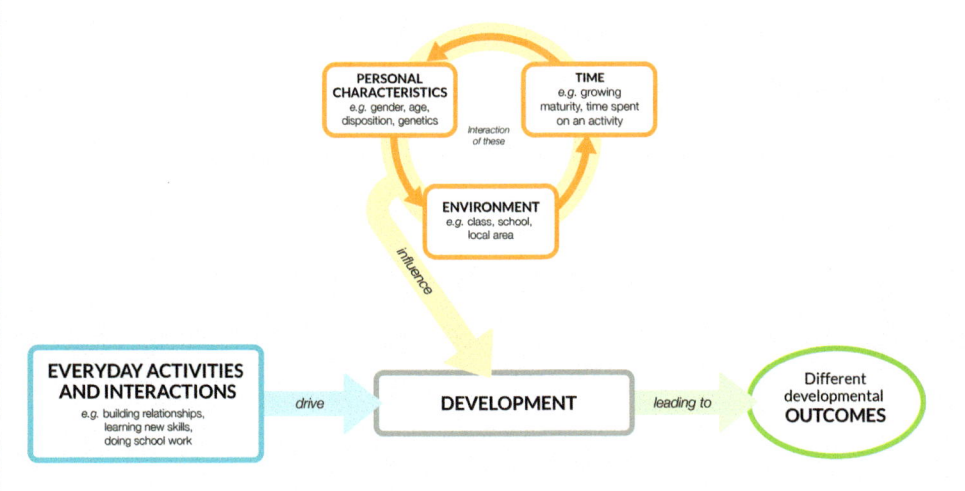

Figure 10.5 EEF (2020) Bronfenbrenner diagram

In the background, the SEND team ran several workshops that were common, individualised, and targeted. 'Tea and Toast Tuesdays' provided staff with key information about the individual pupil and strategies to support him in class. 'Wednesday Workshops' and Continuing Professional Development (CPD) shorts targeted the area of need (SEMH/ADHD) more broadly, as did workshops on emotionally literate classrooms and linking with whole school training on the 'Paul Dix Approach'. Two key areas taken from the Paul Dix Approach being 'emotional currency' (the importance of relationship building with pupils) and 'picking up your own tab' (the importance of negotiating with pupils without them being removed from the

> classroom thus giving the pupil the message that 'I can't deal with you'. This was particularly key in Pupil A's case as he was often receiving this message at home too and was feeling insecure and increasingly untrusting of adults.
>
> Whilst continued layered support remains in place for Pupil A, he is no longer a 'high profile' pupil. There is a good working relationship between home and school and Pupil A is clearly showing that he is using the strategies that he has been taught through emotion coaching and is beginning to identify when he needs 'time out' to re-set rather than being removed from class by an adult.
>
> The current outcomes for Pupil A remain positive, however, EEF Guidance reminds us that 'pupils' development is not linear. As pupils age, the complexity of their needs will change' (EEF, 2020: 5) The Graduated Approach for this pupil will continue, alongside other pupils on the SEND register, and those who may need to be added to the SEND register.

Key to support and active participation of pupils with SEND is the inclusion of clear and individualised outcomes and child-centred support and provision for transition points children will experience. The DfE/DoHSC (2023: 45) outlines their commitment to address this gap:

> the Department for Education is developing good practice guidance to support consistent, timely, high-quality transitions for children and young people with SEND and in alternative provision. This will ultimately look at transitions between all stages of education from early years and will focus initially on transitions into and out of post-16 settings. This includes transitions into employment, adult services and for young people leaving alternative provision at the end of key stage 4, building on learning from the recent Alternative Provision Transition Fund.

Aspirations are important and we need to recognise that our pupils are the next generation of adults and that we are supporting them to realise their potential in the longer term as adults contributing to society. Therefore having an understanding of transition points leading to adulthood is important.

> **Case Study – A Case Study on the Integration of RARPA and Preparing for Adulthood for Students with SEND in Further Education**
>
> **Nikki Townsend**
>
> When planning a curriculum for students with more complex SEND within Further Education consideration must be given to the best approach to use which enables further progression and EHCP outcomes to be met.
>
> Students have often completed a vast range of accredited courses during their schooling, and this can present challenges for Further Education Establishments. Furthermore, for many learners an accredited course is not an appropriate option. To ensure an outstanding learning experience, which is meaningful, progressive and personalised to suit individual needs, some colleges have adopted the Recognising and Recording Progress and Achievement (RARPA) structure (Education & Training

Foundation, 2022). There are six stages which form a cycle and make up the RARPA process:

1. Establishing a starting point via a baseline assessment
2. Target setting
3. Formative review of learning
4. Summative assessment of achievement
5. Planning the next step
6. Setting new targets.

The curriculum is designed around preparation for adulthood and includes the four strands which are:

- Independent living
- Employability
- Community inclusion
- Health.

These help to support young people to transition from childhood into and adult life and prepares them for the changes that they will encounter on their journey.

Independent living – the majority of learners will have access to a house/flat where they can learn vital life skills such as cooking, cleaning and changing a bed.

Employability – students will take part in either a supported/unsupported work experience placement external to college or an experience of work, which is much more sheltered and carried out within the college premises and across vocational areas.

Community inclusion – students have access to the local community, they will undertake shopping for their cooking, access cafes and libraries. In addition to this they may also undertake social action within the college year and give something back to their local community by volunteering of fund raising. Guest speakers are often invited from the emergency services, DSS and local stakeholders.

Health – students take part in personal, social and health education which covers a variety of topics including personal hygiene, sexual and mental health.

This method of integrating the RARPA structure with preparation into adulthood has been extremely successful and has allowed learners to reach their full potential and EHCP outcomes without the rigidity of a prescriptive qualification. For some learners this will include a multidisciplinary approach and individual timetables to allow them to receive the therapies and interventions required.

Reflective Activity

Continue to reflect on ways that person-centred planning is meaningfully embedded into your school practices:

- Make a list of the strengths in you setting with regard to child-centred practice
- Identify any barriers and consider which of these can be addressed
- Make an action plan for addressing the barriers you are able to address to improve practices in your setting.

Concluding comments and reflections

The case studies illustrate the importance of a collaborative approach to embedding child-centred practices in educational settings. There may be pockets of good practice where individuals implement child-centred processes or approaches, however without buy-in from all teachers implementation and outcomes will be hampered. Person-centred planning should be embedded into the ethos of school and SENCOs may be in a position to influence the direction of the school towards this goal at a strategic, senior leadership level. We need to be mindful of working with pupils with more complex SEND to ensure their voices are heard and listened to. Communication happens in different ways and these different forms of communication need to be valued. Poor experiences of school or school systems and processes can hinder communication, for example parents/carers may be less inclined to engage if their experiences in the past have been more challenging. It is important to consider the ways we work with others and how we value them to ensure that we can build the foundation for effective communication with children and young people and their families to improve on person-centre practice and ultimately improve on outcomes.

Individual Reflection

- What new information/learning have you gained from this chapter?
- What are your key reflections?
- What are your next steps/actions as a result?

References

Arnott, L. and Wall, K. (2022) *The theory and practice of voice in early childhood: An international perspective*. Abingdon: Routledge.

Bronfenbrenner, U. (1979) *The ecology of human development*. Cambridge, MA: Harvard University Press.

Council for Disabled Children (2023) https://councilfordisabledchildren.org.uk/ (accessed 1.5.23).

Curran, H., Moloney, H., Heavey, A. and Boddison, A. (2020) *The time is now: Addressing missed opportunities for Special Educational Needs Support and Coordination in our schools*. Available from: https://www.bathspa.ac.uk/media/bathspaacuk/education-/research/senco-workload/National-SENCO-Workload-Survey-Report-Jan-2020.pdf (accessed 1.5.23).

DfE (2017a) *Careers Strategy: Making the most of everyone's skills and talents*. https://www.gov.uk/government/publications/careers-strategy-making-the-most-of-everyones-skills-and-talents (accessed 1.5.23).

DfE (2017b) *SEN Support: A rapid evidence assessment research report*. Coventry: DfE.

DfE/DoH (2015) *Special Educational Needs and Disability Code of Practice for 0 to 25 year olds*. London: TSO.

DfE/DoHSC (2022). *SEND Review: Right support, right place, right time*. Available from: https://www.gov.uk/government/consultations/send-review-right-support-right-place-right-time (accessed 30.5.23).

DfE/DoHSC (2023) *Special Educational Needs and Disabilities (SEND) and Alternative Provision Improvement Plan – Right support, right place, right time*. London: HMSO.

Dix, P. (2017) *When the adults change everything changes*. Williston, VT: Independent Thinking Press.

Education & Training Foundation (2022) *Recognising and Recording Progress and Achievement (RARPA)*. Available from: https://www.et-foundation.co.uk/professional-development/special-educational-needs-disabilities/teaching-and-learning/rarpa/ (accessed 1.5.23).

EEF (2020) *SEN in mainstream schools guidance report.* London: EEF.

Hart, R.A. (1992) *Children's participation from tokenism to citizenship.* Available from: https://www.unicef-irc.org/publications/100-childrens-participation-from-tokenism-to-citizenship.html (accessed 1.5.23).

Helen Sanderson Associates (2023) Person-centred Thinking Tools. http://helensandersonassociates.co.uk/person-centred-practice/person-centred-thinking-tools/ (accessed 1.5.23).

House of Commons Education Committee (2019) *Special Educational Needs and Disabilities.* London: House of Commons.

Rudduck, J. and Fielding, M. (2006) 'Student voice and the perils of popularity'. *Educational Review* 58(2), 219–231.

SENSE (2023) SENSE | For people with complex disabilities. https://www.sense.org.uk/ (accessed 1.5.23).

Simply Psychology (2023) Bronfenbrenner's Ecological Systems Theory. https://www.simplypsychology.org/bronfenbrenner.html (accessed 1.5.23).

United Nations (1989) *Convention on the Rights of the Child.* Available from: https://www.unicef.org.uk/wp-content/uploads/2010/05/UNCRC_united_nations_convention_on_the_rights_of_the_child.pdf (accessed 1.5.23).

Wall, K., Cassidy, C., Robinson, C., Hall, E., Beaton, M.C., Kanyal, M. and Mitra, D. (2019) 'Look who's talking: Factors for considering the facilitation of very young children's voices'. *Journal of Early Childhood Research* 17(4), 263–278.

11 Effective partnership working with parents/carers

In this chapter, we critically examine and explore the following key aspects:

- The importance and value of meaningful partnership with parents/carers
- Recognising and challenging persistent inequalities
- The impact of social capital
- Trust
- Communication skills
- Relationships
- Removing barriers for parents/carers
- Participation models
- Stages of co-production

Key issues

The importance of working with parents/carers as partners is not new, it has been embedded in policy for many years (Warnock, 1978; DfE, 1994; DfES, 2001; DfE/DoH, 2015) but this aspect of practice still presents with challenges. The positive impact on children when parents/carers are engaged is well documented with evidence that it can help to close the attainment gap for children from more disadvantaged backgrounds (Axford et al., 2019). Therefore identifying potential barriers to effective parent/carer engagement, so these can be addressed, is a key area to consider for the role of the Special Educational Needs Coordinator (SENCO).

Issues persist in parent/carer engagement and confidence, despite the reforms of the Special Educational Needs and Disability (SEND) system (Children and Families Act, 2014) aiming to improve on identified cultural and systemic issues. Some of the key issues that will be explored in this chapter include:

1 Understanding the importance and value of meaningful parent/carer partnership
2 Recognising and challenging persistent inequalities in parents/carers' experiences
3 Embedding whole-school approaches to meaningful engagement with parents/carers.

Principles of effective relationships with parents/carers and valuing them as equal partners were evident in Warnock's report (1978: 150), which called for parents/carers' 'full

DOI: 10.4324/9781003033554-11

involvement' in their child's education. There was also recognition of diversity and that parents/carers may 'differ widely in their attitudes, temperament, insight, knowledge, ability and other personal qualities' which may influence 'the extent and nature of the help that they require' (1978: 151). This highlights how critical it is for SENCOs to work closely with parents/carers to be able to accommodate their needs. Yet, this way of working will make demands on the professionals' time and requires genuine opportunity for dialogue with parents/carers, something which is a challenge in the current context with increased workload (Curran et al., 2020). Of course it is also important to recognise that SENCOs are not a homogeneous group and that their experience, knowledge, skills and confidence in the role may vary considerably. It is important that professionals are also appropriately trained and supported to be able to work with parents/carers that may require additional guidance and support.

Current policy/research context

Understanding the importance and value of meaningful parent/carer partnership

Underpinning the need to develop effective systems and processes to support meaningful parent/carer partnership needs to be an embedded understanding and belief in the value of the perspectives and knowledge that parents/carers bring of their own child. As the DfE (2017: 13) identify: 'parents are the best placed individuals to provide details on the health and early development of their child and the support that they have received outside the school system, particularly when a school is first assessing a child's needs'.

Although the principles for effective parent/carer engagement were laid out in 1978, the implementation in practice has given rise to issues. Warnock (1978: 150) warned against this danger, noting that unless effective parent/carer engagement was realised in practice, the 'purpose of our report will be frustrated'. Yet the current context includes persistent issues leading to complex systems, inequalities and mistrust. The proposals in the SEND and Alternative Provision Improvement Plan (DfE/DoHSC, 2023: 6) look to address this: 'we want to ensure that parents experience a less adversarial system and restore their trust that their children will get prompt access to the support they need'.

The Children and Families Act (2014) increased parent/carer rights to support collaborative practice and to provide more choice for parents/carers by mandating 'the importance of the child and his or her parent, or the young person, participating as fully as possible in decisions' as a general principle underpinning practice. The change in language in the Act omits the reference to serving notice on parents/carers when referring to the assessment of need (DES, 1981). Under section 36, the local authority must 'consult the child's parent or the young person' (The Children and Families Act, 2014: 30) which illustrates the shift in language in the legal system towards a more collaborative approach for decision making.

Despite these changes and greater rights for parents/carers, section 36 still specifies 'the authority must determine whether it may be necessary for special educational provision to be made for the child or young person in accordance with an EHC plan' (2014: 30). So, despite empowering parents/carers in the decision-making, this still illustrates the power of the authority in the process. This may therefore continue to limit the level of participation and opportunity for decision making for both parents/carers and schools and can serve to create a 'coproduction illusion' (Boddison & Soan, 2021) because there might be very effective working relationships in schools, which are then essentially overridden by external forces such as State level decisions presiding over parents/carers and SENCOs' intentions. The DfE/DoHSC (2023) proposals for SEND aim to address this through the national system which 'should be co-produced with families, children and young people, so we can build their confidence that the system will meet their needs quickly and effectively' (DfE/DoHSC, 2023: 8).

The EEF (2018: 6) Working with Parents to Support Children's Learning Guidance Report notes:

Schools should be optimistic about the potential of working with parents

- There is an established link between the home learning environment at all ages and children's performance at school.
- Schools and parents have a shared priority to deliver the best outcomes for their children.

It is therefore important to take an optimistic position, to recognise the value gained from parent/carer perspectives and not to view their position as irrelevant or less important. The following highlights how essential some knowledge held by parents/carers is:

Parents are the best placed individuals to provide details on the health and early development of their child and the support they have received outside the school system, particularly when a school is first assessing a child's needs. They can also provide information on whether any difficulties have been noted at home or elsewhere, to help to understand whether they are limited to or exacerbated by the school environment. All of this information is crucial for a thorough assessment of a child's strengths and weaknesses.

(DfE, 2017: 13)

Valuing parents/carers and the contribution they can make to supporting pupils is therefore fundamental.

Recognising and challenging persistent inequalities in parents/carers' experiences

Parent/carer confidence with the SEND system has been a key focus in the past evident in the Lamb Report (2009) but this has really come to the fore recently as an issue (House of Commons Education Committee, 2019; NAO, 2019; DfE/DoHSC, 2022; DfE/DoHSC, 2023).

In recent years, we have seen a significant (more than 80% increase) in the number of Tribunal cases, showing a significant level of parent/carer dissatisfaction and lack of confidence and inequitable experiences of the SEND system (NAO, 2019).

Systems to address the inequities that parents/carers experience within the SEND system are still not effective, with the House of Commons Education Committee (2019: 18–19) identifying the continued 'postcode lottery' of access to support services and advice and ways that the 'complex, awful and often unnecessarily antagonistic experience for parents can prevent them from accessing their entitlements'.

Very importantly, therefore, the discrepancies and inequalities in parent/carer access to information and support has now been openly acknowledged. Disappointingly, this is clearly linked to parent/carer social capital, and not on the underlying needs of the pupil, who should be at the centre of all assessments and decisions about provision. As the House of Commons Education Committee (2019: 77) note:

- 'Social capital plays a huge role in access to information and advice. We were told that some parents cannot access the system at all, and that it could be difficult to know what the next steps were, or what help is available. We heard that paperwork was too complicated and long for some parents and could be difficult to understand.'
- 'One local authority told us that parents and teachers believe that the "EHCP system" favours parents who are wealthy and well-educated, and that other parents can be hard to reach, do not know their rights, and are scared of the system.'

Lack of parent/carer confidence in the wider SEND systems and processes is challenging for the SENCO because SENCOs are often the first point of contact for parents/carers and can also been seen as the gatekeepers to accessing resources in schools as 'the power to decide appropriate provision resides mostly with SENCOs' (Mather, 2016: 7). The gap between parent/carer expectations and the reality of what school can offer can cause tensions in working relationships. If parents/carers lose confidence in the system, then it can be difficult for the SENCO to gain and maintain the confidence of parents/carers at school level.

Trust has been foregrounded as a key factor for effective working relationships with parents/carers. Issues with communication can impact on the level of trust a parent/carer has in the system, school and provisions for their child, which ultimately can lead to lack of trust in relationships with the SENCO. Essentially relationships are key in the current system and Mather (2016: 11) claims trust is key, which comes from an 'open' honest, supportive and co-operative relationship'. The DfE/DoHSC (2023) have shown a commitment to ensuring that parent/carer voice and participation is key to the development of effective SEND practices moving forward. It is essential to be able to regain and build on parents/carers' trust:

build parents' trust: parents and carers experience a fairer, easily navigable system (across education, health and care) that restores their confidence that their children will get the right support, in the right place, at the right time.
(DfE/DoHSC, 2023: 5)

This trust from the parents/carers can empower the SENCO in decision making when parents are confident the SENCO will be implementing the best for their child based on the available resources. These principles were highlighted with the Lamb Inquiry which noted '[g]ood, honest and open communication … requires practitioners who listen to parents and are trusted by them' (Lamb, 2009: 40). The SENCO is a key person in facilitating positive relationships between parents/carers and the school:

The trust that many parents and carers had in their child's schools may therefore have been influenced by their relationship with the SENCo, who appears to play an important role in the building of relationships between parents, carers and schools.
(DfE, 2021, n.p.)

Additionally, the educational choices parents/carers have for their children can be limited by the wider more complex factors which will come into play. Factors such as the demographic, political climate, psychological impact of class or resources available can all influence choices made by parents/carers. Reay (2012: 592) argues that '[e]ducational inequalities are inextricably bound up with social inequalities and cannot be addressed in isolation from them'. The SENCOs being able to signpost or acting as an advocate for those parents/carers who are not able to understand and navigate the complexities is a very important role in combating inequality. Yet this places a significant onus on the SENCO role as the linchpin in the current process:

> In some cases, parental empowerment has not happened. Children and parents are not 'in the know' and for some the law may not even appear to exist. Parents currently need a combination of special knowledge and social capital to navigate the system, and even then are left exhausted by the experience. Those without significant personal or social capital therefore face significant disadvantage. For some, Parliament might as well not have bothered to legislate.
> (House of Commons Education Committee, 2019: 86)

However, when the responsibility then falls on the SENCO, their levels of experience and knowledge may also serve to influence the outcomes for learners in their schools and being able to provide an inclusive education.

Recent reviews have resulted in recommendations for national changes in the SEND system which could help to address some of the issues related to variance in access to services and provisions and the resultant inequalities. The proposals for the future in the SEND and Alternative Provision Improvement Plan (DfE/DoHSC, 2023) include specific reference to clearer systems to improve on provision through working with parents/carers:

> For parents and carers, a national system will provide clarity about what support their children should be receiving without a fight to secure what is appropriate, and without needing to navigate a complex system. This will increase confidence and, in turn, minimise disputes.
> (DfE/DoHSC, 2023: 8)

The hope is that if recommendations are implemented successfully, it will lead to improved systems and processes for schools to work with parents/carers to provide more inclusive education practices in place for learners with SEND. The SEND and Alternative Provision Improvement Plan (DfE/DoHSC, 2023: 75) also set out a commitment to strengthening redress and mandatory mediation. The proposal is to 'refresh the model set for co-production at a local level including clear and transparent communication with parents. This will set out expectations for how local areas should work with families in their area to engage constructively and, as a result, prevent issues from escalating'. The SEN and Disability Code of Practice (DfE/DoH, 2015) will be amended to outline clearer route of escalation when mandatory deadlines or processes have not been met. Furthermore, the tribunal system will be altered in relation to EHCPs to include:

> For appeals about decisions regarding EHC needs assessments and plans, we proposed in the green paper to make mediation a mandatory part of the Tribunal appeals process. The consultation showed some support for mediation and giving it a greater role to play in redress.
> (DfE/DoHSC, 2023: 76)

Embedding whole-school approaches to meaningful engagement with parents/carers

Effective parental/carer engagement requires working in collaboration to ensure there are opportunities to listen and to go beyond listening to share in the important decisions to support children with SEND. This can be challenging, requiring time, professional and personal investment and resources. The Children and Families Act (2014) does not explicitly outline levels for collaboration with parents/carers even though this is such an important and central aspect of practice. Requiring effective collaboration in practice, but without frameworks, training and sufficient resources means that the SENCOs' and parents/carers' efforts to work together are likely to continue to be challenged.

There are different levels of participation and different models to conceptualise working together. Proposed by Arnstein (1969), the ladder of participation illustrates a progressive participatory involvement from non-participatory practices (which could include being manipulated) through to degrees of tokenism (which might include being informed or consulted) and then degrees of citizen power (which may include delegated powers or citizen control). This typology can help to consider the engagement with stakeholders and the ways in which we really involve them in shared decision making and real influence or choice. In addition to considering the levels of engagement in practice, it is important to consider the language we use and what this means. There are a range of terms to describe working together, such as 'informing', 'involving', 'cooperating', 'partnership', 'collaboration' and 'co-production'. However, these terms can have different or nuanced meaning and indicate differing levels of engagement and ways in which we work with others. Roper et al. (2018: 2) refer to co-production as raising the bar in relation to working together because of this move from 'seeking involvement or participation after an agenda has already been set, to seeking consumer leadership from the outset'. This means that if we seek to embed co-production in practice, then co-working between SENCOs and parents/carers has to be integrated at all levels. Roper et al. (2018) claim this includes co-planning, co-design, co-evaluation and co-delivery, which illustrates the very high level of investment necessary to integrate this into systems and processes in school. Working together would need to pervade all aspects of practice so that co-production is an embedded approach, rather than just inviting participation at certain points of a process.

The DfE (2021, n.p.) identified that 'the SENCO played an important mediating and sense-making role for school leaders and their colleagues but also for parents and carers'. If SENCOs are expected to implement 'co-production' this needs to be more explicitly defined in the policy and legislation and frameworks provided to assist with implementation. SENCOs need to be supported with training and appropriate resources. Otherwise we are providing a greater voice, but without the tools to take it forward in practice.

Planning for practice

There are a number of areas for consideration in building effective working relationships with parents/carers, but this section will focus mainly on the following key principles: *collaboration; communication; culture and cultural change;* and *inclusion/inclusive education*. This is linked to how the recent research and *evidence-informed approaches* might inform practices and ways to address some of the identified barriers that hinder SENCOs and parents/carers working together more effectively.

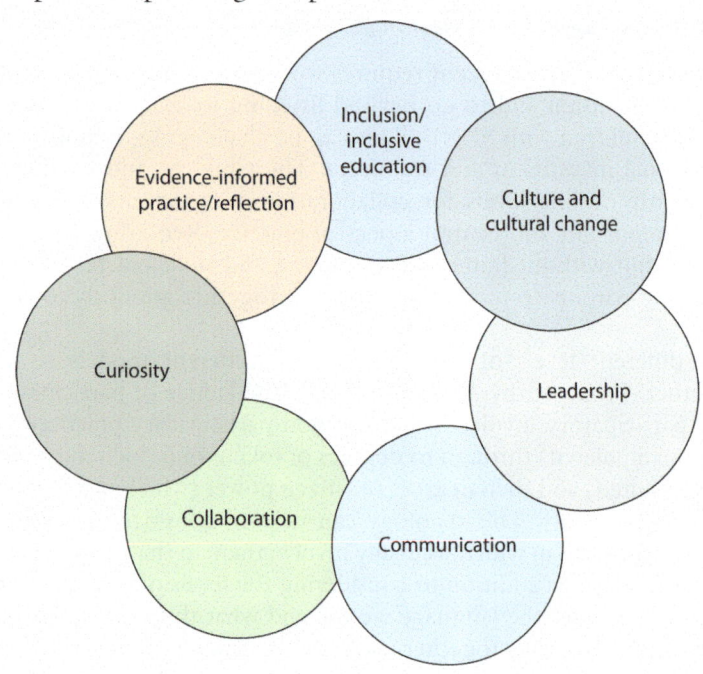

Figure 11.1 Key principles model

Understanding the importance and value of meaningful parent/carer partnership

For too long, the views and knowledge of parents/carers in relation to the education and provision needs of their children have been ignored, or, at best, seen as second rate to the views of the professionals working with their children. Our starting point for effective working with parents/carers, therefore needs to challenge existing practices which ignore the valuable perspectives and knowledge of parents/carers, and moves towards an approach that is more inclusive and collaborative. In this, there is a need to value the unique knowledge that parents /carers have of their own children and value ways of using that key knowledge to inform the planning for support and provision.

Reflective Activity

- Identify a time where there have been differences in expectations between your position as an education professional/SENCO and parents/carers' expectations. Consider the following:
  - Why did this occur?
  - How did you manage the situation? Consider what was positive and what could have been improved.
  - Were other stakeholders involved? Did this help or hinder discussions?
  - If you were in a similar situation in the future, how might you manage this differently?

It is important to consider the frameworks for developing effective relationships with parents/carers, when considering what has worked and what might be most useful in the future. One framework is the 'structured conversations' yet this was linked to an Achievement for All initiative DCSF (2009). The EEF Guidance Report (2018) Working with Parents to Support Children's Learning identifies that communication is key and outlines the following questions to consider:

- Do you know how your parents view the school's communication with them (for example, frequency, content, mode)?
- Does it give them the information they want?
- Are there any time-consuming communications that you currently use? Are these having the desired impact? Are you reaching the parents you want to?
- What do you do for parents who do not speak English or read well?
- What channels do parents have for contacting the school?

(EEF, 2018: 23)

Reflective Activity

It is important to consider our own experiences, skills and knowledge, for example, reflecting on how effective we are as communicators. Based on key features of communication adapted from Cheminais (2015), use Table 11.1 to audit your communication skills. Outcomes from this activity may be useful when we reflect on ways in which we communicate with parents/carers and others we are working with in school:

Table 11.1 Communication skills audit

Communication skill	Examples	My rating 1. Requires development 4. Fully competent	Action for development if rated below 4
Non-verbal cues to put parents/carers at ease			
Attentive – listens actively			
Silence to allow thinking time			
Paraphrasing to check understanding			
Show empathy			
Ask questions to gain a fuller understanding of values, hopes and aspirations			

It is acknowledged that 'parental confidence in the SEN system, and in schools and local authorities in particular, is significantly impacted by the quality of communication and working relationships. This can also affect parents' decisions about whether or not to appeal to the Tribunal' (Lamb, 2009: 79).

As we have seen, this situation has increased significantly in recent years and the House of Commons Education Committee (2019: 3) therefore recommended the introduction of a 'neutral role, the purpose of which would be to arrange meetings, coordinate paperwork and be a source of impartial advice to parents'.

194 *Effective partnership working with parents/carers*

Whilst the suggestion is that this would be a local authority role, it is also important for schools to be mindful of this and to consider what could be done in school to signpost to, or provide, the additional support that is needed to help parents/carers to 'wade through the treacle of bureaucracy' (House of Commons Education Committee, 2019: 3) embedded within the SEND system currently.

Recognising and challenging persistent inequalities in parents/carers' experiences

The gap between parent/carer expectations and the reality of what school can offer can cause tensions in working relationships. The SENCO is often the person who is at the frontline of these discussions.

Parents/carers experience inequalities in their experience of the SEND and education system in many different ways, including in the hierarchical or power relationships that are embedded, or assumed, between professionals and parents/carers. Key to challenging those embedded or assumed inequalities, therefore is about reflecting on ways that parents/carers can feel more relaxed and comfortable talking about their children and their home/family situations. Such opportunities need to ensure that there is a 'no judgement' approach built on positive listening rather than any 'expert' perspective on just telling parents/carers what to do.

We also need to be aware that parents/carers may come with heightened emotions – having to take on an advocate role for their child, and possibly coming from a position of having had to fight to have other professionals listen to them over the years (DfE, 2017). Parents/carers of pupils with SEND may also need and want different information, and have different concerns to other parents/carers (DfE, 2017) – and this needs to be carefully considered so that the school does not inadvertently perpetuate inequalities by not having the information required for parents/carers.

It is also important for us to be aware of the significant 'burden' and 'strain' that parents/carers may experience advocating for the right support for their child. It can be a 'lonely and isolating process that can, and often does, put significant strain on all aspects of a family's life' (House of Commons Education Committee, 2019: 19).

In addition to this strain, it is possible that the parent/carer may also be supporting other family members with similar or different needs, and indeed may have SEND themselves.

The Case Study below provides an insight into the impact that embedded school routines and practices may have on autistic parents/carers as they seek to find ways to manage the stress and overwhelm that they experience to be able to positively support their child though their own educational experiences.

Case Study – Identifying Autism Related Barriers Within Daily School Life and the Impact on Autistic Parents/Carers

Esther Whitney

I am an autistic parent and my child attends a two-form entry primary school in a diverse area of Birmingham.

For some autistic parents/carers, the school environment can often be challenging due to sensory sensitivities, information processing differences, as well as complex social interactions. Many schools acknowledge that the school environment can be at odds with autism, and therefore reasonable adjustments are made for their autistic pupils. However little consideration has been given to the challenges autistic parents/carers face when negotiating daily school life, resulting in being misunderstood, which could lead to assumptions about lack of engagement being made. This appears to be a hidden problem with a large number of autistic parents/carers choosing to home-school their children due to feeling that the education system not being able to meet the needs of their autistic children along with their needs as autistic parents/carers. For autistic parents/carers who are not able to home-school their children, daily school life can be incredibly challenging. Some autistic parents/carers may feel that they are unable to speak out due to the stigma as well as fear of being misunderstood.

This is an ongoing problem within our society, many organisations address the physical barriers of disability, assuming that their services are fully accessible. For those with hidden disabilities such as autism it can often be a tedious never-ending battle in requesting reasonable adjustments from services despite legislation such as the disability discrimination act.

As an autistic parent, one of my many struggles with daily school life was taking my daughter to school in the morning and collecting her in the afternoon. Morning drop offs and afternoon collections caused so much anxiety; cars parked everywhere, parents/carers and children swarming on the pavements heading into the school playground, the roar of parents/carers chatting and children playing on top of that, the dread of other parents/carers trying to talk to you and the fear of being asked if your child would like a play date. This unpredictable chaos resulted in me standing by my front door every weekday morning and afternoon feeling paralysed to leave the house, subsequently my daughter would be late for school. I would be late picking her up, because of the anxiety of the crowds at the end of the school day. For years I suffered in silence, because of fear that I would be misunderstood by the school; until one day I decided to reach out and explain my experiences as an autistic parent. Surprisingly I received a positive response from the school who had never considered the differences autistic parents/carers experience when negotiating daily school life. It was agreed that my daughter could attend the breakfast club which starts 30 minutes before school and avoids the crowds. The school offered an earlier collection time in the afternoon which has led to a much calmer collection. These reasonable adjustments have made a huge difference to us as a neurodiverse family.

Whilst I am grateful of the adaptions suggested I would like to highlight the following:

- I had to reach breaking point to approach the school
- Because I was aware of the legal duty legislation places on services, I was able to articulate my experiences to the school
- The breakfast club costs us as a family £5 per week, I would argue as to whether this is fair, on the basis that if I wasn't an autistic parent/carer morning drop offs would not be a barrier.

Top Tips for removing barriers to engagement for parents/carers

- Acknowledging that for some parents/carers due to disability (visible and hidden) there could be barriers to engagement. Allocating a member of staff who is the official point of contact for parents/carers who require reasonable adjustments and this to be well signposted within the school's literature as well as verbally expressed for those who struggle with reading
- Offering both face to face and online appointments
- Offering the meeting agenda prior to the meeting
- Allow plenty of time, I know school is very busy, being aware that if an autistic parent/carer is coming for a meeting into the school, anxiety is likely to be high which could impact of their ability to process the information discussed
- Be mindful they might need time to acclimatise to the environment prior to the start of the meeting
- After meetings summarise meeting and provide parents/carers with a written and verbal copy
- Being able to automatically adjust one's approach without the need of official diagnosis is also important. Some autistic people will not want to disclose their diagnosis or may not even know they have autism
- The adaptions offered should not have an additional cost to parents/carers.

As the EEF (2018) notes, reducing barriers for parents/carers needs to be considered as part of our practice to ensure that we can be inclusive and provide the spaces to engage with parents/carers. It is so important that we 'Communicate carefully to avoid stigmatising, blaming, or discouraging parents. Focus on building parents' efficacy—that they are equal partners and can make a difference' (EEF, 2018: 7).

Reflective Activity

- Reflect on the systems and processes currently in place to work collaboratively and communicate with parents/carers in your school setting
- Are there any times when there are parent/carer inequalities in terms of access to information/support?
- Why is this?
- How could this be addressed?

Review the Case Study above, which highlights the experience of an autistic parent and consider any ways that established practices in your setting may inadvertently be disadvantaging parent/carer or placing barriers to access and participation in the way of parents/carers being able to participate as fully as they may like to.

Embedding whole-school approaches to meaningful engagement with parents/carers

The need for effective approaches to provide meaningful collaboration and engagement with parents/carers as part of a whole-school approach is essential.

The EEF (2018: 3) Guidance Report – Working with parents to support children's learning, therefore provides a really useful framework for starting to think about and engage with this.

Their recommendations identify the following four key areas for focus:

- Recommendation 1 – Critically review how you work with parents
- Recommendation 2 – Provide practical strategies to support learning at home
- Recommendation 3 – Tailor school communication to encourage positive dialogue about learning
- Recommendation 4 – Offer more sustained and intensive support where needed.

Linked to the first recommendation, the EEF (2018: 6) identify that 'Working effectively with parents can be challenging, and is likely to require sustained effort and support. Most schools say that they do not have an explicit plan for how they work with parents, and fewer than 10% of teachers have undertaken CPD on parental engagement'. It is therefore essential to reflect on what systems and processes we have in place to ensure working with parents/carers is considered fully.

Reflective Activity

Using the EEF Guidance Report (2018), Working with Parents to Support Children's Learning review your whole school approaches for how you work with parents/carers.

In approaching parent/carer engagement, you can start by:

- Developing a clear plan for what you want to achieve;
- Auditing your current practice to assess what is working well and what is not;
- Listening to what less-involved parents/carers would find helpful; and
- Stopping activities without clear benefits.

As we have noted earlier, parents/carers have valuable and unique knowledge and understanding of their child, their behaviour and early development, any support received outside of school (DfE, 2017) and it is therefore essential that we find ways to include and involve parents/carers and ensure that their voice is heard and informs the development of planning for their child.

Effective communication in school is key to successful working relationships (Lamb, 2009). Essentially the SENCO manages the parent/carer expectations during the process and has the responsibility for maintaining a family-led approach. SENCOs are often the main point of contact for parents/carers and in line with the Special Educational Needs and Disability Code of Practice (DfE/DoH, 2015) principle of 'keeping the child's parent or young person informed through a single point of contact wherever possible' (DfE/DoH, 2015: 149) illustrating the central role they hold.

The DfE (2021) identify the quality of the relationship between home and school as critical in ensuring positive outcomes for learners

> A significant component of this relationship is the extent to which schools work to develop co-production with families, a way of working that brings together pupils, parents or carers and education, health and care services when making decisions about how best to support a pupil.
>
> (DfE, 2021, n.p.)

Reflective Activity

- What systems do you currently use to communicate with parents/carers?
- How effective are they?
- How fully do they meet the needs of your parents/carers?
- How do you know?

Evidence suggests that a range of formal and informal channels can be utilised in schools to strengthen working relationships and could include:

> parents' evenings, support plan meetings and contact with the SENCo, but also informal processes such as daily check-ins and home–school books. Some schools used information from families to inform decisions about support packages and, in this way, treated parents and carers as partners in decision-making. In our small sample, collaboration with families, including strong relationships with the SENCo, supported schools in meeting pupils' needs more effectively.
>
> (DfE, 2021, n.p.)

Conversely, where there was weak information sharing this impacted negatively on wider communication between staff and parents/carers. Insufficient knowledge of co-production and how to implement this in practice could support the argument for improved training opportunities. Within the SEN and Disability Code of Practice (DfE/DoH, 2015) it therefore states that 'Practitioners in all services involved in the assessment and planning process need to be skilled in working with children, parents and young people to help them make informed decisions. All practitioners should have access to training so they can do this effectively' (DfE/DoH, 2015: 149).

The SEN and Disability Code of Practice (DfE/DoH, 2015: 61) only refers to 'co-production' once in relation to the local offer. Collaboration with parents/carers is referred to at three points in the document, on other occasions the term 'collaboration' relates to schools and services working together. Increased parent/carer engagement in decision making and parents/carers as being valued in the process continues to be strengthened with the new proposals with one of the five core values as being:

> Co-produced: children, young people and their families will be involved in the decision-making process around the support they receive and in the development of the policy which drives those decisions.
>
> (DfE/DoHSC, 2023: 95)

Similarly, Boddison and Soan (2021) identified there is no direct reference to co-production in the Children and Families Act (2014) and their coding of the Act highlighted the range of terms used for working together. They claim there is a domination of the 'expert' voice limiting equal and meaningful opportunities to work together with families. Without clear definitions in policy on ways in which to work together in practice, this can lead to misunderstandings and different expectations, further exacerbating challenges for both SENCOs and parents/carers.

Reflective Activity

Based on Roper et al. (2018) Stages of co-production in Table 11.2, identify where this could relate to different aspects of your practice and times when you have worked with parents/carers to constructively support their children in a co-productive way, or where you have implemented co-production in processes related to SEND.

Table 11.2 Roper et al. (2018) Stages of co-production

Stage	Different possible examples	My examples from practice
Co-planning	A personalised provision plan that includes both school interventions and parent/carer strategies which have been planned together so it becomes a more coordinated approach to supporting the learner.	
Co-design	Parents/carers reviewing the SEN policy for the school and then working with the SENCO to design more accessible information to be part of the policy.	
Co-evaluating	Provision maps are often shared with parents/carers. Parents/carers could be involved in plans to purchase a new provision mapping tool, so all stakeholders' perspectives are taken into account before making a purchase.	
Co-delivery	Expert parents/carers working with the SENCO to deliver talks to other parents/carers or staff on a topic.	

In the EEF (2020) SEN in Mainstream Schools Guidance Report there is also reference back to the EEF (2018) Working with Parents to Support Children's Learning Guide, as well as some additional prompts that are really useful to consider in terms of reconsidering existing practices in your own school setting. Use Table 11.3 to support your own reflections about practice and aspects that could be developed further.

Table 11.3 EEF (2020: 19) Reflection on practice for working with parents/carers

RAG rate what is currently in place in your setting.	Provide examples of practice- highlighting aspects that currently work well and why	Identify any areas to be developed further, and ways that this could be achieved
Ask parents and carers how the school could communicate more effectively with them, and what type of information they would find most helpful.		
Begin from an understanding that home and school are different environments in which the pupil may behave differently. Comments like 'we don't see that behaviour at school' are counter-productive and may imply deficient parenting skills rather than considering that the pupil may act up at home, rather than at school, because they consider it a safe environment. Be willing to listen, to hear and learn from parents' and carers' accounts of how the pupil behaves at home. Also, remember that parents and carers may not know much about what happens		
How can you be proactive about contacting the pupils' parents and carers to share positive information? Try to include positive contact.		
Engage in genuine two-way conversations to avoid parents and carers feeling that they are being told what to do or that the school is expecting them to 'solve' issues occurring in school, with no discussion or experience of being listened to.		
Be open to learning from parents' and carers' knowledge about the pupil's needs and strengths. Use this to develop knowledge and expertise around the pupil's SEND and share that with colleagues in the school.		
Be proactive about agreeing strategies with the pupil, in consultation with the parents and carers, to support pupils to succeed in school, for example, by including the SENCo in parents' evenings.		

Concluding comments and reflections

SENCOs need to be supported and provided with relevant training and the resources to ensure that effective ways of working with parents/carers are embedded in practice and not dependent upon pockets of practice or individuals' goodwill. This needs to be supported at the whole-school level, because 'Carefully designed school communications can have a positive impact on parents' beliefs and behaviours' (EEF, 2018: 21).

Working effectively with parents/carers across the SEND sector is already in policy and legislation, and has been for many years. It is clear this will not gain momentum in practice without relevant resources, support and training in understanding and implementing co-production and support in managing what sometimes can be very challenging situations and difficult conversations. The commitment in the SEND and Alternative Provision Improvement

Plan (DfE/DoHSC, 2023) aims to drive forward changes that will improve trust, clarity, accountability and opportunities to work with parents/carers more effectively.

> **Individual reflection**
>
> - What new information/learning have you gained from this chapter?
> - What are your key reflections?
> - What are your next steps/actions as a result?

References

Arnstein, S. (1969) 'A ladder of citizen participation'. *Journal of the American Institute of Planners* 35(4), 216–224.

Axford, N., Berry, V., Lloyd, J., Moore, D., Rogers, M., Hurst, A., Blockley, K., Durkin, H. and Minton, J. (2019) *How can schools and early years settings support parents' engagement in their children's learning?* London: EEF.

Boddison, A. and Soan, S. (2021) 'The coproduction illusion: Considering the relative success rates and efficiency rates of securing an education, health and care plan when requested by families or education professionals'. *Journal of Research in Special Educational Needs* 22(2), 91–104.

Cheminais, R. (2015) *Rita Cheminais' handbook for SENCOs 2nd Edition* . CA : SAGE Publications

Curran, H., Moloney, H., Heavey, A. and Boddison, A. (2020) *The time is now: Addressing missed opportunities for Special Educational Needs Support and Coordination in our schools*. Available from: https://www.bathspa.ac.uk/media/bathspaacuk/education-/research/senco-workload/National-SENCO-Workload-Survey-Report-Jan-2020.pdf (accessed 1.5.23).

DCSF (2009) Achievement for All The Structured Conversation Handbook to support training. Available from: https://dera.ioe.ac.uk/id/eprint/2418/1/afa_struct_conv_hbook_0105609bkt_en.pdf (accessed 31.5.23).

DES (1981) *Education Act*. London: DES.

DfE (1994) *Special Educational Needs Code of Practice*. London: DfE.

DfE (2017) *SEN Support: A rapid evidence assessment research report*. Coventry: Coventry University.

DfE (2021) *Supporting SEND: A summary for children and young people*. Available from: https://www.gov.uk/government/publications/supporting-send/supporting-send-a-summary-for-children-and-young-people (accessed 20.12.22).

DfE/DoH (2015) *Special Educational Needs and Disability Code of Practice for 0 to 25 year olds*. Available from: https://www.gov.uk/government/publications/send-code-of-practice-0-to-25 (accessed 20.12.22).

DfE/DoHSC (2022). *SEND Review: Right support, Right place, Right time*. Available from: https://www.gov.uk/government/consultations/send-review-right-support-right-place-right-time (accessed 30.5.23).

DfE/DoHSC (2023) *Special Educational Needs and Disabilities (SEND) and Alternative Provision Improvement Plan – Right support, right place, right time*. London: HMSO.

DfES (2001) *SEN Code of Practice*. London: DfES.

EEF (2020) *SEN in mainstream schools guidance report*. London: EEF.

EEF (2018) *Working with parents to support children's learning guidance report*. London: EEF.

House of Commons Education Committee (2019) *Special Educational Needs and Disabilities*. London: House of Commons.

Lamb, B. (2009). *Lamb Inquiry: Special Educational Needs and Parental Confidence*. Available from: https://dera.ioe.ac.uk/9042/1/Lamb%20Inquiry%20Review%20of%20SEN%20and%20Disability%20Information.pdf (accessed 20.12.22).

Mather, A. (2016) 'Consultation, negotiation and compromise: The relationship between SENCOs, parents and pupils with SEN'. *Support for Learning NASEN* 31(1), 4–12.

NAO (2019) *Support for pupils with special educational needs and disabilities in England*. London: House of Commons.

Reay, D. (2012) 'What would a socially just education system look like?: Saving the minnows from the pike'. *Journal of Education Policy* 27(5), 587–599.

Roper, C., Grey, F. and Cadogan, E. (2018) *Co-production Putting principles into practice in mental health contexts*. Available from: https://healthsciences.unimelb.edu.au/__data/assets/pdf_file/0007/3392215/Coproduction_putting-principles-into-practice.pdf

The Children and Families Act (2014) https://www.legislation.gov.uk/ukpga/2014/6/contents (accessed 20.12.22).

Warnock, M. (1978) *Warnock report: Special Educational Needs, report of the Committee of Enquiry into the education of handicapped children and young people*. London: HMSO.

12 Working effectively with other agencies

In this chapter, we critically examine and explore the following key aspects:

- Professional identity and differences
- Stretched services
- Structural issues and systemic silos
- Communication
- Levels of participation
- Interpreting and using professional reports
- Embedding multi-professional working in practice

Key issues

'Nothing is more important than children's welfare' (DfE, 2018a: 6). Since the original publication of Every Child Matters (DfES, 2003), following the death of Victoria Climbie, the need for professionals from across different services and agencies to work together in joined-up and effective ways has been emphasised. Yet, this remains a complex and problematic practice to embed effectively due to a number of factors which will be explored in this chapter, with the House of Commons Education Committee (2019: 88) highlighting that there is still 'not sufficient emphasis on joint working within the Government'.

The Special Educational Needs Coordinator (SENCO) role involves working with a range of professionals in order to meet children's needs in a holistic way. Although most children's needs can be met through universal provision, there will be children who need more specialist or targeted, individualised intervention. Education, therefore, cannot be managed in isolation. The Special Educational Needs (SEN) and Disability Code of Practice (DfE/DoH, 2015) requires closer working practices between Education, Health and Social Care to meet the needs of children with more complex special educational needs, disabilities or medical needs. Children may need support from wider services and so placing them at the centre of any professional working is key. How we work with other services will be an important factor in ensuring positive outcomes for children and young people.

DOI: 10.4324/9781003033554-12

Multi-agency working has been in practice for some time in legislation, policy and practice, yet challenges continue to persist. Atkinson et al. (2007) identified three key factors that underpin effective multi-agency working:

- **Working relationships:** Issues concerning working relationships were found to be central to multi-agency activity. One of the key issues relates to clarity over role demarcation, a lack of which was highlighted as the most frequently identified challenge. The importance of those involved having commitment to multi-agency working and the development of understanding, trust and mutual respect amongst participants was also emphasised
- **Resourcing multi-agency work:** Adequate resourcing, in terms of funding, staffing and time, was found to be central to the success of multi-agency working. Whilst financial certainty and equity was important, inadequate or time-limited funding was identified as problematic. A rapid turnover of staff, recruitment difficulties and insufficient time allocated for multi-agency activity were also reported to be potential threats to its success
- **Management and governance:** In terms of management and governance, leadership was identified as the key aspect influencing multi-agency work. An absence of clear leadership and a lack of support from upper management were revealed as particularly damaging.

(Atkinson et al., 2007: 3)

This chapter will therefore explore and examine those factors in relation to the following key issues:

1 Professional identity and differences
2 Stretched services in all sectors
3 Structural issues and systemic silos

Current policy/research context

Since the introduction of the Children Act 1989 partnership working has been a focus to support children's well-being. The Children Act 1989 placed an obligation on professionals to work together with children in need and children in need of protection. Yet in 2000, the death of Victoria Climbié led to further changes in legislation (Children Act, 2004) and the Every Child Matters agenda from the preceding green paper of the same name (DfES, 2003).

When Laming (2009) reviewed the progress from the original report (Laming, 2003) it was identified that there continued to be issues regarding lack of resources and training for professionals to be able to work together effectively to safeguard children. It was noted that: 'the challenges of working across organisational boundaries continue to pose barriers in practice' (Laming, 2009: 37). The challenges with professionals being able to physically work together, including being present at multi-agency meetings was reinforced in the House of Commons Education Committee (2019: 57) report 'Schools told us that there was a lack of attendance and engagement, with health and social care staff often not in attendance at meetings and reviews'.

The current SEN and Disability Code of Practice (DfE/DoH, 2015) informed by the Children and Families Act (2014) includes greater duties on working together involving a number of different agencies. Yet the duties are not always clear alongside hampered implementation and challenging context of limited resources. The House of Commons Education Committee noted that (2019: 4) 'Unless health, and social care are 'at the table', we are no further on, and the Education, Health and Care Plan is no more than a Statement by another name'. Their call for greater joint working and a 'joint outcomes framework' (2019: 4) is reinforced by the recommendations in the recent DfE/DoHSC direction (2023) which claims the new national system will outline 'who should be working together, and will enable government to hold delivery partners to account and intervene where expectations are not met' (DfE/DoHSC, 2023: 8).

Professional identity and differences

How we are positioned as professionals and our professional identity will undoubtedly influence how we engage and work with other professionals. There can be quite marked differences in approaches and agendas, as well as misunderstandings or a lack of understanding of each other's roles. If this is not managed it can lead to barriers in communication. It is important to address misconceptions and barriers to communication early on to ensure small misunderstanding do not grow into larger concerns.

Working relationships are fundamental because the professional relationships we develop, maintain and enhance can serve to strengthen provision for children (Atkinson et al., 2007). It can lead to increased capacity in a school when we learn from each other and work together effectively. Understanding what constitutes as a profession is important and would be a foundation for our professional identity. Holding expertise in the field and being sure of the effectiveness of actions or approaches is valuable, however when we work with others our practice is open to scrutiny and could be aligned or misaligned depending upon the circumstances and professionals involved.

It is unrealistic not to acknowledge that conflicts may occur between professionals and this may be triggered by a range of different reasons: professional differences, professional egos, unclear lines of accountability, defensiveness over specialist knowledge, or hierarchical structures, etc. When this occurs it can be difficult to move forward and in some cases the barriers limit the effectiveness of the working relationship. McAuliffe (2014: 12–13) refers to the clash in professions and claims 'many people do not have good knowledge of the value foundations of professional disciplines other than their own, and have little respect or tolerance for difference of opinion'. However, trying to recognise when this happens and why is the first step in redressing it. Difficulties in the working environment can compound these challenges, this was identified in Laming's (2009: 4) report noting: 'anxiety undermines good practice' and is also recognised today with the current state of 'low confidence and inefficient resource allocation' (DfE/DoHSC, 2023: 16).

Fostering a space for open, honest conversations will help to build trust, mutual respect and underpin successful communication and relationships. In an era of accountability, psychological safety and not feeling defensive is important, otherwise we will always be in a position of partial or minimal commitment to working together. This was identified in the House of Commons Education Committee (2019: 57) report because in some cases, we are dependent on the good will of others, rather than operating in a system that facilitates an environment for effective working relationships, 'health and social care input was reliant on personalities rather than clear and fair systems'.

One area to reduce challenges in working together is ensuring clarity over role demarcation. There needs to be improved understanding of roles which would help to build trust and professional respect between agencies and professionals. Professionals might be committed to working with each other, but in some cases there can be issues with differences in professional prioritisation and understanding of the child's needs, coming from their specialist professional perspective. Essentially professionals need to work out what is best for the child which may mean they need to be more flexible in their thinking and approaches.

Differences between professionals are also apparent within the different terminology embedded both in practice and in policy documents. This does not help to unite different professionals around a consistent set of thresholds, understandings and expectations. Differences in terminology such as: 'working together'/'partnership'; 'collaboration'/'cooperation'; 'profession'/'discipline'; 'multi-professional'/'inter-professional' therefore significantly impact on the development of effective collaborative practices.

In this chapter, the term 'multi-agency working' has been used. Hellawell (2019, p. xix) defines this as focusing on 'the structural and strategic relationships between various agencies'. Whereas, 'inter-professional collaboration' is defined as focusing on 'the personal interactions between individual professionals or groups of professionals'. These terms, however, may have other definitions dependent upon the context in which they are used, which can lead to confusion. For example within healthcare 'inter-professional' is often used to refer to the differences of professionals and the unique knowledge they can bring from their disciplines in working together, such as nurses, paramedics, general practitioners, radiographers, etc. (Rizzo Parse, 2015).

In situations where there may be professionals from a range of different disciplines (health, education, psychology, etc.) these nuances of meaning can serve to hinder. Frost (2005: 7) notes that the way in which terms are used interchangeably can also be a barrier, 'fundamentally, there is some confusion and varied usage of phrases such as co-ordination, co-operation, partnership, joined-up thinking and working together'. His review had the aim of providing clarity in relation to these issues. Working together needs a clear basis and foundations that are shared across the professions, which includes the terminology we use. Confusion over terms can lead to blurring of roles and responsibilities, which in turn can lead to issues regarding communication and accountability. Lawson (2004: 225) views this as pivotal to working together stating: 'Imprecise, incoherent and competing conceptions of collaboration plague practice, training, research, evaluation and policy.'

Stretched services in all sectors

The lack of funding and resources in schools and wider services impacts on professionals working together. Support from external services to identify need has been challenging with exceptionally long waiting lists despite children being identified as requiring assessments. Multi-agency working requires time, and investment which is more difficult when the resources and funds are diminished. Schools, special schools and services are having to find creative ways in which to use the resources they have and to work together more effectively when faced with limited resources.

Atkinson et al. (2007: 3) referred to resourcing multi-agency work as a key factor. The current situation is exceptionally challenging with schools facing increased fuel costs (Worth, 2022) and providing more support for families due to the cost of living crisis impacting more widely in society. Services have been under-resourced which has seriously affected ability to work together and meet needs and resulted in limited resources and exceptionally long waiting lists to access services. The OFSTED (2021: np) SEND report noted:

> Even when there was agreement about the need for assessment or appointments, several families and schools felt they did not have sufficient or timely access to local authority and health service provision. This was often attributed to waiting lists for appointments or services not being provided frequently enough. Issues related to a variety of health services, including speech and language therapy, occupational therapy and CAMHS.

Yet the gaps in services were identified two years prior to this report:

> We are seeing serious gaps in therapy provision. We need to see professionals trained and supported so that they are able to support all pupils; these huge gaps in therapy provision across the country are letting down all pupils, but particularly those on SEN Support.
> (House of Commons Education Committee, 2019: 4)

> Some schools were especially concerned about the access to mental health support. We heard that access to Child and Adolescent Mental Health Services (CAMHS) was really difficult and young people were being left without support.
> (House of Commons Education Committee, 2019: 58)

It is evident that services have been stretched for some time now. The pandemic, Brexit and the war in Ukraine are often attributed as reasons for the cost of living crisis. These wider issues may have exacerbated the problem, but they are not the cause for the challenging circumstances we are managing. Resources have been progressively diminishing and in some cases are now at crisis point. This undoubtedly affects outcomes and more concerning, impacts on children's safety and well-being: 'The current reliance on quickly pulling together a team from across overstretched agencies to think and act together to protect a child every time child protection processes are triggered is certainly inefficient and often ineffective' (Child Safeguarding Practice Review Panel, 2022: 10).

A discrepancy in accessing services is now emerging, where it is identified that the 'burden' is now falling to schools and parents/carers to 'fill in the gaps when they were unable to access specialist services and expertise' (OFSTED, 2021: n.p). Parents/carers and schools that are not able to 'fill the gaps' leads to inequity in the provision being offered and widening gap based on those who can and cannot pay for services directly.

Another precious resource for multi-agency working is time. The Workload Report (Curran et al., 2020: 9) highlights SENCOs have limited time to perform their duties and note the budget and financial constraints as a reason for the reduction in time, on respondent stated: 'Due to budget and staffing cuts, my teaching role has increased, and my SENCO time has been halved'. Without the allocation of time to work with professionals, there will not be the opportunity to invest in building quality relationships between school staff and others which underpins effective shared working practices.

Structural issues and systemic silos

The way in which services are structured and resourced can impact on the ways by which professionals work together. Multi-agency working has been hampered by silo working – and this has been driven by issues embedded in practice from the top, in the way that government departments work, or fail to work, effectively together. As the House of Commons Education Committee (2019: 84) identify: 'Nobody benefits when departments avoid accountability and try to pass the buck. The Department for Education, together with the Department for Health and Social Care should develop mutually beneficial options for cost- and burden-sharing with the health and social care sector'.

The ways in which health, education and care are resourced and managed can improve or exacerbate issues related to working together. Organising services so they are physically placed together and the new proposals to standardise and centralise processes related the EHCPs (DfE/DoHSC, 2023) may be a way to address some of the more persistent issues related to working together.

Management and governance is a key factor identified by Atkinson et al. (2007: 3) to support successful multi-agency working. The way in which the services are structured and resourced can impact on the ways in which they can work together. In 2009, Laming (2009: 11) identified that effective multi-agency working 'too often depends on the commitment of individual staff and sometimes this happens despite, rather than because of, the organisational arrangements'. There needs to be strong leadership as identified in the House of Commons Education Committee report (2019: 63–64) 'We heard about the benefits and importance of multidisciplinary working, and how that helped to break down barriers. Unfortunately, we were told it required strong leadership, time and effort, and ultimately was only happening in some areas of the country'.

Siloed working has been challenging to address, and continues to present barriers: 'Arthur and Star's stories tragically illustrate how critical information from multiple sources becomes rapidly fragmented leading to a partial and siloed understanding of children's experiences and lives' (Child Safeguarding Practice Review Panel, 2022: 10). There are structural ways to address silo working, one aspect is to co-locate service where possible. Hellawell (2019: 54) notes 'Where a geographical co-location in response to the new framework has occurred, this can positively contribute to partnership working'. The participant from Hellawell's study commented on the move into one building as facilitating improved communication: 'now, if you have got an issue or anything, you just go and talk to them, and it gets resolved a lot quicker'. These aspects improve mutual understanding which is essential because when it is everyone's responsibility it can be no-body's responsibility. One proposal from the Child Safeguarding Practice Review Panel (2022: 11) was to harness expertise in 'proposed new Multi-Agency Child Protection Units to deliver excellent practice' (Child Safeguarding Practice Review Panel, 2022: 11). This forming of 'units' may serve to facilitate improved communication and mutual understanding to strengthen multi-agency leadership and accountability.

The current system for EHCPs is an example of a structural process that has led to divisiveness and inequity. The new proposals acknowledge that the complex, bureaucratic system needs to be addressed to 'ensure that parents do not endure lengthy, adversarial and costly processes' (DfE/DoHSC, 2023: 9).

The ways in which services are structured and the budgets allocated to the different services will need to be addressed in order to facilitate improved mechanisms for services to work together. The House of Commons Education Committee Report (2019) identified disparity in the provisions available across regions and budgetary constraints when one organisation holds the budget and another organisation is responsible and accountable for providing provision:

> Many local authorities told us that the complexity of Clinical Commissioning Groups (CCGs) made it hard to work together. Kent County Council told us that not all Clinical Commissioning Groups commission the same services, which meant that in some cases only some of the local authority's population could access specific types of support. The local authority told us that it was illogical that therapists were employed by the NHS, that budgets were held by the Clinical Commissioning Group, but that responsibility for ensuring provision is in place sits with the LA. We did hear that joint commissioning could be successful as Coventry City Council told us that joint commissioning between the Clinical Commissioning Group and the local authority had funded speech and language therapy included in part F of Education Health and Care Plans.
> (House of Commons Education Committee, 2019: 60)

Different systems, priorities and timescales across services were further aspects identified as prohibitive to offering appropriate support for children:

> Local authorities also told us about challenges working with social care and health. They described challenges around information sharing because agencies have different systems, and challenges around meeting timescales because it was not clear what took precedence and each agency was working to their own timescale, with health and social care seeing requests for assessment advice as lower priority than their own direct work.
> (House of Commons Education Committee, 2019: 59)

The proposed National SEND and Alternative Provisions Standards (DfE/DoHSC, 2023) claim to clarify which budgets will be used to pay for support which is essential because how budgets are managed and how services are organised at a macro level will need to be part of the solution. The new proposals aim to include a systemic change to the processes in place which are not currently working, yet this was the aim of the SEND reforms in 2014. It is absolutely crucial that the changes proposed for 2024 onwards are implemented effectively, which is acknowledged in the document:

> National Standards will not deliver change on their own. Standards will only be translated into reality through efficient funding, effective accountability and an appropriately resourced and skilled workforce.
> (DfE/DoHSC, 2023: 31)

Planning for practice

Working effectively with other agencies to ensure not only educational outcomes, but also the safety and well-being of all pupils requires a commitment to **communication**. We need to challenge where **communication** is weak to reduce and remove barriers to working together. Developing innovative ways to **collaborate** and foster **curiosity** serves to address reduced resources and limitations of the way services are currently structured. Looking to the future, **culture and cultural change** is already identified as fundamental (Lamb, 2009; House of Commons Education Committee, 2019; NAO, 2019; DfE/

DoHSC, 2023) if services for children with SEND are to improve. It is important we are also mindful of this in our settings as we build spaces for more transparent, honest and open conversations with others.

All of this will also be dependent on clear **leadership** founded on shared ***inclusive values*** and a strong moral purpose focused on providing the best outcomes for pupils with SEND and their families.

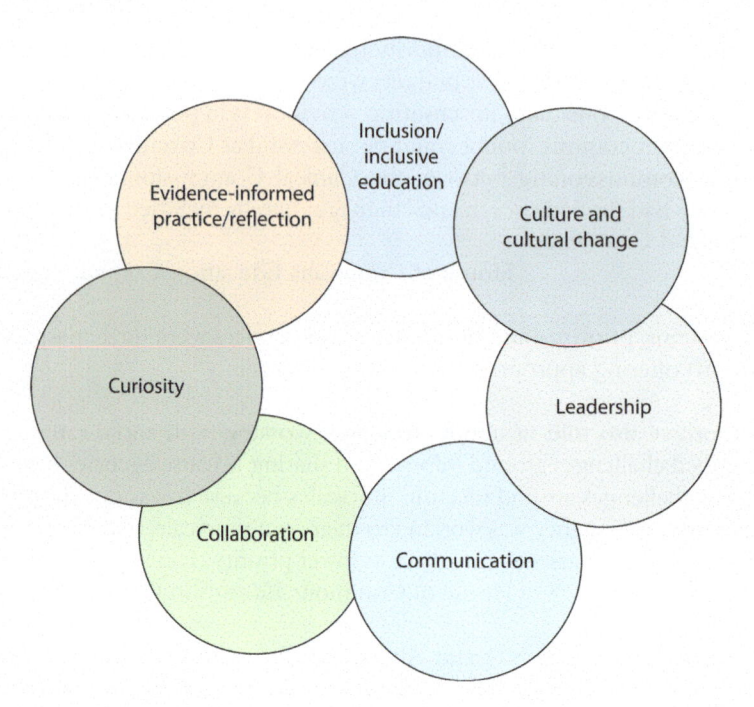

Figure 12.1 Key principles model

Professional identity and differences

How we develop our professional identity and our understanding of other professional roles and identities is important in how we relate to and work with other professionals. This can be difficult for the SENCO role due to often being the only SENCO in the school. The SENCO also often works with so many professionals from diverse disciplines, it can provide opportunities to engage in different ways of perceiving situations and can sometimes shine a light on how we are positioned professionally. ***Communication*** is a key underlying principle to enable us to build and maintain relationships with others.

Communication enables us to have improved clarity over roles, responsibilities and areas of expertise. Lack of knowledge of other professional roles can therefore lead to misunderstanding and possible barriers to communication that could negatively impact on professional relationships and outcomes for children. For example, a parent/carer might visit a medical practitioner who suggests they should ask the school to apply for an Education Health and Care plan. Parents/carers contact school to request this and school might have a very different perspective. This places the professionals involved and the parents/carers in a difficult situation. Improved knowledge of the professionals roles and responsibilities as well as a clear shared understanding of the ways in which we work together would combat these situations occurring. A shared framework for working together might serve to improve practice or embedding multi-agency working as part of the pre-service and in-service training of professionals would be another possible approach to address issues.

Through an innovative initiative called Action for Collaborative Transformation (ACT), academics in a higher education institution in the South East of England have adapted professional courses to include training elements for both pre-service and in-service professionals. This aims to upskill knowledge of other professions they may work with and reduce misconceptions. Projects have included a wide range of professionals for example, GPs, TAs, teachers, SENCOs, social workers, speech and language therapists, nursing, radiographers, etc. The overarching aim is developing an interdisciplinary community of learning and research (Delahunt et al., 2020) Through communication and respect, projects have had tangible outcomes to support professionals, for example an event for in-service teachers in managing medical conditions in school (Hughes et al., 2016).

Reflective Activity

Use the reflective questions below to start to consider ways that you understand your own professional identity and the professional identity of other professionals that you work with.

Consider what impact this has on the development of effective and collaborative practices moving forward.

- How do you see yourself professionally? Are you confident in multi-agency meetings? Are there areas you feel less confident? In what ways could you address this? For example recognising the limits of our own expertise and being open and honest about what we can bring to meetings that is valued.
- What could you do in practice to understand the role of other professions in more depth?
- If you had an opportunity for a secondment to a different role or service to aid your professional understanding, which profession would you choose and why? Is this because you know little about the profession or is it because you feel more comfortable with that profession?
- When did you last notice conflicting values when working with professionals from different disciplines?
- What were the main barriers you noticed?
- Why do you think this occurred?
- How did you manage the situation?
- What would you do the same, and what would you do differently, next time you are in a similar situation?

Consider the terminology you have used in a meeting with others. Are there differences in language, e.g. use of acronyms and are these addressed? What could be done to ensure there is clarity in meetings where professionals might use specialist terms or the language use might differ?

List at least five points to address this issue and select one approach to trial in the next suitable meeting.

Frost's (2005: 13) conceptualisation for professionals working together is presented as a hierarchy and could be a useful way to consider the levels of involvement when working together:

Level 0 – no partnership – uncoordinated, free-standing services
Level 1 – co-operation – services work together towards consistent goals and complementary services, whilst maintaining their independence
Level 2 – collaboration – services plan together and address issues of overlap, duplication and gaps in service provision towards common outcomes
Level 3 – co-ordination – services work together in a planned and systematic manner towards shared and agreed goals
Level 4 – merger/integration – different services become one organisation in order to enhance service delivery.

Reflective Activity

- Using Frost's (2005) levels of participation consider a couple of the working relationships you have with professionals.
    - Where would you place these and why?
    - If the relationships do not reach higher levels why is this?
    - Is this due to barrier/s?
    - Or it may be appropriate to work at lower levels for some tasks and then higher for others.
- How might you improve working with others in a more integrated way to enhance service delivery?

Stretched services in all sectors

As the House of Commons Education Committee (2019: 56) have identified, 'advice and information [from other professionals] are in short supply ... As services fail to deliver, distrust of professionals grows, and advice is sought elsewhere'.

There is, therefore, a need to ensure that any input available from other professionals is fully utilised to support the development of practices, not only for the individual pupil, but also, as applicable, to support increased knowledge and understanding to inform the development of practices across the whole school setting. Where we have been able to benefit from input and assessment from other professionals, there is, therefore, a real need to develop effective practices to fully utilise and implement strategies and recommendations from their professional reports into practice.

Unfortunately, all too often, reports from other professionals are not valued as much as they should be to inform the development of strategies. One reason for this can sometimes be the inclusion of high levels of professional jargon in some reports, which can impact on the understanding of education professionals and parents/carers.

Reflective Activity

- Think carefully about the range of professional reports that you have received to support the development of understanding about pupils needs in your school setting.
- How is the information on the reports shared with all – teachers and support staff working with the pupil, and parents/carers to inform the development of practices?
- Are there any examples of professional jargon or standardised scores that you do not fully understand and which require further interpretation and explanation from the other professional?
- How do you positively address this to ensure that the report received is used directly to influence and inform practice?

Managing the funds available more effectively is one way to address the challenges of very limited resources. **Collaboration** and *curiosity* to try new ways of working can lead to opportunities to provide more effective intervention and support for pupils. It also can improve on capacity in school as professionals learn from each other. Daniels (2011: 40) noted that 'boundary-crossing suggests that expertise is also developed when practitioners collaborate *horizontally* across sectors'. The following Case Study illustrates a new way of working between a SENCO and Speech and Language Therapist which resulted in improved expertise, provided a more cost-effective way to use resources and a model that could be scaled up in school.

Case Study – Multi-Agency Working in a Secondary School Context

Judith Stephenson

The focus of the case study was an innovative way of working collaboratively in a mainstream secondary school to address the needs of pupils with Speech, Language and Communication Needs (SLCN). This involved a pilot project between a GCSE English teacher and a Speech and Language Therapist (SALT). Children with poor language skills find it more difficult to understand new words and concepts, instructions, and feedback, leading to lower academic achievement (Snowling and Hulme, 2011). This mainstream secondary school in the south of England had a large proportion of pupils on the SEND register with a significant number of these having speech, language and communication issues. Traditional models of speech and language therapy delivery do not always allow a young person to generalise language skills to classroom learning.

The teacher involved in the pilot was also the SENCO who showed an interest in managing the needs of pupils on the SEND register. The SALT was the link therapist for the school working there one day a week. Therefore exploring ways to have the greatest impact for the limited time in school was important. Rather than a traditional model of working with children identified on the caseload, this project involved the teacher and SALT selecting a Year 11 GCSE class who were preparing for their exams. The SALT and teacher worked together for a term to jointly plan lessons and jointly deliver the lessons. The pilot was designed to increase pupils' functional use of language by giving them skills that would have an impact on their learning in the classroom.

After each lesson the SALT and teacher met to evaluate the lesson plan and delivery which would inform the next lesson. The joint planning sessions involved looking at the existing lesson plans from the teacher and adapting these to provide communication friendly ways of understanding the subject content, e.g. one example is using visuals and pre-teaching of subject specific vocabulary.

This project was necessary as pupils with speech, language and communication difficulties (SLCN) have pervasive difficulties which affect their ability within the classroom. Some research has shown that language of older children with SLCN can be enhanced through working in the classroom (Joffe, 2011). The SALT was working for a local NHS team and worked in link secondary schools one day a week and in this school there was a large caseload. The teacher found it difficult to prepare the children for exam questions because despite differentiation the pupils really struggled to understand key concepts (e.g. analyse or summarise, etc.) to support them in being able to access and respond to exam questions. These difficulties cannot be addressed by just targeting the language skills in isolation and pupils need a therapy model which encourages generalisation to the classroom environment. The model also fits with a coaching method which allows a therapist to facilitate others to meet the needs of pupils with SLCN.

The pilot working resulted in a number of benefits for the school, staff and pupils. Following the pilot the teacher reported feeling empowered and upskilled to meet the needs of pupils in all of her classes with language difficulties. The pupil understanding and engagement within the GCSE lessons improved. The teacher also reported feeling empowered to spread the practice within the department. The SALT was able to meet the demands of the caseload in a functional way.

Systematic reviews of the literature considering speech and language intervention in the school setting promote a collaborative approach to intervention (Elksnin, 1997; Steele & Mills, 2011; McGinty & Justice, 2006). One empirical study conducted by Throneburg et al. (2000) found that class based intervention was the most effective means of addressing vocabulary for primary aged pupils. The EEF promotes that the development of subject specific language at secondary school can be supported by targeted vocabulary instruction. Yet, there is an argument for further evidence on the short- and long-term effectiveness of or organisation wide interventions in Secondary Schools.

Reflective activity

- Which professionals/services do you currently work with?
- How effective are existing working practices?
- Could they be developed to improve efficiency at a time when all services, including the workload of school staff/SENCOs, is stretched?

Use Table 12.1 to consider ways in which you work with services and areas where you could made some further changes to improve on efficiency and outcomes. The first row has been completed as an example of what you might focus on in practice.

Table 12.1 Tool to audit ways of working with services

Service or agency	Identified area or priority	Identified tasks to work on together	Desired outcomes for school	Benefits/outcomes for the partner	How we will measure the impact
SALT	GCSE class – understanding of key terms on the exam papers	Collaborative planning of a unit of work – joint delivery for identified lessons	Improved language outcomes for identified pupils – improved exam results	More cost effective use of time. Able to support pupils with applying their understanding in class	Pupils' exam results Teacher/SALT/Pupil feedback

Addressing systemic silos

Culture and cultural change as well as **leadership** are key principles in addressing issues related to systemic silos. The OFSTED SEND report (2021n.p) refers to networks as a way to improve multi-agency working:

> Local leaders in both areas felt that school networks provided opportunities for them to share and develop inclusive approaches. The SEND lead in local authority 2, for example, said that meeting with other leads allowed 'real champions of inclusion' to push for best practice. This was echoed by the lead for behaviour and exclusions in local authority 1, who also commented that school leaders who took part in similar types of collaborative groups challenged each other to be more inclusive.

Developing a culture for safe spaces where practice can be supported and challenged is important to enable change going forward. There will always be constraints and boundaries to our circle of influence, but taking a lead on fostering open, honest and transparent conversations to further practice is a step towards an environment where professionals can value what they contribute as complementary to what others contribute. The current attempts at multi-agency working may be ideological, if there are no clear changes and improvements in practice to ensure children can access the holistic support that should be available to them. In addition to multi-agency working for meeting the needs of children requiring educational, health and social care support, safeguarding is often undertaken by SENCOs. Working Together to Safeguard Children (DfE, 2018a: 6) makes it clear that: 'Everyone who comes into contact with children and families has a role to play'. Yet, there are persistent issues with ensuring all are involved working collaboratively to meet children's needs. The House of Commons Education Committee (2019: 57) noted:

> Schools and colleges told us that there had been no increase, or even a decrease, in health and social care support. We heard that there was little co-operation or collaboration, or the onus was on the school to bring services together. Some felt that health and social care bodies were playing 'catch up' with the reforms, meaning all that was currently happening was the maintenance of the status quo.

There are wider implications impacting on the services being able to work together as identified in the OFSTED SEND report (2021: n.p) which referred to schools' challenges with multi-agency working and the 'frustrations with bureaucracy in the SEND system that could lead to challenges for collaboration and partnership working'. Therefore, despite changes in legislation to increase the duties on education, health and social care to work together and developments in policy to implement improved working together (DfE, 2018a, 2018b) unfortunately the worst of outcomes from failures result in Serious Case Reviews. This was highlighted during the pandemic with the tragic outcomes for Arthur Labinjo-Hughes and Star Hobson (Child Safeguarding Practice Review Panel, 2022):

> Despite the intentions of recent reforms (and most recently the Children and Social Work Act 2017), multi-agency safeguarding arrangements are not yet fit for purpose everywhere. This results too often in blurred strategic and operational responsibilities, creating fault lines in practice arrangements. This has major consequences for the ability of practitioners across different agencies to work together skilfully and purposively to protect children.
> (Child Safeguarding Practice Review Panel, 2022: 5)

> There needs to be much greater focus on creating the optimum conditions and environment for what is very complex and high-risk decision making. The perennial problems of sharing, seeking and using information about a child and a family persist. This must be tackled. We cannot afford to revisit these problems again and again; new approaches are required.
> (Child Safeguarding Practice Review Panel, 2022: 6)

These tragedies necessitate *cultural change* in how we organise the structures and systems at a macro level as well as within schools to ensure children are kept safe and well. Good communication is considered as fundamental to successful multi-agency working. There is a need for clarity of purpose through the establishment of clear and shared aims and objectives. Establishing common systems is not enough, what is required is a shared understanding of how to work together towards the shared goals which are centred around the child, as outlined in the Child Safeguarding Practice Review Panel (2022: 10) which noted: 'Trust, shared values, and identity are crucial behavioural factors in frictionless sharing of information between professionals'.

Reflective Activity

Review again the list of professionals that you currently work with:

- Which professionals do you feel more aligned to in practice?
- Reflect on why you have stronger relationships with some professionals and not others.
  - Is this due to common professional values?
  - Is this due to relational aspects such as personality?
  - How can you reduce any possible unconscious bias?

Physical space and structural aspects are important to working together and need to be considered going forward. The OFSTED SEND report (2021: n.p) refers to location of the services as having an impact on how well the services operate together:

> Some representatives from both the local authority and CCG discussed how the location of services could have an impact on the strength of collaboration. The physical proximity of different teams, either within the same buildings or through the creation of multi-team meetings or working groups, was felt to have a beneficial impact. Representatives saw this as a way of enabling staff to access each other and of building trust between partners.

The Multi-Agency Safeguarding Hubs (MASH) include a number of benefits by being co-located services:

1. More accurate assessment of risk and need, as safeguarding decisions are based on coordinated, sufficient, accurate and timely intelligence
2. More thorough and driven management of cases. Some felt that this was the key benefit of multi-agency hubs, as it avoids cases getting 'lost' in the system, and ensures leads are chased up
3. Better understanding between professions, both in terms of the terminology used and the general approach to safeguarding
4. Greater efficiencies in processes and resources

(Home Office, 2014: 8–9)

It could be argued that too much time is being 'wasted' trying to get different professionals to be able to collaborate with each other, when they could potentially do a better job working separately completing their part of the process, and their specialist role. Yet, with this position, it could entrench further separatist views and further distance between what is known and what we think we know about other professional roles. The MASH review (2014) shows that when working together is supported and happens as a collaborative venture rather than a siloed experience of operating in your own area of influence or expertise, the outcomes provide much improved judgements, communication, accountability and value for money.

Reflective Activity

- Consider the ways in which you could co-locate or organise the resources or services in school to improve on communication and effectiveness.
- Consider also the Case Study that follows in this section and reflect on any ways that aspects of the practice outlined could be of benefit to the development of practices in your own school setting.

Case Study – Embedding Multi-Professional Understanding and Working in a Primary School Setting

This Case Study is based on the development of practices and professional working relationships within a primary school in an area of high social deprivation over a two year period.

The SENCO and senior leaders in the school context had reflected on the barriers to successful access to education for pupils and families in their school community. Whilst some barriers and factors were linked to the need for more consistent staffing and the implementation of specific evidence-informed intervention approaches, a significant majority of barriers related to wider aspects of practice impacting on the pupil and their family. These included:

- Poor housing
- Lack of money/food
- Poor educational experiences
- High levels of adult illiteracy
- Low aspirations
- Unemployment
- Poor health
- Drug and alcohol abuse
- High levels of teenage pregnancy – many of the pupils attending the school had very young parents
- Low levels of engagement

The SENCO and senior leaders reflected that they would not be able to address all of those factors by themselves, but started to put together a picture of the amount of different services and agencies that were working – separately – with the families that they were supporting.

The school therefore hosted an initial multi-agency meeting – to bring together all of the different professionals working with the pupils and families attending their school. This included representatives from:

- Community Police
- Social Care
- Health Visitors
- Midwives
- Adult Education Services
- Housing
- GP Services
- Job Seekers and Employment Service
- Adult and Young Peoples Mental Health Services
- Religious groups
- Food and Clothing Banks.

> Over a period of two years, regular multi-agency meetings were held – located in different venues to help to increase understanding of the different professional contexts within which the different professionals worked.
>
> Initially, the focus of the meetings was just on developing a shared understanding of the role and remit of the different professionals and their services.
>
> Gradually, this was then able to be extended into more effective discussions about shared priorities and ways that the professionals could collaborate together to address shared trends and areas of priority, or to support particular families or pupils.
>
> At this point, an important step forward was the introduction of parents/carers into the multi-agency group to discuss and plan collaborative approaches to community needs, so that the needs of the local community could be fully understood from their own perspective, rather than from the perspective of the professionals.
>
> As a result of the work that was undertaken, professional trust and understanding increased – with a significant impact in collaborative working practices to secure successful outcomes for the families and pupils within the catchment area of the school.

To be able to effectively take forward meaningful multi-agency working requires a commitment to the benefits of the approach and an open understanding of any challenges that continue to need to be overcome.

To support with this, review Table 12.2 as a planning format to consider aspects of practice that currently work well to support multi-agency working in your school setting, and any challenges that remain, and ways to positively address those. Develop this further to add on any additional examples of aspects of practice that currently work well, or challenges/barriers to overcome relevant to your own school setting.

Table 12.2 Review of multi-agency working

What is working well? RAG* rate the effectiveness of positive aspects of practice to support multi-agency working currently in place	Examples of practice	Ways to develop this further
• Attending multi-agency meetings/conferences		
• Developing relationships: knowing people by name		
• Building a Directory of Services to improve knowledge and understanding about different services		
• Accessing training from other professionals		
• Working together with other professionals to build a holistic picture of the child		
• Building pastoral roles within the school setting to support collaborative working with families and other professionals		
• Opportunities for secondments between professionals to aid professional understanding		

(*Continued*)

Table 12.2 (Continued)

Remaining challenges RAG* rate the impact of the challenges/barriers on practices in your school setting currently	Examples of practice	Ways to positively overcome those challenges/barriers
• Lack of access to other agencies		
• Lack of response/attendance by other agencies		
• GDPR – ways to effectively share information between professionals		
• Lack of training/understanding/knowledge about different systems and processes		
• Time		
• Shared understanding of thresholds/expectations		

* Red = Not evident in practice; Amber = some aspects evident in practice; Green = Fully evident in practice.

Concluding comments and reflections

Is multi-agency working a good idea when we stop to look at the many barriers and challenges faced by professionals? It is difficult to argue against what is fundamentally the 'right' principle, and although the current attempts at multi-agency working can appear to be ideological, in reality the consequences of not working together effectively is too often identified as the weaknesses leading to serious case reviews.

It is difficult to see a clear improvement in practice, when there are still so many persistent barriers which in some cases are outside our realms of influence to address. However it is important to recognise that legislation has been strengthened to include greater duties on services working together such as with the Children and Families Act (2014). There have also been key initiatives and political agendas to drive forward change, such as the Every Child Matters agenda (DfES, 2003) and most recently the SEND and Alternative Provision Improvement Plan (DfE/DoHSC, 2023) which also includes reference to the development of the National Standards for SEND in collaboration with the Department of Health and Social Care and NHS England. The fact that the current proposals from the government are presented as a collaborative venture between the DfE and DoHSC reinforces the commitment to working together at the macro level. A cultural change is required at all levels alongside the investment in resources, systems and structures if we are going to ensure that working together will have the desired improvements for all.

Reflective Activity

- What new information/learning have you gained from this chapter?
- What are your key reflections?
- What are your next steps/actions as a result?

References

Atkinson, M., Jones, M. and Lamont, E. (2007) *Multi-agency working and its implications for practice: A literature review.*

Child Safeguarding Practice Review Panel (2022) *Child Protection in England.* Available from: https://assets.publishing.service.gov.uk/government/uploads/system/uploads/attachment_data/file/1078488/ALH_SH_National_Review_26-5-22.pdf (accessed 20.5.23).

Children Act (2004) Available from: https://www.legislation.gov.uk/ukpga/2004/31/contents (accessed 20.5.23).

Children and Families Act (2014) https://www.legislation.gov.uk/ukpga/2014/6/contents (accessed 20.12.22).

Curran, H., Moloney, H., Heavey, A. and Boddison, A. (2020) *The time is now: Addressing missed opportunities for Special Educational Needs Support and Coordination in our schools.* Available from: https://www.bathspa.ac.uk/media/bathspaacuk/education-/research/senco-workload/National-SENCO-Workload-Survey-Report-Jan-2020.pdf (accessed 1.5.23).

Daniels, H. (2011) The shaping of communication across boundaries. *International Journal of Educational Research* 50 (1), 40–47.

Delahunt, T., Le Moine, G. and Soan, S. (2020) 'Challenges of multi-professional working within one English higher education institution: 'we hit a giant': Is this a shared experience?' *Practice* 3 (1), 58–66.

DfE (2018a) *Working Together to Safeguard Children: A guide to inter-agency working to safeguard and promote the welfare of children.* Available from: https://www.gov.uk/government/publications/working-together-to-safeguard-children-2 (accessed 20.5.23).

DfE (2018b) *Information sharing: Advice for practitioners providing safeguarding services to children, young people, parents and carers.* Available from: https://assets.publishing.service.gov.uk/government/uploads/system/uploads/attachment_data/file/1062969/Information_sharing_advice_practitioners_safeguarding_services.pdf (accessed 20.5.23).

DfE/DoH (2015) *Special Educational Needs and Disability Code of Practice for 0 to 25 year olds.* Available from: https://www.gov.uk/government/publications/send-code-of-practice-0-to-25 (accessed 20.5.23).

DfE/DoHSC (2023) *Special Educational Needs and Disabilities (SEND) and Alternative Provision Improvement Plan – Right support, right place, right time.* London: HMSO.

DfES (2003) *Every child matters.* London: Crown Copyright.

Elksnin, L.K. (1997) 'Collaborative speech and language services for students with learning disabilities.' *Journal of Learning Disabilities* 30 (4).414–426

Frost, N. (2005) Professionalism, partnership and joined-up thinking: a research review of front-line working with children and families. *Research in Practice* www.rip.org.uk

Hellawell, B. (2019) *Understanding and challenging the SEND Code of Practice.* London: SAGE Publications Ltd.

Home Office (2014) *Multi agency working and information sharing project final report.* Available from: https://assets.publishing.service.gov.uk/government/uploads/system/uploads/attachment_data/file/338875/MASH.pdf (accessed 20.5.23).

House of Commons Education Committee (2019) *Special Educational Needs and Disabilities.* London: House of Commons.

Hughes, L., Durrant, J. and Le Moine, G. (2016) 'Skilling up for health and well-being – The professional development challenge'. *Professional Development Today* 18(4), 16–25.

Joffe, V.L. (2011) Secondary school is not too late to support and enhance language and communication. *Afasic newsletter*, Winter Edition. Afasic

Lamb, B. (2009). *Lamb Inquiry: Special Educational Needs and Parental Confidence.* Available from: https://dera.ioe.ac.uk/9042/1/Lamb%20Inquiry%20Review%20of%20SEN%20and%20Disability%20Information.pdf (accessed 20.12.22).

Laming (2003) *The Victoria Climbie Inquiry*. Available from: https://assets.publishing.service.gov.uk/government/uploads/system/uploads/attachment_data/file/273183/5730.pdf (accessed 20.5.23).

Laming (2009) *The protection of children in England: A progress report*. Available from: https://assets.publishing.service.gov.uk/government/uploads/system/uploads/attachment_data/file/328117/The_Protection_of_Children_in_England.pdf (accessed 20.5.23).

Lawson, H.A. (2004) 'The logic of collaboration in education and the human services'. *Journal of Interprofessional Care* 18(3), 225–237.

McAuliffe, D. (2014) *Interprofessional ethics: Collaboration in the social, health and human services*. Port Melbourne: Cambridge University Press.

McGinty, A.S. and Justice, L.M. (2006) 'Classroom-based versus pull-out language intervention: An examination of the experimental evidence'. *EBP Briefs* 1, 3–26.

NAO (2019) *Support for pupils with special educational needs and disabilities in England*. London: House of Commons.

Ofsted (2021) *Supporting SEND*. Available from: https://www.gov.uk/government/publications/supporting-send/supporting-send (accessed 20.5.23).

Rizzo Parse, R. (2015) 'Interdisciplinary and interprofessional: What are the differences'. *Nursing Science Quarterly* 28(1), 5–6.

Snowling, M. and Hulme (2011) 'Interventions for children's language and literacy difficulties'. *International Journal of Language and Communication Disorders* 47(1), 27–34.

Steele, S. and Mills, M. (2011) 'Vocabulary intervention for school-age children with language impairment: A review of evidence and good practice'. *Child Language Teaching and Therapy* 27(3), 354–370.

Throneburg, R., Calvert, L., Sturm, J., Paramboukas, A. and Paul, P. (2000) 'A comparison of service delivery models: Effects on curricular vocabulary skills in the school setting'. *American Journal of Speech-Language Pathology* 9, 10–20.

Worth, D. (2022) '£63K a month bills: Soaring energy prices hit schools'. *TES Magazine Online*. Available from: https://www.tes.com/magazine/news/general/ps63k-month-bills-soaring-energy-prices-hit-schools (accessed 20.5.23).

13 Concluding comments

> In this chapter, we provide some conclusions to the book as a whole, focusing on the following aspects:
>
> - A summary of the current situation and challenges
> - Ways to move forward – a timeline for the new proposals
> - Models to implement change
> - Use of evidence-informed practice:
>
>   Action Research
>   Lesson Study
>   EEF Guidance Reports
>
> - Use of Continuing Professional Development (CPD)
> - Principled approaches to the development of effective practices

The current situation and challenges

As we have explored throughout the book, the situation with the Special Educational Needs and Disability (SEND) system in England currently remains a challenging one. It is challenging for parents/carers who continue to experience adversarial and inequitable situations and responses when trying to navigate the SEND system to achieve the best outcomes for their child; challenging for pupils with SEND who continue to experience barriers to access and participation which exclude them from opportunities to learn and develop alongside their peers and to focus on outcomes that are directly relevant to their experiences; and challenging for the education professionals – teachers, support staff and SENCOs who are desperately trying to do their best within a SEND system that is still not yet fit for purpose (House of Commons Education Committee, 2019; DfE, 2022; DfE/DoHSC, 2023).

Whilst the House of Commons Education Committee (2019) and DfE/DoHSC (2023) identify that the SEND reforms are the right ones, yet it is clear that change is essential, and actually this relates to the education system as a whole, not just the

SEND system struggling to operate within it. As Fullan (2020: 61) notes – 'The status quo – the way schools are – is no longer fit for purpose. Almost 4 out of 5 students are disengaged from school learning, inequality is rapidly on the rise, anxiety and stress among the young of all socioeconomic groups is steadily increasing. All signs point to change'.

Whilst the pandemic was hugely challenging in so many ways, it is a shame that the opportunities presented by the pandemic have not been fully utilised to provide the 'principled interruption' (Ainscow et al., 2006) to our thinking about how schools and the education system should function, and the impact that the traditional school system and environment that we continue to place children within has on our pupils. Many important lessons were learnt during that period and as pupils returned to schools, the opportunities to fully learn from those experiences to change embedded practices in positive ways seem to have been missed.

As Fullan (2020) identifies – change is absolutely necessary. Yet, as we have explored, change is a challenging and unsettling thing.

Since the House of Commons Education Committee (2019: 83) called for immediate action from the government to 'move swiftly to address the many other problems that we identify in our report. A generation of children depends on it', there have, therefore, been further stresses and strains placed on teachers, families and children trying desperately to navigate the system. Some of the persistent wider challenges have been referred to in the book in relation to specific areas of practice. Here they are explored further in their own right.

The financial challenge

Challenges with resources and sufficient funding to meet the needs of pupils with SEND, as well as the cost of living crisis and the impact this has on families has been referred to throughout the book. However, the deep rooted challenges with funding are significant. The current system is unsustainable (NAO, 2019), with 81.3% of local authorities overspending their high-needs budget in 2017–2018. Most local authorities were transferring money from their school block of funding to their high-needs block of funding (NAO, 2019), which served to draw away funds that would ordinarily be available for supporting inclusive practices in mainstream, possibly exacerbating the challenges of providing high-quality, well-resourced, inclusive provisions to avoid children having to be placed in specialist provision.

In the current system pupils' needs are not being met in a timely way due to the long clinical waiting lists owing to stretched services. The responsibility for meeting this gap is falling upon the schools and parents (DfE, 2021a). Some parents/carers are resorting to paying for services directly, which is leading to an inequitable two-tier system for pupils who have the most complex needs – those who are able to pay can access services and those who do not have the financial capability or social capital to navigate the complex systems are having to wait to access the support.

In 2014, the Department for Education did not fully evaluate the costs involved in the implementation of the SEND reforms and 'did not complete a formal regulatory impact assessment, but published an evidence pack to support the passage of the Children and Families Bill. It had not, at that stage, completed its evaluation of the local pathfinders' (NAO, 2019: 35). Furthermore, 'decisions by the Department for Education to allow local authorities to spend their implementation grant with little or no oversight or safeguards' (House of Commons Education Committee, 2019: 12).

Therefore the implementation of the SEND reforms was at a disadvantage financially from the start. The expectation of the 2014 SEND reforms was for an improved process with parents/carers as co-producers to build confidence in the system and reduce the number of costly statutory assessment requests (DfE, 2011). Yet, requests for EHCPs have since increased and 'between January 2014 and January 2018, the number of pupils in special schools and alternative provision rose by 20.2%' (NAO, 2019: 8).

The proposal to build confidence in the system is echoed again in the planned new changes (DfE/DoHSC, 2023: 5–6) as noted below:

> This will give families and providers clarity, consistency and confidence in the support that is ordinarily available, in order to be responsive to children's needs. With these expectations, and improved mainstream provision, more children and young people will receive the support they need through ordinarily available provision in their local setting. Fewer will therefore need to access support through an Education, Health and Care Plan (EHCP).

Too many times, it has been noted that more money will not have the desired impact, there has to be a change in culture. Confidence needs to be gained in the system, but with cultural change at a systemic level to be able to utilise resources more effectively.

> unless there is a systemic cultural shift on the part of all parties involved, additional funding will make little difference to the outcomes and experiences of children and young people with SEND.
> (House of Commons Education Committee, 2019: 12)

The teacher training challenge

Throughout the book, teacher levels of knowledge, skills, competency, confidence and self-efficacy have been referred to. These aspects are important to consider in relation to the wider context of Initial Teacher Training (ITT).

There have been issues identified with ITT (Carter, 2015: 57) in relation to preparing the teaching workforce to meet pupils' needs: 'a number of organisations have raised concerns with us about how ITT inadequately prepares new teachers to address SEND in the classroom'. This led to the recommendation that 'Special educational needs and disabilities should be included in a framework for ITT content' (Carter, 2015: 58). This was adopted with the introduction of the Core Content Framework (2019a) and the Early Career Framework (2019b) which includes a two year induction period for teachers who achieve Qualified Teacher Status. The extended induction (which was previously one year) supports the new teacher with training and guidance as they progress, which is important because teaching is a profession that we continue to improve on. This developmental nature is noted by Fletcher-Wood and Zuccollo (2020: 1): 'Teachers improve gradually through experience, particularly if they teach the same course content for several years (Kini & Podolsky, 2016). This increase in effectiveness is considerably faster in a supportive professional environment'. Fletcher-Wood and Zuccollo's (2020) report undertook a detailed review of the evidence on the impact of teacher professional development. A central claim was that high-quality training and development would boost pupil attainment and may also address retention problems in the profession. Therefore, not only the initial training, but effective Continuing Professional Development (CPD), is important to get right.

Whilst there is a mandatory requirement for CPD in schools, this is determined by the school and can therefore be quite variable. Furthermore with the evident variability in SEND training identified in ITT (Carter, 2015) the current workforce may need very targeted support and training to ensure they are able to meet the needs of pupils with SEND. This includes a requirement to monitor and manage the training needs related to the staff knowledge of SEND in the Special Educational Needs (SEN) Information Report (DfE/DoH, 2015). Some of the Case Studies shared in the previous chapters have provided insights into how some schools and SENCOs are approaching the need to embed critical thinking and understanding about SEND and inclusion into CPD opportunities to support their staff to develop effective practices and fulfil their statutory responsibilities for SEND.

The current proposals to address high-quality training in the teaching profession and CPD includes a government commitment to improvement by 2024 focused on 'giving all teachers and school leaders access to world-class, evidence-informed training and professional development at every stage of their career' (DfE, 2022: 8). The reported progress to date by the government claims:

> Every teacher and school leader now has access to a golden thread of high-quality, evidence-based training and professional development at every stage of their career. By providing training on areas that are fundamental to high-quality teaching like behaviour management, adaptive teaching and curriculum design, these reforms will help teachers and leaders to support all pupils to succeed, including those identified with SEND.
>
> (DfE, 2022: 17)

There are aspirational plans outlined with regard to training which include

> Working closely with the Education Endowment Foundation, the Institute of Teaching will be England's flagship teacher development provider, delivering cutting-edge training.
>
> (DfE, 2022: 21)

Whilst this is indeed pleasing to note, the recent NASUWT (2023) research on the quality of training exposed the following findings. 'Almost three quarters of respondents who received SEN/ALN/ASN-related training or CPD in the last two years received just one day or less in total' (NASUWT, 2023, n.p.). Additionally, 'Teachers report that their school does not have enough money to fund training/CPD and that external training/CPD is often very expensive' (NASUWT, 2023, n.p.).

Furthermore, the training that was being delivered was often not fit of purpose:

> Most training/CPD is delivered by a member of school staff. Local authorities are still a major provider of CPD/training across the UK but, increasingly, schools are obtaining CPD/training from consultants and private providers. This is often expensive and there are concerns that programmes are 'glitzy' rather than focused on what teachers need.
>
> (NASUWT, 2023, n.p.)

It would seem that the aspirations outlined by the Department for Education (2017) are not yet embedded in ITT and with the Market Review leading to a new accreditation process for Initial Teacher Training Providers, there are further developments taking place to assure the training is of high quality (DfE, 2021b) The new SEND proposals (DfE/DoHSC, 2023) for change have noted the importance of training that needs to be addressed at the start of a teachers' career and their ITT course:

> We heard, however, that we need to go further if we are going to achieve the aim of improving mainstream provision so that it is more inclusive of children and young people with SEND. Respondents consistently highlighted the need for ongoing teacher training – and when children and young people who are in alternative provision were asked what would have helped them stay in their mainstream school, the most common answer was teacher training in SEND.
>
> (DfE/DoHSC, 2023: 54)

The recruitment and retention challenge

There are less teachers training to enter the profession now, than in past years. Government 2022–2023 statistics based on the Initial Teacher Training Census note:

> In total there were 28,991 new entrants to ITT in 2022/23 compared to 36,159 in 2021/22[1], 40,377 in 2020/21 and 33,799 in 2019/20.
> Percentage of ITT recruitment target reached 93% Primary subjects (down from 131% in 2021/22)
> Percentage of ITT recruitment target reached 59% Secondary subjects (down from 79% in 2021/22)
> Percentage of ITT recruitment target reached 62% EBacc subjects (down from 84% in 2021/22)
>
> (Gov.uk, 2022)

The recent (2022–2023) strikes over pay and conditions for teachers have served to highlight in the media the challenges faced in schools. This has included high-workload, poorly maintained facilities, budget cuts and lack of teachers as some of the reasons for taking industrial action (Adams, 2023). These conditions undoubtedly have an impact on retention. The National Education Union (2022: np) noted that:

- 44% of England's state-school teachers plan to quit by 2027, according to the latest NEU poll. Half of those (22%) intend to leave within two years
- Schools are struggling to fill vacant posts, leading to a doubling up of roles. 73% of teachers say this has worsened since the start of the pandemic.

Additionally, findings from the Special and Additional Educational Needs (NASUWT, 2023, n.p.) report identified

> Teachers try to do the best for the learners they teach. However, they are not always equipped with the knowledge, skills and expertise to meet the needs of learners with

SEN/ALN/ASN. Increasing pressures and workloads, including those arising from other education reforms, have consequences for teacher morale, teacher wellbeing and teacher retention.

The retention of staff is also being keenly felt within posts for SEND where workload, stress and well-being are factors. As the NASUWT research has identified 'The findings raise major concerns about the retention and future recruitment of SENCOs/ALNCOs/ASN Co-ordinators' (NASUWT, 2023, n.p.), but also for the recruitment and retention of Teaching Assistants (TAs) and support staff working in schools to support meeting the needs of pupils.

The issue of recruitment and retention has been identified in the government proposals (DfE/DoHSC, 2023: 55) where it is noted that more needs to be done to ensure teaching is an attractive profession:

> Continuing to attract, retain and develop the highly skilled teachers we need is one of our top priorities, as set out in our Teacher Recruitment and Retention Strategy. That is why we are delivering 500,000 training and development opportunities by the end of 2024, alongside a range of resources to help schools address teacher workload issues, prioritise staff wellbeing and introduce flexible working practices.

The continuing contradictions challenge

There are a number of tensions identified in the book. Some of these contradictions remain in systems and processes related to SEND, despite government proposals (DfE/DoHSC, 2023). These contradictions need to be carefully considered if we are to make progress towards an education which meets the needs of all. One consideration is the necessity for a separate SEND system. With fully inclusive approaches from the State level, through the education system and processes, it could be argued that an entirely separate system to meet the needs of some learners (based on a negative model of difficulties rather than differences) is not required. Some of the continuing contradictions are noted below (see Table 13.1).

Table 13.1 Contradictions in the DfE/DoHSC (2023) proposals

Performance targets – 'a national and local inclusion dashboard that will present timely performance data across education, health and care' p. 71	Versus	Celebrate success in all forms – 'Our vision is to create a more inclusive society that celebrates and enables success in all forms' p. 7
Long clinical wait times – Recognising the 'challenges presented by long waiting times and staff shortages when it comes to receiving support from specialists' p. 61		Early intervention – A focus on 'early identification of needs and intervention' p. 5
Standardisation: a single set of National Standards – 'new evidenced-informed National Standards' p. 5		Personalisation – the need to recognise that pupils have 'unique needs and these will depend on their personal circumstances and backgrounds' p. 27
Less bureaucracy – The proposals will ensure that 'the experience of seeking support at every stage is less bureaucratic' p. 9		Increased bureaucracy and new systems – Introduction of new systems 'single national system based on the new National Standards will be delivered locally, through new local partnerships and an improved EHCP process' p. 9

Reflective Activity

'We are confident that the 2014 reforms were the right ones. We believe that if the challenges within the system—including finance—are addressed, local authorities will be able to discharge their duties sufficiently' (House of Commons Education Committee, 2019: 84).

- Having reviewed the information in this book and in relation to practice in your own area and school setting, how far would you agree with the statement above.
- What, if any, are the remaining barriers and challenges to enabling this to move forward?

Moving forward

We are at a critical time for SENCOs and those who are working with children and families of children with SEND. In 2014, the SEND reforms were referred to as the 'biggest change' – yet in reality almost 10 years on, there has been little improvement and some would argue a more complex, adversarial system is now operating.

In order for change to occur it is not simply policy or legislation changes that need to take place. In all aspects there needs to be a principled values-informed approach underpinning the system and everything we do. The Government proposals (DfE/DoHSC, 2023) could be viewed as including some really positive developments to address the current challenges outlined earlier in this chapter and through the book as a whole. However, it is absolutely vital that the implementation of these reforms do not proceed in the same manner as the SEND reforms of 2014. Otherwise, implementation, appropriate training and support for culture change will be severely hampered again.

Table 13.2 provides some of the changes proposed by the Government (DfE/DoHSC) that are likely to impact on practice in school. Look at the proposed change and the timeline to then consider the possible implications for practice.

Table 13.2 Review of proposed changes (DfE/DoHSC, 2023)

Proposal in SEND and Alternative Provision Improvement Plan (DfE/DoHSC, 2023)	When?	Possible implications for practice
Change Programme	Commences in 2023	
Regional Expert Partnerships	Commences in Spring 2023	
Standard EHCP template	Supporting guidance and processes from 2025	
National Standards	Commences in 2023, initial publication in 2025	
Local SEND and alternative provision partnerships	Non-statutory guidance to be issued in Autumn 2023	
Evidenced-based local inclusion plans	Commences in 2023 and agreed by the end of 2024	
Digital requirements for EHCP systems	Test and design commences in 2023, and dependent on the digital solutions, roll-out commences in 2025	
An amended version of the SEND Code of Practice	Not specified but consultation aligned to the introduction of the new National Standards	
Review of Children's Social Care to introduce a Children's Social Care National Framework	Framework published on 2/2/23 for consultation	
New leadership level SENCO (Special Educational Needs Coordinator) NPQ (National Professional Qualification) for schools	Notes that further details on the timings will be provided in due course.	

Models to implement change – use of evidence-informed practice

Clearly, we are at a point of change and transition, and, as we have identified throughout the book and as one of our key principles underpinning the discussions as a whole, meaningful engagement with evidence-informed and reflective practices are essential to support effective changes and developments within our school settings.

Change, however, as we have identified, is challenging and can be fraught with emotional responses and there is therefore a need for schools to utilise existing, and new, models for leading change in effective ways.

There are a number of different models to support schools to be able to plan and lead change, and in this concluding chapter we want to focus on four in particular:

1 Action Research as a structured model to embed evidence-informed approaches to school development and change
2 Lesson Study
3 The EEF's Guidance Reports and key recommendations – particularly the EEF (2019) Guide to Implementation – Putting Evidence to work, which provides a very structured and evidence-informed approach to understanding how to plan and implement changes, both large and small
4 Quality CPD for staff.

Action Research

There has been a drive recently for schools to undertake research. The DfE (2017) reviewed progress towards an evidence-informed teaching system, and noted that

> School leaders' support for engagement with research is the most important driver. Whether schools are completely disengaged or highly engaged with research evidence, school leaders can make positive changes to increase engagement.
> (DfE, 2017: 9)

Therefore, to foster a culture that supports research in schools will require Senior Leadership support.

> Teachers' use of research evidence was prompted by a need to solve a practical problem: for the more research-engaged teachers, research was part of the evidence base they used to achieve this.
> (DfE, 2017: 6)

The National Award for SEN Coordination is a current requirement to be a SENCO and is currently a masters level qualification. Many courses include practitioner research (an example of Action Research is included in Chapter 8). Providing opportunities to engage in research in this way is important to build teachers' knowledge skills and confidence as noted in the DfE (2017: 6) finding:

> Most teachers interviewed did not feel confident in engaging with research directly, or feel able to judge its quality, relying on senior leaders and other organisations like

the Sutton Trust and the Education Endowment Foundation (EEF). The exceptions were those undertaking higher level academic study.

(DfE, 2017: 6)

Action Research is a model that can be used in schools to research a range of processes and approaches. For example, it might investigate the implementation of a new policy, it may focus on the effectiveness of current interventions for literacy, it may explore the impact of a new intervention, etc. Vulliamy and Webb (1992: 14) note that 'Action research is always a form of self-reflective enquiry. It is an approach which requires teacher-researchers to use evidence to identify issues and gain understanding of problems with which they are directly concerned'.

Action Research is essentially an ongoing, cyclical process to inform and improve on practice. Elliot describes the process of: 'review, diagnosis, planning, implementation, monitoring effects – is called action research, and it provides the necessary link between self-evaluation and professional development' (1981, p. ii). This aligns well with the Graduated Approach outlined in the SEN and Disability Code of Practice (DfE/DoH, 2015) and referred to in Chapters 7 and 8. Importantly, like the Graduated Approach 'It requires not only the critical reflection on practice and theory–practice conversation, but also it designates ongoing and evolving action as part of that process' (McAteer, 2012: 12).

In some settings Action Research has been utilised as 'an important component of a school's overall management and staff development strategy' (Vulliamy & Webb, 1992: 17). INSET in schools can also be an opportunity to build collaborative Action Research projects for whole school development.

Lesson Study

Lesson Study was originally developed in Japan with a long history related to examining teaching practices to inform improvements (Takahashi & Yashida, 2004). It is a method of professional learning where small groups of teachers undertake an enquiry involving a cycle of 'study-plan-do-review' activities to improve pedagogical knowledge and strategies and ultimately improve on pupil learning and progress.

Despite some variations in Lesson Study practice, the basic principles involve:

1 Collaborative design of lessons or units of study,
2 Execution of the design with observation,
3 Reflection on the product with a view to its improvement.

(Norwich et al., 2020: 1)

Lesson Study for Assessment: Introduction and Guidelines (Norwich, 2014: 6) provides a useful overview and guide on how to implement this in practice as well as including all the templates to be able to conduct the Lesson Study process. Figure 13.1 outlines the cycles used in a project:

232 *Concluding comments*

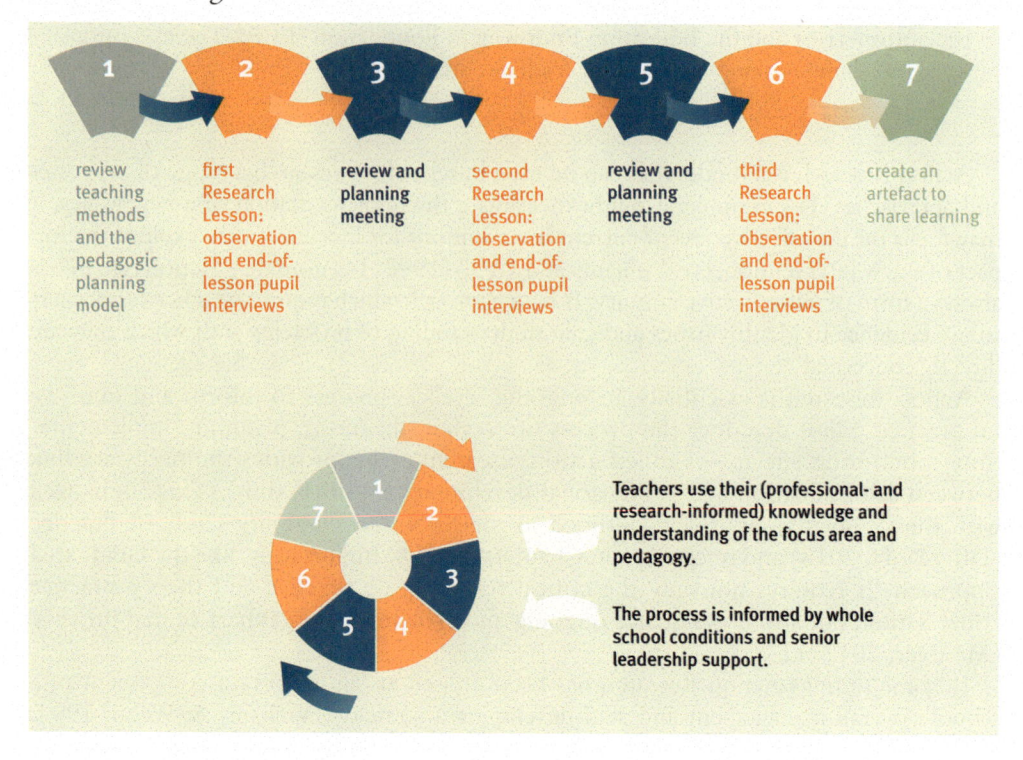

Figure 13.1 Lesson Study process

Source: https://blogs.exeter.ac.uk/lessonstudysend/files/2017/09/LSfA-guidance-booklet-pdf-.pdf (accessed 4.6.23).

The EEF (2023) reviewed the effectiveness of Lesson Study as an approach and although they were not able to determine measurable outcomes related to pupil attainment, they did identify the value it has in supporting CPD and improved practice in schools:

> Teachers felt Lesson Study was useful professional development, valued the opportunity to collaborate with colleagues in a structured way, and reported several changes to their practice as a result of the programme.
>
> (EEF, 2023, n.p.)

A useful resource to find out more about Lesson Study and how this has been used in relation to supporting Special Educational Needs and Inclusive Education is available on the following website: https://www.lessonstudysend.co.uk/

Use of the EEF Guidance Reports and key recommendations

The EEF Guidance Reports provide a wealth of accessible evidence-informed information to support meaningful reflection, review and development in our schools. Rigorous use of them, embedding the recommendations in practice by using them to form individualised

Action Plans in your school context will support the effective development of understanding and practices.

In particular, the following EEF Guidance Reports are particularly relevant to our work in SEND, although others (e.g. Metacognition and Self-Regulated Learning, 2018c; Using Digital Technology to Improve Learning, 2019b) also include really useful recommendations and evidence-bases to inform planning for developments to support all learners in our schools:

- Special Educational Needs in Mainstream Schools (EEF, 2020)
- Effective Professional Development (EEF, 2021)
- Putting Evidence to work – A School's Guide to Implementation (EEF, 2019a)
- Making best use of Teaching Assistants (EEF, 2018a)
- Working with Parents to support Children's Learning (EEF, 2018b).

The EEF (2020) SEND key questions tool (https://d2tic4wvo1iusb.cloudfront.net/production/eef-guidance-reports/send/ SEND_key_questions_tool.pdf?v=1695043976) provides a really useful tool to support a review of SEND practices across the school setting. This tool is based on the five recommendations from the EEF (2020) SEN in mainstream schools Guidance Report and provides question prompts for school leaders to reflect on in relation to existing practices in their school setting.

Using tools like this will support a principled approach to 'making the familiar unfamiliar' (Delamont & Atkinson, 1995), providing 'principled interruptions' (Ainscow et al., 2006) to existing practices and enabling real reflection about how effective those practices are.

In addition to the recommendations and evidence-informed information provided in the EEF (2020) SEN in Mainstream Schools Guidance Report, the evidence-informed approach to effective implementation – Putting Evidence to work – A School's Guide to Implementation (EEF, 2019a) provides some really important and valuable models and information to support schools in thinking about how to engage more effectively with research and evidence-bases to plan and embed effective change moving forward.

In particular, the following models – the Implementation Process diagram (see Figure 13.2) (EEF, 2019a: 5) and the Six Recommendations for effective implementation (see Figure 13.3) (EEF, 2019a: 6–7) are particularly helpful.

Reflective Activity

- How far have you/your school setting engaged with the EEF Guidance Reports so far?
- How far do you think that the recommendations and evidence-informed information from the Guidance Reports are fully embedded?
- Would it be worth revisiting any with staff to ensure that there is full understanding and ownership of the recommendations so that they can be actively embedded in practice to support developments moving forward?
- How fully is the EEF (2019a) Putting Evidence to Work – A School's Guide to Implementation used and embedded in practice in your school setting?
- How do you think that this could be developed further to support and improve the implementations of any changes that need to be made?
- Who would you like to involve in this?

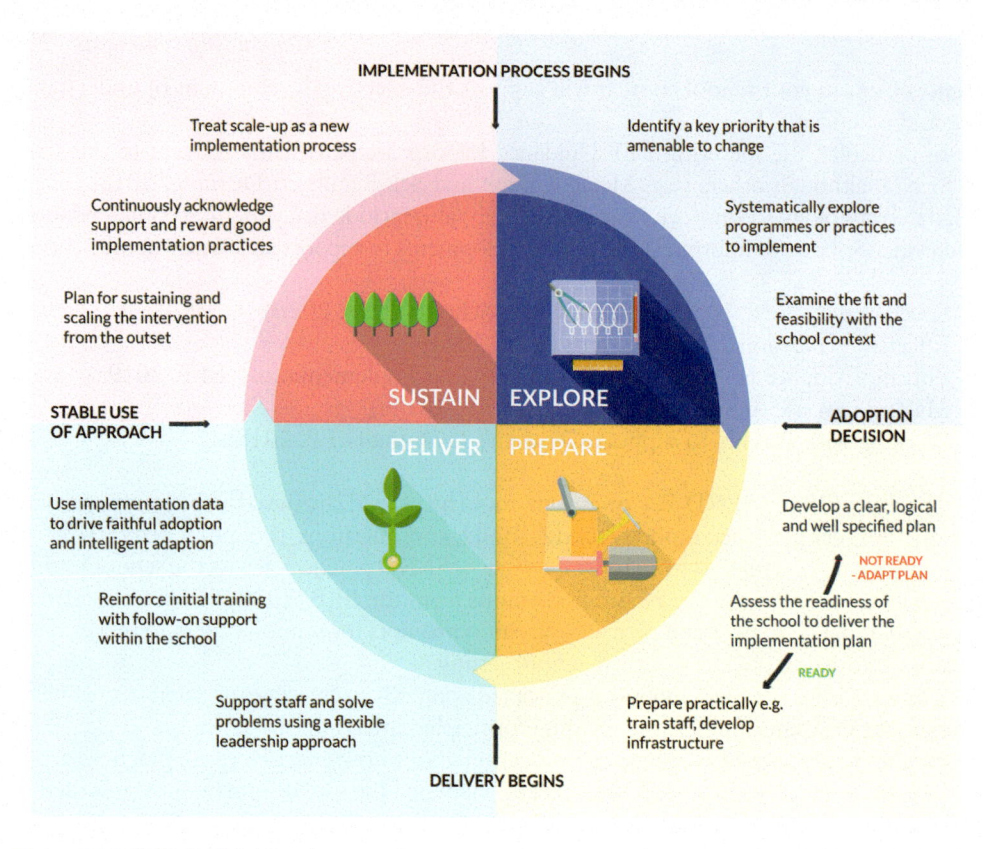

Figure 13.2 EEF (2019a) Implementation Process diagram

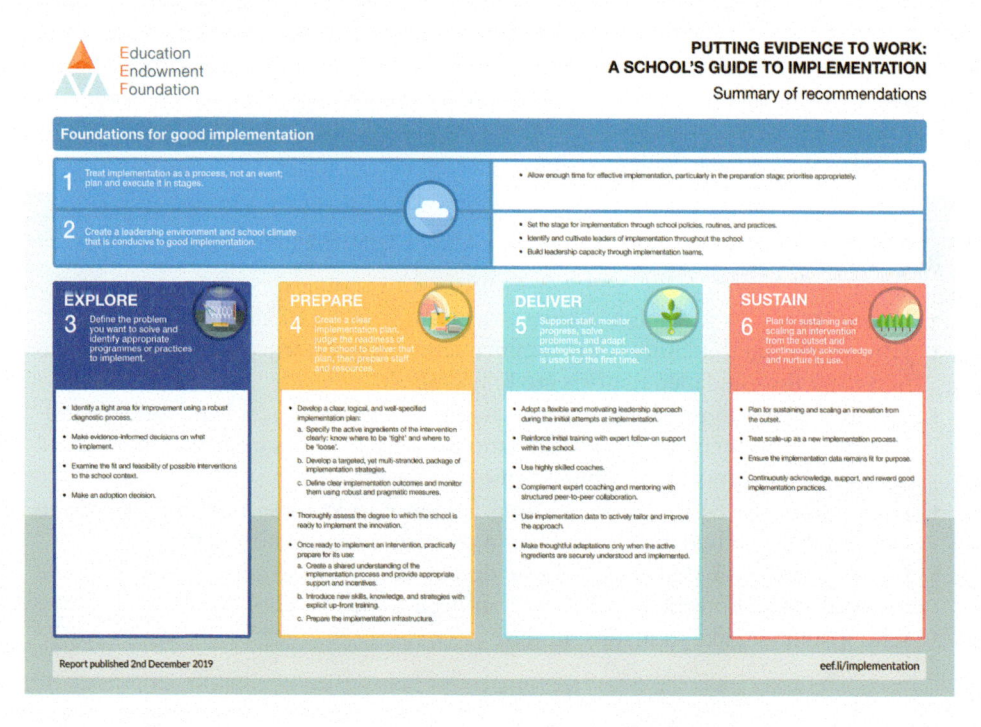

Figure 13.3 EEF (2019a) Six Recommendations for effective implementation

Use of CPD

Central to being an effective leader and being able to lead successfully in a culture of change, is the notion of everyone, including leaders, becoming 'Lead Learners' (Fullan, 2020: 60). The practice of being a Lead Learner involves '6 overlapping aspects:

1. Participating as a learner
2. Listen, learn, and lead, in that order
3. Be an expert and an apprentice
4. Develop others to the point that you become dispensable
5. Be relentlessly persistent and courageous about impact
6. Focus on the "how" as well as the "what" of change' (Fullan, 2020: 60).

Lawrence (1996, p. xi) refers to the discovery in educational psychology that 'people's level of achievement are influenced by how they feel about themselves'. Training and guidance for supporting children with SEND is an area SENCOs are often involved in to ensure that colleagues have the resources and knowledge to meet needs. Insufficient training, will impact on confidence and teachers' levels of self-efficacy, which will in turn influence the outcomes for pupils in the class:

> It is the emotional impact of not feeling able to cope with the needs of some children that can undermine a teachers' sense of themselves as a professional, and from this their levels of self-efficacy (Ellis, Tod, and Graham-Matheson 2008), which can then negatively impact on their confidence to meet the needs of other children with SEN, even if they do hold the skills and resources necessary to do that.
>
> (Ekins et al., 2016: 239)

It is therefore really important to ensure that good quality training through CPD is available to staff. The Special and Additional Educational Needs Report (NASUWT, 2023, n.p.) notes the following key features for successful, quality training: 'a strong focus on learner outcomes; extended learning (usually lasting at least two terms); follow-up and consolidation activities; opportunities to experiment in the classroom; opportunities for peer learning and peer support; and opportunities to analyse and reflect on what has been learned. High-quality CPD also takes account of individual teachers' starting points and their day-to-day experiences'.

The EEF (2021) Effective Professional Development Guidance Report includes Recommendation 2: 'Ensure that professional development effectively builds knowledge, motivates staff, develops teaching techniques, and embeds practice'. They identify that effective CPD requires the four essential elements outlined below:

A **Build knowledge**
  - Managing cognitive load
  - Revisiting prior learning

B **Motivate staff**
  - Setting and agreeing on goals
  - Presenting information from a credible source
  - Providing affirmation and reinforcement after progress

C Develop teaching techniques

- Instruction
- Social support
- Modelling
- Monitoring and feedback
- Rehearsal

D Embed practice

- Providing prompts and cues
- Prompting action planning
- Encouraging monitoring
- Prompting context specific repetition

(EEF, 2021: 14)

Figure 13.4 illustrates why it is important to have a balanced approach which includes all the elements identified for effective CPD as outlined above.

Building knowledge	Motivating teachers	Developing teaching techniques	Embedding practice	Likely outcome
✓	✓	✓		If embedding practice is missing, a teacher may understand the content, be motivated to improve, and have the techniques to do so but—after a period of time—may revert to old habits.
✓	✓			When developing techniques and embedding practice are absent, this could lead to the 'knowing, doing gap'. Here, a teacher may be fully aware of what they need to do and be motivated to do it; unfortunately, they do not know how to do so, nor do they have the tools to deliver.
✓				Here teachers may have effectively built the knowledge but lack the motivation and skills to implement.
	✓	✓	✓	In this instance, while teacher motivation and implementation may be present, they may have misunderstood and misapplied the initial knowledge.
✓	✓	✓	✓	Where professional development features a mechanism from each group, it may be more likely to be effective.

Figure 13.4 EEF (2021) Continuing Professional Development balanced approach

Source: https://educationendowmentfoundation.org.uk/education-evidence/guidance-reports/effective-professional-development

Reflective Activity

Think back to the last time you delivered CPD to staff. Use Figure 13.4 to evaluate if your training included the following elements:

1 Building knowledge
2 Motivating teachers
3 Developing teaching techniques
4 Embedding practice.

The EEF Effective Professional Development Guidance Document (2021) includes some examples for each of these areas if you need some examples to help you reflect more effectively.

Identify if your training was balanced. If it wasn't balanced, what will you do next time to make sure your CPD session is more effective?

Principled approaches to the development of effective practices

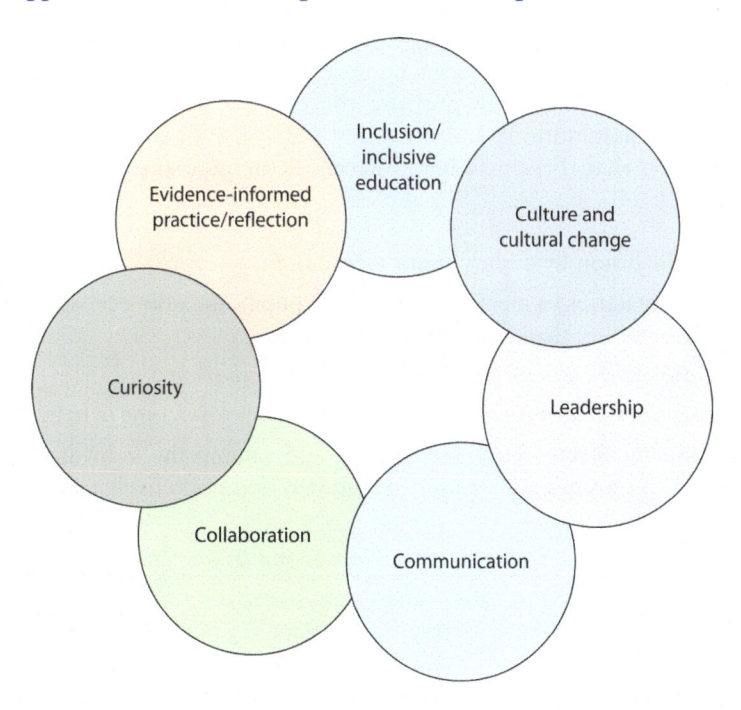

Figure 13.5 Key principles model

We firmly believe in the importance of principled approaches in the development of effective practices. Without clear, understood and shared principles to underpin the development of practices, change processes can become forced and not focused on a broader understanding of the changing needs and context of the whole school community. Hopefully the discussions, reflective activities and case studies throughout the chapters will have raised questions for you and will have helped you to start to identify areas of practice pertinent to your own school setting that you want to focus on and develop in some way.

We are in a time of change and unrest involving policy change, political change, an unprecedented pandemic, the war in Ukraine, a cost of living crisis and uncertain developments for SEND. Due to this uncertainty, it is more important than ever that we keep a principled, values-led approach as central to our understanding of effective ways to support pupils through outstanding leadership of SEND in our school contexts.

Key to this, as we have evidenced through the book, is the need to continually be critical and curious – to identify and challenge embedded assumptions and practices which may perpetuate inequitable and exclusionary practices and attitudes; to ensure that our practices become 'inclusive by design' – so that inclusive practices and approaches are *built in* to the development of our schools, rather than *bolt on* amendments when the needs of all pupils are not met within the core offer.

The key concepts of 'making the familiar unfamiliar' (Delamont & Atkinson, 1995) and 'principled interruptions' (Ainscow et al., 2006) to give us the space and opportunity to review and reflect on existing practices are therefore essential.

Reflective Activity

Running through the book have been a number of underpinning key critical questions.

Review the questions below and use these as an aid to consider your own understandings, assumptions and attitudes and those of others in your school setting and ways that these may be positively challenged and developed moving forward:

- *What does 'inclusion by design' mean to you and in your school setting?*

  How far are practices to meet the needs of all pupils, including those with SEND, fully 'built in' rather than 'bolt on'?

- *How are differences understood by you and in your school setting?*

  Are 'differences' still seen negatively as 'difficulties' to be overcome or to be eradicated?

  Or are differences celebrated, recognising and valuing the individuality of each person and the strengths that they individually and collectively can bring to the school community?

- *How is the concept of SEND understood by you and in your school context?*

  Is the term SEND used to 'label' differences, to explain/excuse/justify poor progress/outcomes and to remove responsibility for key pupils from the class teacher to the SENCO?

  Or is it understood as a problematic concept, one that is socially constructed without clear definition which therefore requires careful reflection and use of the term?

- *How do we know how effective practices are in including all – pupils, parents/carers, staff?*

  What systems, practices and approaches do we have for engaging with the authentic voices of those whom we are trying to work with?

  What assumptions do 'we' make about 'the other' and what is best for them?

> And how far do we ensure that we actively listen to and engage with the authentic voice and experiences of those people (pupils, parents/carers, other staff members) that we are trying to work with?
> - *What is meant by 'participation' in your school setting?*
> Is it full and active participation, enabling co-production, co-design, co-planning and shared ownership of new developments – or are the systems and processes to encourage participation simply tokenistic?

We hope that this book has provided you with clear information and guidance about the current policy context, as well as activities to help you to critically consider existing practices and understandings for you and in your own school setting. We hope that the Case Studies and examples that have been shared are useful in supporting the development of effective practices in your schools and that, through the embedded use of the Key Principles that we identified at the start of the book and which run throughout all of the chapters, you feel supported to take forward a principled approach to the leadership of SEND in your own school setting.

We also hope that this book about SEND and the effective leadership of SEND has actually started to challenge your thinking about the underpinning concept of SEND and to encourage a more principled approach to the understanding and acceptance of difference. In this, whilst we are both dedicated to and passionate about improving the processes and the experiences of children, parents/carers and professionals within the existing SEND system, we remain absolutely committed to a more inclusive understanding of difference and stand with Barth (1990: 514–515, cited in Loreman et al., 2010: xv) in firmly believing that:

> Differences hold great opportunity for learning. Differences offer a free and abundant renewable resource. I would like to see the compulsion for eliminating differences replaced with an equally compelling focus on making use of these to improve schools. What is important about people and about schools is what is different, not what is the same.

For us, it is just disappointing that more than 30 years on, society and the education system is still 'stuck' with its focus on eliminating rather than celebrating and positively valuing differences.

Finally, thank you for your ongoing work to help to develop more inclusive and effective school settings and practices to support the needs of all pupils, including those with SEND. Thank you for your commitment to the development of outstanding leadership of SEND in your schools. We hope that this book has helped to reinforce your understandings and that the discussions, Case Studies and examples throughout the book inspire you to re-evaluate some of the existing practices, assumptions and attitudes which may be held in your school and support you to find effective ways to challenge and develop them so that we can move further forward into building more inclusive schools and societies for the future.

As a final activity, complete Table 13.3 to consider how confident and competent you feel with each principle in the book. We will naturally have strengths and limitations based on our own abilities, experience and leadership in each of these principles, and it is therefore important to recognise this in ourselves and also to be able to draw on the support of others who may be able to complement our skills set.

240 Concluding comments

Table 13.3 Review of principles

Principle	Description	Confidence rating 5 = very confident 1 = no confidence	Competence rating 5 = very competent 1 = no competence	My actions to address lower levels of confidence and competence
Inclusion/inclusive education	'We believe that inclusion and the development of inclusive practices is an ongoing and dynamic process, not something that can simply be "achieved". It is fundamentally concerned with the identification and removal of barriers, and the presence, participation and achievement of ALL students' (UNESCO, 2021).			
Culture and cultural change	School culture is literally defined as 'the way we do things around here' – it is everywhere, in the attitudes, values, practices, relationships and communication embedded in the school.			
Leadership	To effect the culture change that is required demands strong strategic leadership. Leadership that is embedded with inclusive values, with a knowledge and understanding of the change process, and ways to enable and empower all staff working within the school context to understand, own and take responsibility for the changes to practice, provision, attitude and approach to SEND that is required.			
Communication	Effective communication and relationships need to embed everything that we do. All too often communication systems are not fit for purpose for the people (pupils, parents/carers, colleagues, other professionals) that we need to include.			
Collaboration	Collaborative practice indicates a commitment to working together, in some cases, for pupils with more complex SEND this is fundamental to be able to support their progress.			
Curiosity	For us, professional curiosity is a central factor in the development of inclusive practices and schools. In our work in schools, there is therefore a need to develop professional curiosity. This helps us to challenge existing or embedded assumptions – leading us to ask questions rather than base new ideas on pre-existing knowledge and 'truths' which may actually not reflect the actual situation or reality for the pupils, families and colleagues with whom we work.			
Evidence-informed practice and reflection	Where change is needed, and to support with the reflection, evidence-informed approaches and practices which consider the research evidence about what works in what type of setting and under what conditions are really important.			

References

Adams, R. (2023) *Schools across England close as teachers vow to continue strikes*. Available from: https://www.theguardian.com/education/2023/apr/27/schools-across-england-close-as-teachers-vow-to-continue-strikes (accessed 1.6.23).

Ainscow, M., Booth, T. and Dyson, A. (2006) *Improving schools, developing inclusion*. Abingdon: Routledge.

Barth (1990) – reference not required because this is cited in Loreman et al., 2010

Carter, A. (2015) *Carter review of initial teacher training*. Available from: https://www.gov.uk/ (accessed 1.6.23).

Delamont, S. and Atkinson, P. (1995) *Fighting familiarity: Essays on education and ethnography*. Cresskill, NJ: Hampton Press.

DfE (2011) *Support and aspiration: A new approach to special educational needs and disability*: a consultation. Norwich: TSO.

DfE/DoH (2015) SEN and Disability Code of Practice. London: Crown Copyright.

DfE (2017) *Evidence-informed teaching: An evaluation of progress in England: Research report*. Available from: https://www.gov.uk/government/publications/evidence-informed-teaching-evaluation-of-progress-in-england (accessed 1.6.23).

DfE (2019a) *ITT Core Content Framework*. Available from: https://assets.publishing.service.gov.uk/government/uploads/system/uploads/attachment_data/file/974307/ITT_core_content_framework_.pdf (accessed 1.6.23).

DfE (2019b) *Early Career Framework*. Available from: https://assets.publishing.service.gov.uk/government/uploads/system/uploads/attachment_data/file/978358/Early-Career_Framework_April_2021.pdf (accessed 1.6.23).

DfE (2021a) *Supporting SEND: A summary for children and young people*. Available from: https://www.gov.uk/government/publications/supporting-send/supporting-send-a-summary-for-children-and-young-people (accessed 20.12.22).

DfE (2021b) *Initial teacher training (ITT) market review: Overview*. Available from: https://www.gov.uk/government/publications/initial-teacher-training-itt-market-review (accessed 1.6.23).

DfE (2022) *Opportunity for all: Strong schools with great teachers for your child*. London: Crown Copyright.

DfE/DoHSC (2023) *SEND and alternative provision improvement plan*. London: HMSO.

EEF (2018a) *Making best use of teaching assistants*. London: EEF.

EEF (2018b) *Working with parents to support children's learning*. London: EEF.

EEF (2018c) *Metacognition and self-regulated learning*. London: EEF.

EEF (2019) Putting evidence to work: A school's guide to implementation. London: EEF.

EEF (2019a) *Putting evidence to work – A school's guide to implementation*. London: EEF.

EEF (2019b) *Using digital technology to improve learning*. London: EEF.

EEF (2020) *Special educational needs in mainstream schools*. London: EEF.

EEF (2021) *Effective professional development guidance report*. London: EEF.

EEF (2023) *Lesson Study*. Available from: https://educationendowmentfoundation.org.uk/projects-and-evaluation/projects/lesson-study (accessed 1.6.23).

Ekins, A., Savolainen, H. & Engelbrecht, P. (2016) An analysis of English teachers' self-efficacy in relation to SEN and disability and its implications in a changing SEN policy context, European Journal of Special Needs Education, 31:2, 236–249, DOI: 10.1080/08856257.2016.1141510.

Elliott, J. (1981) *Action-research: A Framework for Self-evaluation in Schools*. Cambridge: Schools Council 'Teacher-Pupil Interaction and the Quality of Learning' Project, Working Paper No. 1.

Fletcher-Wood and Zuccollo (2020) *The effects of high-quality professional development on teachers and students: A rapid review and meta-analysis*. Available from: https://epi.org.uk/publications-and-research/the-effects-of-high-quality-professional-development-on-teachers-and-students/ (accessed 1.6.23).

Fullan, M. (2020) *Leading in a culture of change* (2nd Edition). Hobeken, New Jersey: Jossey-Bass.

Gov.uk (2022) *Initial Teacher Training Census*. Available from: https://explore-education-statistics.service.gov.uk/find-statistics/initial-teacher-training-census/2022-23 (accessed 1.6.23).

House of Commons Education Committee (2019) *Special Educational Needs and Disabilities*. London: House of Commons.

Lawrence, D. (1996) Enhancing Self-Esteem in the Classroom. London: PCP Ltd.

Loreman, T., Deppler, J. and Harvey, D. (2010) *Inclusive education: Supporting diversity in the classroom*. Abingdon: Routledge.

McAteer, M. (2012) Action research in Education. London: SAGE

NAO (2019) *Support for pupils with special educational needs and disabilities in England*. London: House of Commons.

NASUWT (2023) *Special and Additional Needs*. Available from: https://www.nasuwt.org.uk/advice/in-the-classroom/special-educational-needs.html (accessed 31.5.23).

National Education Union (2022) *State of Education: The Profession*. Available from: https://neu.org.uk/press-releases/state-education-profession (accessed 31.5.23).

Norwich (2014) Lesson Study for Assessment: Introduction and Guidelines. Available from: https://blogs.exeter.ac.uk/lessonstudysend/files/2017/09/LSfA-guidance-booklet-pdf-.pdf (accessed 31.5.23).

Norwich, B., Benham-Clarke, S. and Lin Goei, S. (2020) 'Review of research literature about the use of lesson study and lesson study-related practices relevant to the field of special needs and inclusive education'. *European Journal of Special Needs Education* 36(3), 309–328.

UNESCO (2021) *Reaching out to all learners – A resource pack for supporting inclusion and equity in education*. Geneva: International Bureau of Education.

Takahashi, A. and Yashida, M. (2004) 'Ideas for establishing lesson-study communities.' *Teaching Children Mathematics*, (10) 9 436–443.

Vulliamy, G. and Webb, R. (1992) *Teacher research and special education needs*. London: Routledge.

Index

Note: Pages in *italics* refer to figures and tables.

accountability 2–3, 31–36, 148, 205–206, 208–209
Achievement for All initiative 193
adaptations 82, 84–85; adaptive teaching 71, 82, 226; review of *86*
'Assess, Plan, Do, Review' process 27, 63, 103, 107–109, *108*, 112, 131
assistive technology 139
Attention Deficit Hyperactivity Disorder (ADHD) 23, 40–41, 114, 180
autism/autistic people 8, 15, 41, 95, 173, 194–196

belonging 68, 180
Bronfenbrenner model, EEF 25, 90, *90*, 179–181, *181*

Care Quality Commission (CQC) 3, 34, 37
case studies 21, 23; autistic parents/carers 194–196; delivering quality CPD to support staff 26–27; The Equality Act (2010) 41–43; identifying children's needs 95–96; inclusive school cultures 76; interventions 144; multi-agency working: in primary school 218–219; in secondary school 26–27, 213–214; person-centred planning 174–175, 180–182; professional identity of SENCO 51–53; SENCO-Teacher relationship (Graduated Approach) 114–116, *115*, *116*, *117*; solution focused approach 97–98; staff understanding of statutory responsibilities for SEND 77–79; TAs teaching the teachers 162–163; tiered model of provision 119–120
child-centred practice. *see* person-centred planning
The Children and Families Act (2014) 39, 187, 191, 199, 204, 220, 224
Children and Social Work Act (2017) 216

Child Safeguarding Practice Review Panel 208, 216
Class Profile system 98, 101, 103
Clinical Commissioning Groups (CCGs) 33, 209, 217
collaboration/collaborative practice 7, 20, 32–33, 36, 49, 54, 74, 98, 112, 150, 171, 184, 187, 191, 198, 206, 209, 213–214, 216–217, 219–220
communication 7, 20, 36, 49, 54, 74, 93, 98–103, 112, 153, 168, 171, 174–176, 184, 189, 191, 193, 197–198, 200, 205–206, 208–211; communication skills audit *193*; formal/non-formal types of 176; and interaction 22–23, 119, 122, 125, 131, 133–134, 139, 149, 172
continuing professional development (CPD) 25–26, 53, 63, 76–78, 138, 147–148, 153, 181, 197, 226, 232, 235, 237; balanced approach 236, *236*; elements for effective 235–236; and training approaches for TAs 148–149, 154–155, 157
coordination of provision 105, 125, 129; Case Study 114–116, 119–120; effective/accessible systems 106–107, 112; evaluating provisions 125–126; Graduated Approach. *see* Graduated Approach; inclusion in action model *107*; provision mapping 106, 120–124, *122*, *124*; review of existing processes *113*; tiered model of provision 109–112, *110*, 117–119, 122
co-production 32, 170, 188, 190–191, 198–199, 225; stages of *199*
cost of living crisis 31, 48, 64, 206–207, 224, 238
Council for Disabled Children 167
Covid-19 pandemic 42, 49, 133–134, 207, 216, 224, 238

Index

culture/cultural change 6, 36, 49, 54, 74, 136, 174, 191, 209, 215–216, 220, 225, 229
curiosity (professional) 7, 20, 54, 74, 93, 112, 153, 162, 171, 174, 209, 213

deficit-led model of SEND 16, 17
Delivering Better Value programme 4, 32, 48
The Department for Education 2, 31, 33–34, 38, 182, 208, 224, 227
Department for Health and Social Care 208, 224
digital technology *140*
disability discrimination 40

Education Act (1981) 15
Education Act (2008) for SENCOs 50
Education Endowment Fund (EEF) 6, 8, 17, 23, 49, 70–71, 95, 135–136, 147–148, 160, 196, 226, 231–232; Areas of Need 22–23, *24*, 25; aspect of practice for working with parents/carers *200*; audit tools 74, *75*; Bronfenbrenner model 25, 90, *90*; digital technology to improve learning guidance report *140*; Effective Professional Development Guidance Report 25, 27, 235, 237; 'Five a Day' principle 82, *83*, 84, 155, *156*; guidance reports for TAs 148, 150; implementation process *60*, *234*; ineffective/effective deployment of TAs *161*; Making Best Use of Teaching Assistants Guidance Report 150, 157, *157*; planning quadrant 180; planning targeted intervention *137*; Report SEND in Mainstream Schools 63; on scaffolding 84, 114; A School's Guide to Implementation 233; SEND Key questions tool 233; SEND recommendations 71, *72*, 73–74, 95; SEN in Mainstream Schools Guidance Report 6, 8, 68, 71, 74, 90, 120, 147, 150, 176, *180*, 199, 233; tiered approach to educational support 129, *129*; visioning exercise tool 161, *162*; Working with Parents to Support Children's Learning Guidance Report 188, 193, 197, 199
Education, Health and Care Plan (EHCP) 2, 15, 17–19, 32, 40, 84, 105, 108, 135, 167–168, 170, 175, 182, 189–190, 205, 208–210, 225; lack of effective engagement between agencies and services 32–33
Emotional Literacy Support Assistant (ELSA) 63, 134
employability 183
English as an Additional Language (EAL) 163

The Equality Act (2010) 39–42; direct disability discrimination 40–41; discrimination in consequence of disability 40; failure to make reasonable adjustments 40–42; legal recourse to commence proceedings 39–40
Every Child Matters agenda 203–204, 220
evidence-based teaching 71, 111
evidence-informed approach 7–8, 20, 27, *28*, 74, 82, 111, 133, 135–136, 141–143, *142*, *150*, 191, 218

'Five a Day' principles 82, *83*, 84, 155, *156*
formative assessment 95, 109
fully distributed approach 68
Further Education Establishments 182

GL Dyslexia Screener 96
Graduated Approach 79, 106, 112–114, 117, 182; 'Assess, Plan, Do, Review' model 107–109, *108*, 112, 131; SENCO-Teacher relationship (Case Study) 114–116, *115*, *116*, *117*

high-quality teaching 71, 82, 98, 106, 111, 120, 128, 130–131, 145, 152, 164, 226
holistic system 98
House of Commons Education Committee (HoCEC) 3, 18–19, 31–35, 37, 44, 50, 108, 167, 172, 188–189, 203–205, 208, 212, 215, 223–224

identification of children's needs: challenges of 88–89, 93–94; communication systems 98–103; dilemmas of difference reflection tool *94*; identification dilemma 14, 89, 93–94; identifying SEND 100–101; inclusive approaches to identifying needs 89–91, 94–95; register of pupil's individual characteristics and needs *99*; solution-focused approaches 96–97
inclusion by design 73, 76, 79, 238
inclusion in action model 107, *107*
inclusion/inclusive education 5–6, 14, 20, 27, 36, 48, 54, 68–69, 74, 93, 112, 129, 136–137, 152, 153, 171, 177, 190, 191, 210, 224
inclusive technology 139
Individual Class Inclusion Map 124
Initial Teacher Training (ITT) 226–227; Census 227; Core Common Framework 82, 225; Early Career Framework 225; Initial Teacher Training Providers 227
instructional apps 139
inter-professional collaboration 206

interventions, planning and delivering 128, 131–135, 138–140, 150, 154; audit for gaps in knowledge/skills of staff *141*; Case Study 144; effectiveness and impact of 131–135, 138–140; cognition and learning 132–133, 139; communication and interaction 133–134, 139; sensory and physical 134–135; social, emotional and mental health 134; evidence-informed approaches 135–136, 141–143, *142*; key principles 128–131, 138; child-centred practice 130, 145; graduated approach 131; high-quality teaching 131; inclusive values 130–131; lifestyle model of intervention 129, 135; straightforward 132, 137; strategies to support memory *143*; tiered approach to educational support 129, *129*

Kent Mainstream Core Standards 96

ladder of participation model 168, *169*, 191
Lamb Report (2009) 188–189
leadership 6–7, 13, 20, 45–46, 54, 65–66, 74, 153–154, 161, 170, 177, 210, 215, 238–239; Case Study 51–53, 62–64; of change 49–50, 57–58, *58*; school's change and implementation process 59, 60, *60*; tools for supporting effective change 58; effective leadership, principles of 46, 48–49, 54–56; Fullan's framework for leadership 56; inclusive leaders, traits of 47–48; ley leadership task 47; Lone Ranger leadership styles 49; moral purpose 45, 56; school leadership 46–48, 50–51, 151; SENCO as strategic leader 50, 54, 61–62, 64–65; senior leaders/leadership 1, 6, 46, 49–50, 52, 62, 98, 115, 123, 154–155, 184, 218, 230; understanding 46–49, 54, 57
lifestyle model of intervention 129, 135
local authorities 2–4, 19, 30–39, 49, 51, 53, 92, 123, 126, 135, 175, 187, 189, 209, 224–225

making the familiar unfamiliar 7, 61, 233, 238
Maximising the Impact of Teaching Assistants (MITA) website 155
medical models of SEND 16, 25
multi-agency working (working relationships) 174, 204; audit tools *215*; gaps in therapy provision 207; Multi-Agency Child Protection Units 208; multi-agency safeguarding hubs (MASH) 217; in primary school 218–219; professional identity and differences 205–206, 210–212; review of *219*; in secondary school 213–214; structural issues and systemic silos 208–209, 215–217, 220;

support from external services 206–207, 212–213

NASEN Whole School SEND approach 38
The National Agreement and School Workforce Remodelling 148
National Award for SEN Coordination (NASENCO) 50–52, 62, 141, 143, 230
National Curriculum Inclusion Statement 67
National Development Team for Inclusion (NDTI) 69
National Standards for SEND 4, 17, 19, 35, 37–38, 71, 92, 135, 149, 209, 220
National Strategies (1997–2011) 109, 121
non-instructional apps 139
non-verbal communication 176–177
NPQ (National Professional Qualification) 48, 51, 62
Nurture Group 63–64

Ofsted 3, 31, 34, 37, 79, 111, 131, 132, 207; Inspection Framework 79, 111, 132; OFSTED/CQC Inspections 37, 39; Ofsted SEND report 207, 215–217

parental confidence in SEND system 19, 35, 193
parents/carer partnership 7, 19, 35, 37, 41–42, 63–64, 78–79, 91, 95, 102, 108, 117, 163, 166–167, 175, 181, 184, 186–187, 207, 210, 223–225; aspect of practice for working with *200*; autistic 194–196; importance and value of 187–188, 192–194; recognising and challenging inequalities in 188–191, 194, 196; whole-school approaches to 191, 197–199
person-centred planning (child-centred) 166–168, 172–174, *178*, 184; across school 170–171, 176–179, 182; case studies 174–175, 180–182; factors for supporting children's participation *178*, 178–179; inclusive culture 172; involving and valuing individuals 168–170, 174, 176; Talking Point Posters 179, *179*
Person-centred Thinking Tools, Helen Sanderson Associates 174
principled interruptions 7, 61, 112, 224, 233, 238
Professional Standards for TAs 154
provision mapping (Provision Maps) 106, 120–124, *122*, *124*
Pupil Progress Review Meetings 64, 123

quality first teaching approach 64, 71, 96

Rapid Evidence Assessment Research Report 90
respect 5, 54, 93, 206, 211

scaffolding 82, 84–85, 114; review of 85
school culture 6; inclusive 68–69, 74
screening assessments 95, 125
self-efficacy, staff 69–70, 77, 79
SEN and Disability Code of Practice (DfE/DoH, 2014, 2015) 1–3, 15, 17–18, 35–39, 50–51, 53, 67–68, 70–71, 77–78, 111, 120–121, 134–135, 140, 166–167, 171, 188–189, 191, 197–198, 203–204, 220, 224, 230–231; Areas of Need: cognition and learning 22–23, 62, 119, 122, 125, 131–132, 138, 139, 149; communication and interaction 22–23, 119, 122, 125, 131, 133–134, 139, 149, 172; physical and sensory 22, 119, 122, 125, 138; social emotional and mental health difficulties 22–23, 119, 122, 134
SEND and Alternative Provision Improvement Plan 1, 17, 20, 37, 46, 48, 51, 68–69, 71, 77, 106, 170, 187, 190, 200, 209, 220
Sentiments, Attitudes and Concerns about Inclusive Education (SACIE) 70
Serious Case Reviews 216
social capital 189–190, 224
Social, Emotional, and Mental Health (SEMH) 62–64, 125, 180
solution-focused approaches 96–98
Special and Additional Educational Needs 227, 235
Special Educational Needs (SEN) 1, 5, 8, 13–16, 25, 29, 31, 46, 50, 70, 91, 128, 130, 193; definition of 16; levels of 18–20, 27; SEN Information Report 109, 140, 226; SEN Pathfinder projects 2, 19; SEN Register 122, 213; SEN Support 15, 18–19, 34, 91, 100–101, 103, 105–106, 132, 135–136, 207
Special Educational Needs and Disability (SEND): Areas of Need 22–23, 24, 25, 119, 122, 138; challenges 3, 14; contradictions 228, 228; financial challenge 224–225; implementing threshold criteria 15–18; recruitment and retention 227–228; reductionist interpretations 14–15, 20; teacher training 225–227; change and transition using evidence-informed practice 229–236; action research 230–231; implementation process 233, 234; lesson study 231–233, 232; review of proposed changes 229; use of CPD 235; use of EEF Guidance Reports 232–233; data 18; identifying needs of pupil 91–92; impacts on effective implementation of 31–32; key principles model 4–5, 5, 20, 36, 54, 73, 92, 111, 136, 153, 171, 192, 210, 237, 239; review of 240; SEND Reforms of 2014 33–34, 36, 108, 209, 224–225; SEND Register 15, 40, 101–103, 102, 130; SEND Support 18, 37, 106; social models of 17, 25; thresholds for identifying 22–25
The Special Educational Needs and Disability Regulations (2014) 39
The Special Educational Needs and Disability Tribunal (2017) 39–42
Special Educational Needs Coordinators (SENCOs) 1–2, 6, 8, 21, 27, 31, 36, 39, 46, 61, 63–67, 76–78, 84, 96, 100, 106–107, 121, 123, 131, 133–135, 139–140, 147, 149, 153, 162–163, 166, 170–171, 176, 181, 184, 186, 188–191, 197, 199–200, 203, 207, 210–211, 218, 223, 228–229; action research (interventions) 144; developing professional identity of 51–53; and Graduated Approach 109, 113; Learning Outcomes 147; National Award for SEN Coordination (NASENCO) 50–52, 62, 141, 143, 230; NPQ for 48, 51, 62; role in supporting TAs 149; SENCO I 63; SENCO–Teacher relationship 114–116, 115, 116, 117; as strategic leader 50, 54, 61–62, 64–65
specialist teachers 98, 134
specialist technology 139
specific, measurable, achievable, realistic and time-bound (SMART) 139
Speech and Language Therapist (SALT) 63, 98, 100, 211, 213–214
speech-generating apps 139
Speech, Language and Communication Framework 133–134
Speech, Language and Communication Needs (SLCN) 213–214
spiral of inquiry strategic approach 62
Statements of Special Educational Needs 19, 148
statutory responsibilities for SEND 30, 66, 86, 109; Case Study 41–43; consistent implementation of 33–35, 38–39; focus on accountability 34–35; inclusive education culture 76; local offers 36–38; reach of 30–33, 36–38; SEND law and 35–36, 39, 43; teacher and staff self-efficacy 69–70, 77–79
systemic cultural shift 3, 33, 225

Talking Point Posters 179, 179
Teaching Assistants (TAs) 130, 147–148, 211; Case Study 162–163; collaboration of teachers-TAs 150, 157; CPD and

training approaches for 148–149, 154–155, 157; EEF Guidance report 148, 150; effective deployment in schools 148–153, 160–162, *161*; Higher level teaching assistant (HLTA) 149; targeted in-class learning support 151; targeted intervention delivery 152–153; whole-class support 151; Health Check 155; inclusive cultures 154; 'The Incredible Five Point Scale' 163; index for inclusion 154, *154*; Making Best Use of Teaching Assistants Guidance Report 150, 157, *157*; as 'Mum's Army' 148; observation schedule 155; Performance Management cycle 163; preparation and training school self-review 155, *155*; Professional Standards for 154; rise of TAs in England 148; SENCO's support for 149; TA Deployment Review Guide 159; TAs questionnaire 159, *160*; teachers' questionnaire 159, *159*; Teacher-TA agreement template 157–158, *158*; training in schools 149

total communication approach 175–176
Tribunal system 35, 39–43, 188, 190, 193

The United Nations 168
United Nations Conventions on the Rights of the Child (UNCRC): Article 12 167; Article 13 170
Universal, Targeted and Specialist model 109–111, *118*

values-based approach 167
visioning exercise tool 161, *162*

Warnock Report (1978) 1, 13, 15, 187
Waves of Intervention 109, *110*
whole-school approaches 67, 91, 111–112, 117, 124, 161, 170; case studies *114–117, 119–120*; developing whole-school inclusive pedagogy 71, 73, 82, 84, 86; inclusive school cultures 68–69, 74, 79; meeting needs of children *80–81*; parental/carer partnership 191; teacher and staff self-efficacy 69–70, 77–79
Working Together to Safeguard Children 215
Workload survey report 170–171